GUNS AND GANDHI IN AFRICA

For Moira and Don
best wishes
Bill Sutherland

More Comments about GUNS AND GANDHI IN AFRICA

It is time to begin learning from Africa, not just about it–and this book is the vanguard of a fresh stream of writing from which a wholly new understanding of the possibilities of nonviolence in apparently hopeless situations will emerge.

–Dr. Elise Boulding, former Secretary-General of the International Peace Research Association; Professor Emerita of Sociology, Dartmouth University

About the Authors

Bill Sutherland, a World War II conscientious objector born in the U.S., has lived in Africa for the past five decades, tirelessly recording and participating in efforts for social change on both continents. As co-founder of the Congress of Racial Equality, Americans for South African Resistance, World Peace Brigades and countless other organizations, he served as a special assistant to the Sixth Pan-African Congress in Tanzania, and has been a leading figure in fostering Pan-African relations for all of his adult life.

Matt Meyer, multicultural coordinator for New York City's Alternative High Schools and Programs, has traveled and written extensively on education and political struggles in Africa, Latin America, and the U.S. As national co-chair of the consortium on Peace Research, Education and Development, Matt has helped bring together university-based professors and students, primary and secondary school teachers, and community-based activists for transformative approach to social change. He also co-chairs War Resisters International Africa Working Group, and is an editor of and contributor to the volumes *Children of War: Children of Hope, Puerto Rico: The Cost of Colonialism,* and *Multicultural Voices in Action.*

GUNS AND GANDHI IN AFRICA

PAN-AFRICAN INSIGHTS ON NONVIOLENCE, ARMED STRUGGLE, AND LIBERATION

BILL SUTHERLAND AND MATT MEYER

Africa World Press, Inc.

Africa World Press, Inc.

First Printing 2000

Book design: Krystal Jackson
Cover design: Debbie Hird

Library of Congress Cataloging-in-Publication Data

Sutherland, Bill.
Guns and Gandhi in Africa: Pan-African insights on nonviolence, armed struggle and liberation / Bill Sutherland and Matt Meyer.
p. cm.
Includes bibliographical references and index.
ISBN 0-86543-750-5. -- ISBN 086543-751-3 (pbk.)
1. Africa. Sub-Saharan--Politics and government--1960- 2. Passive resistance--Africa, Sub-Saharan--History--20th century. 3. Insurgency--Africa, Sub-Saharan--History--20th century. 4. Pan -Africanism--History--20th century. 5. Sutherland, Bill. 6. Meyer, Matt. I. Meyer, Matt. II. Title.
DT352.8.S88 1999
967.03's--dc21 99-29191
CIP

CONTENTS

ACKNOWLEDGEMENTS AND DEDICATION

So many individuals and organizations helped support the process of travel, discussion and editing that went into this project and book. First and foremost, Ginny Hill deserves our gratitude and more. As the chief transcriber, as a thoughtful editor and observer of the African political scene, and on a personal level, she is the "unindicted coconspirator" without whom this book would not have been possible.

The A. J. Muste Memorial Institute provided, from the outset, a fiscal and organizational basis for our outreach and development in the U.S. Within and outside of their framework, a number of people remained consistent in the giving of their advice, funds and contacts, including: Charles Alexander, Michael Andregg, Bill Barrett, Tom Betrand, Karl Bissinger, Marie Bloom, Elise Boulding, Dorie Bunting, Jim Cason, Jon Cohen, Andres Thomas Conteris, Jack Caroli, Ralph DiGia, Sam Diener, Maire Dugan, Dan Duwees, Carol Berstein Ferry, David Gilbert, Sandy Gold, Anne Houston Harte, Connie Hogarth and Art Kamel, Bob Henschen, Russell Herman, Joshua Hornick, George Houser, Joe Iosbaker, Rob Jones and Whitney Tymas, Joel Kovel, Bob Lederer and John Reilly, Felicia Leon, Bob Lepley, Diane and Elliott Liebowitz, Elmer Maas and Kairos/Plowshares New York, Elspeth Meyer, Betsy Mickel, Mara Miller, Janet and Bob Moses, Walter Neagle, Chris Ney, Dennis O'Neil, Esther Pank, Greg and Donna Payton, john powell, Clayton Ramey, Caroline Rioux, Craig Simpson, Gail Snowden, Susan Steinberg, Jill Sternberg, Michael True, Barby and Vic Ulmer, Helen Vukasin, Vera Williams, Dorie Wilsnack, Gloria Weinberg, Beverly Woodward, Rev. S. Michael Yasutake, Sherry Zekowski, Bob Zuber, and Jean Zwickel. A special thanks goes to Arlene Hinds for various administrative tasks. Special recognition also goes out to Vincent Harding, for whom this work will hopefully fulfill his longterm faith in the need for such a project. The offices and officers of the War Resisters League provided ongoing administrative assistance.

Our travels together throughout Africa, taking place over a six year period, were only possible because of the generosity and creative use of resources of a number of our friends and colleagues. We must, of course, thank all those who gave their valuable time, often in the midst of extremely pressured schedules. Those who were included in our extensive dialogues, and who make up the better part of the text of this book, deserve no less than a byline of coauthorship. Their names appear throughout the chapters, and so will not be repeated here; their contributions have been too great to list. It is our sincere hope that they will find the results of our cumulative effort rewarding and useful.

The logistical support during our African encounters was no less than extraordinary. We were able to see a great many people during relatively short visits, due mainly to the contributions of: J. P. Addy and the Volta River Authority, Dr. Robert Lee, David Acquah, Aki Sawyerr, Ad'Obe Obe, Ambassador Lopes Tembe Ndlana, Mary Tandon, Ruvimbo and the Southern African NonGovernmental Development Organizations Network; David Martin, Mutizwa Mukute, Flavia Gema and the Southern Africa Research and Documentation Center; Ibbo Mandaza, Sandy Katz, Francis Christie, Arturo Jossefa Jamo, Jose P. Tembe, Janet Mondlane, Prexy Nesbitt, Nan Cross, David Bruce, Paul Puritt, Adele Kirsten and Karl van Holdt, Halton Cheadle, Devon Pillay, Richard Steele and Anita Kromberg, Julie Frederikse and Stelious Comninos, David Gallagher, Mose Tjitendero, Peter Katjavivi, Chris Davids and the UNICEF Policy Monitoring Unit, Vicki Ehrenstein ya Toivo, Howard Jeter, Ambassador Agbuzu, Bright Mwansa Chunga, Hilda and Alex GwebeNyirenda, Joan Wicken, Paul Rupia, Joseph Butiku, Colin Forbes, Jan Van Criekinge, Janine EdelOtte, Brigitte Djionadji and the organizers of Tchad Nonviolence; Mawina Sowa Kouyate, Tumika Daima and the AllAfrican Peoples Revolutionary Party; Vasu Gounden, Hayden Allen, Timothy Lind, Sue Britton, Ivan Toms, Stanley Hermans; Laurie Nathan and the Center for Conflict Resolution; Margaret and Colin Legum, and Lavinia Browne.

The support of loving families has served to sustain us both in spiritual and in material ways. We return that love, with much admiration, to Marilyn Meyer, Sylvia Meyer, William Starr, Jr., Bill Starr III, Esi Sutherland, Ralph Sutherland, and Amowi Sutherland. A constant source of critical analysis, of challenging perspectives, of patient and caring commentary, and of encouragement to continue the work came from comrade and partner Meg Starr.

Finally, a number of our supporters over these years are no longer with us, unable to read this finished product. We trust, however, that--as they have passed on to join with the ancestors--their own contributions to our ongoing lifework continue to nurture and guide us. Our thoughts turn to Jim Bristol, Kenneth Boulding, Sybil Claiborne, W. H. Ferry, Mollie Lehrenbaum, Simon Meyer, Suzanne Starr, Efua Sutherland, Kwame Ture, and Mwalimu Julius Nyerere. It seems fitting, therefore, to dedicate this book to two groupings: to all those who have gone before us, in love and in struggle, and to the next generation of resisters, of community builders, of revolutionaries.

M.M. (New York) and
B.S. (Dar-es-Salaam)
May 1999

FOREWORD

by

The Most Reverend Desmond Mpilo Tutu, D.D. F.K.O.
Anglican Archbishop of the Church of the Province of Southern Africa
1984 Nobel Peace Laureate

When thinking about introducing this volume on *Guns and Gandhi in Africa,* I cannot help but reflect upon a concept which is neither Western nor Indian in it's origins, but uniquely African. *Ubuntu,* a difficult word to render precisely in English, seeks to describe the essence of what it means to be human. You know when it is there and when it is absent. It speaks about gentleness, hospitality, putting yourself out on behalf of others, being vulnerable. It embraces both compassion and toughness. It recognizes that my humanity is bound up in yours, for we can only be truly human together.

Ubuntu is relevant to this book because, in their discussions about the African process of liberation and social change, Bill Sutherland and Matt Meyer have looked beyond the short-term strategies and tactics, which too often divide progressive people. They have begun to develop a language that looks at the roots of our humanness beyond our many private contradictions. By challenging us to better understand concepts often seen as opposed to one another--like nonviolence and armed struggle--they help to focus our attention on the larger struggles we must still wage, united: for economic justice, for true freedom and equality, and for a world of lasting peace.

In chairing South Africa's Truth and Reconciliation Commissions (TRC), one of the difficult tasks was dispelling the many myths and erroneous notions about the nature of reconciliation. Reconciliation, as we so forcefully found out, is not about being cozy; it is not about pretending that things were other than the way they were. Any attempt at reconciliation, which does not face up to the past, including sometimes uncomfortable realities, is not true reconciliation at all and will not last. There are similar myths and misunderstandings about the history of nonviolence and armed struggle on our continent, which Bill and Matt--in conversation with many proponents of one or the other of these options--try to dispel.

When some of us, in the dark days of apartheid, proclaimed our belief that all violence was evil but not equal--that some violence was borne of a horrible choice between continued oppression or a violent overthrow of the oppressive regime--there was much misunderstanding about that position. Were we adherents of Gandhi, whose notions of soul force (by the way) were not only developed in South Africa, but were based on some concepts he learned in South Africa? Were we apologists for the guerrillas, who were, of course, labeled terrorists by the real terrorists of the world: those who promote injustice and structural violence and the militarism and repression that are necessary in maintaining it?

The policies of the new South Africa help explain our responses to the violence of the past, such as our constitution that guarantees human rights, coexistence, and development opportunities for all, irrespective of color, race, class, belief, or sex. Even policies of our new Defense Forces allow for the rights of conscience, ending conscription in our land. The importance of Bill and Matt's book is that they too help us examine the subtleties between rough questions and all-too-easy answers; they help us probe the relationship between cause and effects, between means and ends.

On a personal note, I cannot help but share that I know Bill Sutherland for a long, long time. An early and persistent builder of organizational links between Americans and South Africans, Bill has distinguished himself as a vital ally to our cause, and as a friend. In his capacity as an expatriate, living all these years on the frontlines in Tanzania, Bill has provided hospitality, support and encouragement for untold numbers of people the world over, demonstrating the truest of Africa spirits. It is exciting, finally, to read some of his perspectives, and draw on his experiences.

In concluding the report of the TRC, we wrote, "Reconciliation does not come easily. It requires persistence. It takes time." We recognized that it would take great commitment, especially by those who have benefited and who continue to benefit from past discrimination, to transform a society based on unjust inequalities and dehumanizing poverty. I think of these words in the context of this book because, as we reflect upon five decades of Africa's struggle for freedom, we know that it will take great persistence and commitment in the new millennium to transform this planet into one of true peace. God's Shalom, peace, involves inevitable righteousness, wholesomeness, and fullness of life, participation in decision-making, goodness, laughter, joy, compassion, and sharing. Real peace will come to us, when we proclaim justice to all the inhabitants of this beautiful world of ours.

CHAPTER 1

WHY EXAMINE VIOLENCE AND NONVIOLENCE IN AFRICA?

As we enter the twenty-first century, how can we break the cycles of violence–both militaristic and institutional–that are plaguing humanity all over the world? What could we do if we really tried? What does one do when power is in one's grasp? How has lasting social change really been made–behind the scenes and at the grassroots level? What do we all need to do in order to build a society in which everyone can live in dignity and peace?

In April of 1960, a little known event took place which, for a brief moment, achieved what world revolutionaries of the twentieth century dream about even today–a conference in which broad groupings and individuals from the South and the North came together to respond to two major crises of common concern. The Africa of 1960 was mainly under European domination; only a handful of countries had wrestled free from the chains of colonialism. The British colony of the Gold Coast, which led the way towards independence under the stewardship of Kwame Nkrumah, had transformed itself into the sovereign state of Ghana, a center of anti-colonial and Pan-African activity. Several years into Nkrumah's presidency, the unique Positive Action Conference was to be a space for the nonviolent advocates of the North to meet the African liberationists of the South; the relevance of pacifism and "positive action" to the independence movements was to be openly addressed.

The first crisis to which the conference sought to respond was the explosion of a French nuclear bomb in the Sahara desert; the second was the situation in South Africa after the Sharpeville Massacre, which had just taken place the previous March. The French nuclear test took place in spite of an international campaign that culminated in an attempt to reach the planned test site by a group of nonviolent direct actionists. In South Africa, the liberation movements had called for a peaceful protest in Sharpeville Township, which resulted in a demonstration where hundreds of people were shot in the back, and wounded or killed. The Sharpeville Massacre was the decisive factor in the conclusion by principal leaders in the South African liberation movement that nonviolence could no longer work.

In the beginning of the planning for the Positive Action Conference, it did seem as though the leadership–and Nkrumah in particular–was very open to a pacifist approach about what needed to be done. In fact, Nkrumah had instructed a small group of advisors to invite anybody they wanted whom they thought could make a contribution to the ongoing struggle. One of those advisors was Bill Sutherland, an African American advocate of Gandhian nonviolence living in Ghana since 1953. This was the first time in Bill's experience that a government leader was calling for strategists from the international nonviolent movements.

A.J. Muste, the dean of the U.S. peace movement and Executive Secretary of the religious pacifist Fellowship of Reconciliation, was astounded: here was a conference to which he and Rev. Ralph Abernathy, chief assistant to Martin Luther King, had come from the United States, leading pacifists had come from France, England, and Japan, and theoreticians and organizers had come all the way from India. Nkrumah had arranged for all of these advisors to come to the capital of Accra, with expenses paid by the ruling Convention Peoples Party. It was Nkrumah's gamble to find a way to keep the drive for the liberation of the African continent on the right track. With the death of Pan-Africanist George Padmore just prior to the conference, he had lost his most trusted advisor on African affairs. He undoubtedly felt pressure to continue to give forceful leadership in a maelstrom of competing ideologies, unbridled ambition, and intrigue. Ever the strategist, Nkrumah seized upon the momentum created by the world interest in nuclear disarmament and the interest of people of African descent in new developments on the continent, to serve his one great passion–political independence and unity for all the peoples of Africa.

"This is your conference," Nkrumah told the advisor group. "Let's see what you can come up with."

* * *

Bill Sutherland's life history epitomizes the bridge between Pan-Africanism and Gandhian nonviolence. He was introduced to both at an early age. His family were pioneers in racial integration, and Bill and his sisters experienced a great deal of ostracism and discrimination in the white community into which they moved. In fact, his oldest sister never fully recovered from the psychological trauma she suffered as the first lonely African American child in a very hostile environment. By the time Bill and his second oldest sister, Muriel went to school, the atmosphere was less hostile, and some of the teachers tried to make life more tolerable. But it was crystal clear to Bill and his sister that it was the African side of their African American ancestry that made them outcasts. In different ways, this experience determined the direction of both their lives. Muriel and her husband founded Freedom House Community Center in the heart of the African American community in Boston, and the MacArthur Foundation awarded her a genius grant. She was also a trustee at the University of Massachusetts, and had been on the Board of Overseers at Harvard University. At his late sister's funeral in Harvard chapel, Bill used a biblical analogy: "The stone the builders rejected became the cornerstone of our lives."[1]

Other earlier experiences aroused Bill's interest in nonviolence. One Sunday evening, his father took him to a small African American church in a neighboring town, where the speaker was a fiery Indian nationalist describing Gandhi and the movement for the independence of India. When Bill reported on this the next day in social studies class, the teacher entered into a long apologia for British rule–Bill's first inkling of "white folks united." On the other hand, another teacher, in 1935, made a point of giving him a copy of the book Black Reconstruction by W.E.B. DuBois, and the Young People's Society of the white Congregational Church also invited him to become a member. Incidentally, the director was a young white southerner who was a pacifist and a socialist. Throughout his high school days, Bill was active in the junior National Association for the Advancement of Colored People (NAACP), as well as in youth groups that focused on international relations and socialism.

At Bates college in Maine, Bill continued his activities for racial justice and pacifism through work in the New England Student Christian Movement, where he met David Dellinger, who would later become one of the leaders of the national anti-war movement and a member of the Chicago Seven. Dellinger was also the principal founder, in 1940, of the Newark Ashram–a community center based on the Gandhian approach and located in a blighted African American neighborhood. Upon graduation, Bill volunteered for the student peace service of the American Friends Service Committee (AFSC), later joined the Newark Ashram, and also became the field secretary of the Youth Committee Against War. About the time of his graduation in 1940, the draft was instituted, and Bill decided to become a conscientious objector. One of his friends, class valedictorian Frank Coffin (who was to later become a Congressman and federal judge), predicted that Bill would be imprisoned by June of 1942. He was off by only one month!

In July 1942, Sutherland was sentenced to four years in prison and was sent to Lewisburg Federal Penitentiary where fellow war resisters Dave Dellinger, Ralph DiGia, and others later arrived. Determined to maintain their political commitment in prison, they participated in strikes against segregation in the prison system, and against mail censorship. Getting out of Lewisburg in 1945, Bill helped to found the New York office of the Congress of Racial Equality (CORE). His interest in Africa, however, developed during travels throughout Europe with the Peacemakers project.

In 1950, the Peacemakers organization–a group of radical war resisters against the Korean War–began speaking out about their beliefs on city street corners. They were often challenged by pro-war citizens, shouting "Tell it to the Russians!" That seemed like a valid challenge, and the idea of a bicycle trip came up. Dave, Ralph, Quaker Art Emory, and Bill would bike from New York to Moscow, challenging the concept of the Iron Curtain, and call upon the young men on both sides to lay down their arms and refuse to fight. In London and Paris, heading east, they happened to meet African students whose enthusiasm about their struggles back home was contagious. They were so gung-ho about the possibilities for liberation on the African continent, and Bill was inspired by their passion. "Back in the U.S.," Bill thought, "the possibilities of progressive social change looked rarer and more remote, but in Africa it seemed that there was a real possibility to put the values we were talking about into practice."

Bayard Rustin, an African American conscientious objector colleague and student of A.J. Muste, managed to get himself to Africa first. Bayard headed for Nigeria and met with Nnamdi Azikiwe, who published a regional newspaper, the *West African Pilot*. Azikiwe was a primary leader in the liberation movement in Nigeria, and was very partial to African Americans. He had attended Lincoln University in the U.S., several years before Kwame Nkrumah of Ghana attended the same African American college. Azikiwe was a prime example of the inaccuracy of the picture so often painted that Africans somehow don't like or don't understand African Americans. His secretary was an African American, and he believed in the technological transfer of information from one society to the other. So there was Bayard–young, dynamic, charismatic–and Azikiwe thought that he could really be very helpful. But in San Francisco, Bayard was arrested on a charge of homosexuality, and was kicked out of the Fellowship of Reconciliation. Though Bayard eventually became Executive Secretary of the War Resisters League after some months, at the time he suggested that Bill Sutherland go to Nigeria in his stead to assist in the editing of the *West African Pilot*.

"Everybody was knuckling under to McCarthy," Bill recalls, "and I had a vision of Africa so idealistic that it almost prevented me from getting there!" Bill's view was that the Western and Northern world had made it's greatest contribution in technology (the "world without"), while the Eastern world had reached its highest attainment in the development of a deep spirituality (the "world within"). Africa itself, in his view, had both of these elements present, but would contribute a new dimension of human warmth–a warmth which still remained after centuries of slavery and colonialism.

Not everybody agreed with Bill's vision. A.J. Muste, for example, felt that Bill had gotten off on the wrong foot. According to A.J.'s analysis, Africa would have to go through various social and economic stages, including industrialism, before Africans would be ready to reach a revolutionary potential.

"The process of social change in the U.S. or Africa," Bill suggested, "was not as clear as all that–not as clear as conventional Marxist analysis. I compared A.J.'s logic to playing the piano. He was reading music and playing on the white and black keys; I was going to try to play not on the keys, but in the cracks."

Meanwhile, in England, *Peace News* editor Hugh Brock, who was active with the Movement for Colonial Freedom, had introduced Bill to the Pan-African doyen George Padmore.[2] Padmore was a Trinadadian by birth, an intellectual who had become a mentor to the burgeoning West African freedom movements. A leading Marxist in the 1920s and '30s, Padmore lived in Moscow as a distinguished member of the Comintern, but broke with the Soviets in the years prior to World War Two over their "united front against fascism" position; he argued that the struggle against imperialism in Africa should not be sacrificed to the struggle against fascism in Europe. To George Padmore, Bill's idealistic visions about Africa's indigenous spiritual/scientific mix were ridiculous. The only way forward was to beat the colonists at their own game: use them, get their technology, steal their power as they had stolen ours.

"Luckily for me," Bill observed wryly, "Padmore also had a sentimental streak: a Pan-African of whatever stripe might prove useful to the cause!" During the first Lancaster House Conference on Nigerian Independence, Azikiwe came to London, and Padmore appointed Bill to be the correspondent for the *West African Pilot*. He began to do the job that he planned to continue in Nigeria, fully expecting to get a travel and work visa.

But there were unexplainable delays. Bill's applications simply would not get processed. The British colonial office was still in charge of all migration to and from Nigeria. Eventually, it became clear that they had a dossier on Bill and didn't want him to be in their colonies. During the waiting process, Padmore brought Bill "into the fold," introducing him to other Pan-Africanists and setting him up to be what they called a "back-room boy," helping out behind the scenes.

"One memorable afternoon," Bill recalls, "Padmore had me meet him at a sidewalk café in Paris, where he was discussing politics with African American author Richard Wright. Wright had just begun working on the book that was to become *Black Power*, and was filled with exciting stories about his recent trip to the Gold Coast."

Bill himself was still waiting to reach the shores of Africa.

* * *

As the twentieth century draws to a close, the computer and telecommunications advances of the present generation portend potential changes for the next generation that are truly revolutionary in scope. From the breakdown of national boundaries to the shifting of material resources and financial structures, the focus of grassroots progressive movements for social change must surely be re-thought. Though the interconnected roots of violence throughout the world–racism, sexism, capitalism, heterosexism, ageism, and the like–seem to carry on without pause, one must ponder whether the prediction of the great scholar and activist Dr. W.E.B. DuBois will hold true even into the next millennium; whether the problem of race will still play a key role in twenty-first century society.

Still, as a young white man from New York City, a Jewish boy of East European ancestry with no recent lineage to

Africa save the centuries of servitude in Egypt and the bond all humans share to that cradle of advanced civilization, it seemed presumptuous of me to want to develop such a close collegial relationship with Pan-Africanist Bill Sutherland. In the 1990s especially, with all the hoopla regarding troubled Black–Jewish relations, such a bond should apparently have been at least a little strained. Yet these last years of work and travel, throughout Africa, the U.S., and the Caribbean, have only seen our collaboration strengthen, with this book, as it's primary goal. In some ways, our connection has been based on politics before personality, on our ideology and experiences, though developed from different perspectives at very different time periods.

My name, Matt Meyer, became known in New York left circles when I decided to publicly resist the Selective Service registration program enacted by President Jimmy Carter years after the formal draft had been stopped in the 1970s, in response to the massive U.S. anti-war movement. Carter, in his bid for re-election, was trying to prove that, despite his reputation as a liberal, he too could be tough on the Russians. Registration, like Carter's presidential bid, was an abject failure, with hundreds of thousands of eighteen-year-olds quietly defying registration in one way or another. The ineffective program remains on the books to this day, despite bipartisan objections and a general ignoring of the process, but back in 1980 it was a big deal to publicly announce one's plans to resist. There was no sense that the few of us "going public" wouldn't become government examples of bad behavior, and be subject to the five years and ten thousand dollars fine that the federal felony of resistance held with it. In fact, a little over a dozen of us ever served any time at all, but television interviews and photos in *Rolling Stone* magazine[3] had made me a minor movement celebrity amongst the predominantly white peace groups.

I introduce myself because, in providing the context for the pages that follow, some sense of the cast of characters is necessary. My participation in this book began largely because of my draft resistance, which led me to the national office of the War Resisters League, that seventy-five-year-old organization committed to nonviolent direct action and a

Gandhian philosophy of which Bayard and Bill had both been active adherents. Immersing myself in movement activities, I struggled to find relevance in the undergraduate courses I was enrolled in at the time. Attending the 1982 War Resisters International (WRI) Triennial in Italy was my turning point: here I would meet resisters from every corner of the globe.

Much to my naive amazement and chagrin, however, almost no representatives were present from outside of Western Europe. No comrades from Africa, Latin America, or Asia were in attendance–save for two outspoken Indian activists from the land of Gandhi himself! This not-very-international Triennial, combined with the critiques I was hearing back at home from groups like the Black Veterans for Social Justice, convinced me of the racism and divisions so deeply embedded within our peace efforts. My academic studies turned toward African history and politics, while my activist work turned, in part, to the search for historical or practical bridges that could be built or strengthened. In time, I was led to Bill, the man with whom I remain honored to share this book's authorship.

* * *

Though Bill and I have both observed and participated in the political scene from a number of different vantage points and time periods, the decision to make this book a collection of stories and experiences rather than a detailed historical review grew out of our own self-acknowledged strengths and weaknesses. Viewing ourselves primarily as activists, we quickly moved away from an attempt to re-visit the story of the decolonization of the African continent from a strictly chronological and scientific point of view. Our approach has been experiential and eclectic, moving from personalities and places in a somewhat idiosyncratic way.

On the other hand, this is not fundamentally a collection of the experiences comprising the life of Bill Sutherland. Despite pleas for such a book from diverse and sundry corners of the globe, Bill would have none of it. In his evaluation, there are enough dull biographies of this type on the market; adding another would not significantly contribute to the movements he's committed his life to building. In addition, early on in the writing process Bill insisted (in no uncertain terms) that I take on the role of narrator; one learns at a young age, in African society at least, to respect one's elders! Though Bill's stories provide the central design through which this tapestry is woven, the book chronicles the experiences of the African leaders, with a focused eye on philosophies, strategies, and tactics employed in achieving freedom.

We began the discussions in the early 1990s, noting that past sacrifices and present suffering, misery, and death in many parts of the continent cried out for a sober assessment of strategies, tactics, and goals of the last five decades of struggle. The lessons learned by the elder statesmen and grassroots activists who led these struggles could provide vital analysis for a more stable, peaceful, and productive future. We believed then, and continue to believe, that a candid review of the importance of methods of revolutionary struggle–including nonviolence and non-military alternatives–is needed if we are to achieve a humane society of justice and peace. This perspective has been put forward by Bill throughout his own fifty years in Africa, and provides a framework for the questions we asked of the leaders we were able to talk with.

We have used Bill's life and his life-long relationships as a backdrop for creating dialogues with those leaders whom he or we have been in closest contact. Dialogue, in fact, is the center point of what this project means to us: both in the process of creating and in the process of distributing this book. If Bill's experiences provide the book's spine, then our open dialogues are its life-blood and voice. What we have learned and continue to learn, and what we most hope to share, has come from the creation of meaningful spaces for frank discussion.

Due to several factors involved in experiential writing, we have been both graced with rare access and limited by personal and logistical roadblocks. Our ability to spend long hours at the homes of Julius Nyerere and Kenneth Kaunda, or to take hours away from the matters of state pressing on Zimbabwean Foreign and Labor Minister Nathan Shamuyarira or Namibian President Sam Nujoma were undoubtedly connected to Bill's long personal histories with these people long before any of them were in positions of national or international power. Save for some Ghanaian contacts made by Bill's oldest daughter Esi, former Deputy Minister of Education, and for some connections of my own in South Africa and Mozambique, all of the discussions were arranged through Bill's ever-present and all-inclusive green box of index cards.

Because of the nature of the network of elder statesmen, however, it is true that the majority of interviews we taped were with the men who led their organizations and governments. The extraordinary work done in maintaining and building those struggles and countries on the local level–sometimes by men, but more often by women–were a minor part of our base of current contacts. In addition, an increasing number of new grassroots efforts, often small but politically significant, of women's organizations and women leaders of environmental, human rights, and party groupings, have come to our attention. For similar reasons, much of French-speaking Africa has not been at the center of these conversations.

The realities of where Bill has been and who he knows and has known serve both to deepen and to limit this work. A comprehensive review of nonviolent social change throughout the continent is not the subject of this book, though these authors would like to openly encourage the writing of such a collection.

Nevertheless, over the course of the last eight years, in visiting over a dozen countries, we have held meetings with over a hundred activists and leaders. Our questions have not been based on a strict formula, though our basic outline and focus has remained the same. We attempted to ground our own and our hosts' reflections on a number of questions. What is the relationship between means and ends? What strategies, we pondered, were most effective in obtaining the truest forms of lasting liberation? What were the consequences, if any, of certain tactics as compared with others? Which strategies or philosophies were or were not employed and why?

What role did locale, colonial history, and historical moment play in all this? What has national independence meant for the ordinary African person? What has been or will be the role of the modern nation-state in Africa? What visions exist for the future of Africa? How, specifically, were the methods of nonviolence and/or armed struggle used in various circumstances? In what ways, we wondered, were they essentially unconnected or contradictory options? In what ways were they fully complementary or strategically co-exisistant?

In many instances, these questions led us to a series of additional questions regarding the uses of the military in society or the role of violence in society more generally. In some conversations, those we were interviewing went off on tangents that seemed fascinating, but only faintly related to our topics. Still other times left us reviewing discussions with quite different answers and perspectives from one another. It is our intention that the richness of these diversions and disagreements come out in the text presented.

Though this book impressionistically reflects upon contemporary events, it is clearly not a journalistic accounting of our times. No broad dialogue on forty-plus years of struggle could both present the often subtle and far-reaching analysis included herein and adequately present the latest facts, figures, and fortunes. We have no doubt that relevant and exciting new developments will be taking place on the very topics touched on in this book, just as the print is being laid on the pages. We similarly expect, however, that the general attitudes and underlying issues at the roots of peace and conflict and freedom will remain fundamentally the same.

* * *

Just as some of our political goals are centered upon bridging the gaps between diverse peoples, so too this book aims at appealing to several different audiences. On the one hand, the unique experiences of an African American who has truly and successfully lived the Pan-African experience, who has made of his life and politics an experiment in the ideals of struggle, unity and peace, these stories, we hope, will provide insight and interest for the many Americans of African descent, in search of a deeper sense of identity.

In addition, though not a scholarly text, we expect that the frank discussions contained herein will be of interest to academics and African political leaders. Snippets of behind-the-scenes conversations, never reported upon considerations, or new reflections on the parts of public leaders, should provide some useful insights for Africanists in the university and the parliamentary sectors.

We have also made a conscious attempt to write this book in a widely accessible fashion, such that those who have little or no knowledge of African history can still find some fascination here. Our focus upon strategy and tactics, with a special emphasis on nonviolence, suggests that grassroots activists–especially those espousing pacifist viewpoints–might look closely at the examples and questions raised throughout these chapters. Though the organized peace movements of the north have generally ignored African politics and history, it is apparent that the reverse does not hold true. The uses of nonviolence–at least on a tactical level–are documented here, with a focus upon evaluating their effectiveness vis-a-vis alternative modes of struggle. As progressive movements throughout the world seek to redefine their ideologies, tactics and strategies, we hope and expect that activists well beyond the African solidarity variety will find much to discuss and critique through these pages.

If the publication of this book can make a small contribution in furthering dialogues between broad groupings of people–from Africa to the Americas, from academia to the activist sector–we will indeed feel like we have accomplished one of our primary goals.

* * *

Ghana, as the first country to obtain post-World War Two independence, where Bill had settled several years prior to the landmark transition of power, and the country his three children still call home, seemed an appropriate place to start our journey. There were two main perspectives we wanted to explore. First, the campaigns of Kwame Nkrumah, leading Pan-Africanist and first Ghanaian President, were largely based on what he called Positive Action, his version of Gandhi's soul-force nonviolence. Though Nkrumah was overthrown by a military coup, and later took the position that armed struggle would be necessary in uniting the continent against colonialism and neocolonialism, the effects of the early pivotal freedom struggles on later generations needed further investigation. The often undocumented coming together of the African, European and us movements to protest the French testing of nuclear weapons in the Sahara is described in detail. In addition, the more recent politics of current President Jerry Rawlings seemed a necessary source for a more complete understanding of this key West African nation. The reports on these explorations make up our second chapter, "Pan-Africanism, Ghana, and the Politics of Positive Action."

Our third chapter, Mwalimu, Tanzania, and the Meanings of Freedom, takes us chronologically through Bill's travels from Ghana to Tanzania in the early 1960's. With the shift in continental focus from West to East Africa, Tanzania became the center of Pan-African liberation forces beginning in this period. Reviewing Bill's memories of the mid-1960's, we focused our dialogues around the premiere African statesman, former Tanzanian President Mwalimu Julius K. Nyerere. Looking not just at Tanzania, but at the developments throughout the turbulent decades, this chapter links closely with our fourth, "Kenneth Kaunda, Zambia, and the Riddles of Violence and Nonviolence." Kaunda, more than any other head of state, spoke and wrote extensively of his philosophical commitment to nonviolence. His questions and critiques of absolute pacifism, documented in his own book *The Riddle of Violence* and in our discussions together, are essential for an understanding of the practical obstacles faced in Zambia and beyond.

With political tides shifting in the latter 1960's towards a greater adherence of the practices of people's war, our fifth chapter covers the countries of southern Africa, which developed liberation movements utilizing various types and degrees of armed resistance. "National Liberation and the Struggles Against Colonialism in Southern Africa" looks at the examples of Mozambique, Zimbabwe, and Namibia in particular, comparing the pre-independence policies and outcomes especially as they relate to strategies used. The post-independence reflections of the leaders of these movements and others proved to be most fascinating, dispelling many common myths and misunderstandings. The complexities and contradictions of the case of pre- and post-apartheid South Africa serve to highlight our sixth and largest chapter, "Turning Points: South Africa and the Process of Liberation." Employing a wide range of philosophies, strategies and tactics amongst a diverse grouping of people in what was the continents longest fight for political freedom, the case of South Africa provided an affirmation that the series of questions we were raising were truly timely and relevant given today's changing definitions of revolutionary struggle.

"The Pan-African Experience: Glimpses through the Decades," the seventh chapter, brings us back to the Pan-African vision that began Bill Sutherland's life journey. In addition to chronicling his personal interactions with Martin Luther King, Malcolm X, Robert Franklin Williams, and others, it provides his own insights and experiences with the Pan-African Congresses that have been held over the past forty years. Be it on the inter-governmental level, such as through our dialogue with Salim A. Salim, Secretary General of the Organization of African Unity (OAU), or on the people-to-people level of local action, the state of modern Pan-Africanism is assessed with an eye on our basic concerns. "Pan-Africanism Continues!," chronicles some recent international experiences effecting peace research and action throughout the continent.

Our conclusion, "The Future of Nonviolence, and Revolution in Africa," attempts to draw out these concerns in a clear and summarized manner, and to state our varying analysis on the ways forward for progressive social change. We provide examples of positive ways in which we believe people can make a difference, and help to build a better tomorrow.

* * *

The themes of this book are multi-faceted and interconnected, and grow primarily out of our political principles and perspectives. While advocates of the power of nonviolence, we have never been among those who equate nonviolence with non-action, or who see nonviolence as the opposite of revolution. Just as pacifism has been confused by some with a form of passivity or pacification, we are uncomfortable with the negativism in the word "non-violence" itself, preferring the more positive approach of Gandhi's Satyagraha.[4] A nonviolence that ultimately upholds or excuses the status quo is fundamentally false; it helps perpetuate violence. Our main concerns have been the overwhelming structural and institutional roots of conflict–such as racism, sexism, and capitalism–which in themselves constitute the greatest violence of our times.

As commonly defined, nonviolence is no more than a momentary tactic, which can therefore be used for both revolutionary or reformist efforts. But as far as we are concerned, the creation of a truly nonviolent world would call for total global revolution. In this light, we have often identified with Che Guevara's assessment that one cannot be a true revolutionary without great feelings of love. Our own perspective is not that far off from Mao Tse Tung's assessment that weapons are not the decisive factor in determining victory or defeat: "it is people, not things, that are decisive."[5] We agree with the Chinese and Indian notions that no revolution, whatever the methods used, can take place without the spiritual transformation of the people.

We strongly believe that the institutionalized violence of society cannot be eradicated without revolutionary social upheaval, and we are also well aware of examples of narrow-minded reformists among both the pacifist and armed-struggle camps. If we are to achieve our goals, we believe that dialogue is essential, especially among all those searching for truly revolutionary alternatives.

Defining our terms–the true meaning of nonviolence, armed struggle, or revolution–must be taken more seriously. Looking at the reality rather than the rhetoric of what has been done and of the relationship between cause and effect is an ongoing task. We have tried to be careful and objective in our use of language, recognizing the cultural, linguistic, and political complexity of the issues involved.

* * *

"OBI NKA BI"–a stylized image of two fishes or centipedes attempting to bite each other's tails, one of the symbols used in the Adinkra cloths of the Akan peoples of West Africa–is the closest phrase Amowi Sutherland Phillips could come up with on short notice. During a brief stay on the Caribbean island of Jamaica, where Bill's daughter and son-in-law live and work, dinner conversation turned to the meaning of nonviolence, and to the words that one might use to express this concept in Amowi and Allen's native Ghanaian language of Fanti. "One Love"–the unity of peoples, especially African peoples–is more easily heard in this land of Bob Marley, where the rhythms of reggae sway with the trees and most people still remember Marley's ability to join the hands of the political leaders in fierce opposition–Manley and Seaga–on stage in concert for a momentary display of togetherness. But nonviolence in any language is a tougher concept to express or demonstrate or define.

In English, nonviolence has always been an inadequate expression of the Gandhian term Satyagraha, roughly translated from Hindi as "soul force." For Gandhi, spiritual power is the strongest force in the universe and the basis of all transformation, social and personal. His struggle to keep his deeply held beliefs from becoming dogma is reflected in the title of his autobiography, *The Story of My Experiments with Truth*. But his experiments, like all others worthy of the name, were carried out as though the premise were absolutely true. The best known examples of satyagraha have been the strikes, boycotts, fasts, and mass demonstrations associated with the civil disobedience campaigns to free India from British domination. Gandhi, however, made the foundation of his movement human relations and development at the local level. For him, real and lasting social change would come about through the establishment of what he called "village republics." At this level, it was not necessary to achieve independence from Britain for the people to institute fundamental changes.[6] We have difficulty in relating to a number of his experiments in the areas of health and personal morality, but we fully identify with his basic premise that real and lasting change can come about only through struggle rooted in the positive aspects of the values and cultures of the people involved.

Some aspects of the present movements that we can identify with, apparently coming from the North and West (pro-democracy, environmentalism, women's liberation, human rights), can actually be found in the history of Africa. This aspect of their history, all too often, is being rejected by Africans in their rush to "catch up" with the more industrialized nations, and has long been ignored and denied in Europe and the U.S. But what of these roots of democratic and peaceful structures and processes in Africa and the so-called Third World? As far as nonviolence is concerned, Allen Phillips' answer is quick but common: "There is no such equivalent concept to be found in Fanti."

"OBI NKA BI," the creatures locked in connection with one another's tails, translates roughly as: "Bite not one another." It has been used for centuries as a warning against backbiting and to advocate harmony, peace, unity, forgiveness, and fair play.[7] Some interpretations suggest that the symbol represents the call to not attack unless unduly provoked, to not begin the cycle of biting. But, Amowi asks, isn't nonviolence the commitment to not bite under any circumstances whatsoever? Nonviolence, Bill replies, is not about a commitment to non-confrontation; confrontation is absolutely necessary for truly revolutionary soul-force action. The difference lies in the manner of biting! And so the dialogue continues.

Unity–"one love"–at this juncture of time may seem like a utopian vision. The break-up of traditional republics throughout the world, the ethnic fighting that seems to be taking place by tribes in Europe and around the globe, continues simultaneously with the consolidation of international capital. All of the movements that we are affiliated with or dialogue with share in a search for a way out of this morass. We hope that you will find this book a contribution to ongoing dialogues–towards the search for unity and a vision of peace with justice–upon which we believe our very survival depends.

NOTES

1. Interview/dialogue with Bill Sutherland, September 9, 1993, Brooklyn, New York.

Note: As a large part of the book relies upon direct quotes or information from primary sources, these endnotes will cite the beginning of an interview section only. All further quotes from that section are to be assumed as taken from the same cited interview.

2. *Peace News for Nonviolent Revolution* still publishes on a monthly basis, at: 5 Caledonian Road, London N1 9DY, Britain. A recent issue (*Peace News*, No. 2434, February 1999, p. 10) chronicles Hugh Brock's commitment to justice in Africa, as commemorated in the opening of a Hugh Brock Collection library on nonviolence at the Mindolo Ecumenical Foundation in Zambia (P.O. Box 21493, Kitwe, Zambia).
3. Susan Jaffe, "Is Reagan Dodging the Draft?" *Rolling Stone*, No. 350, p. 9, Straight Arrow Publishers, New York, August 20, 1981.
4. M.K. Gandhi, *An Autobiography* or *The Story of My Experiments With Truth*, Navajivan Publishing House, Ahmedabad, 1927. Gandhi attributed the birth of the term Satyagraha to struggles in South Africa, around 1906. He noted that Europeans interpreted the term "passive resistance" too narrowly, and stated that "it was clear that a new word must be coined by the Indians to designate their struggle." (p. 239). Later, his developing thoughts were compiled in *The Science of Satyagraha* (edited and published by Anand T. Hingorani), Bharatiya Vidya Bhavan, Bombay, 1970.
5. Mao Tse Tung, *On People's War*, Foreign Language Press, Peking, 1967. The full quote, "Every Communist must grasp the truth, 'Political power grows out of the barrel of a gun,'" comes from Mao's essay "Problems of War and Strategy," November 6, 1938, *Selected Works*, Vol. II. Earlier that year, Mao had written: "Weapons are an important factor in war, but not the decisive factor; it is people, not things, that are decisive. The contest of strength is not only a contest of military and economic power, but also a contest of human power and morale" (from "On Protracted War," May 1938, *Selected Works*, Vol. II). An interesting review of the strategic implications of these quotes took place as A.J. Muste replied to the writings of Chinese Communist

Minister of Defense Marshal Lin Piao in his famous essay, "Who Has The Spiritual Atom Bomb," *Liberation*, November 1965. As Muste noted. The phrase "spiritual atom bomb" was actually coined by Lin Piao; this essay was recently reprinted and is available in pamphlet form from the A.J. Muste Memorial Institute, 339 Lafayette Street, New York, NY 10012.

6. Bharatan Kumarappa, *Capitalism, Socialism or Villagism?*, Sarva Seva Sangh Prakashan, Rajghat, 1945. This volume, with a foreword by Gandhi, details the Indian movement's views on the village republics. These ideas were adapted for post-independence issues in Jayaprakash Narayan's *Towards Total Revolution: India and Her Problems*, Popular Prakashan, Bombay, 1978.
7. W. Bruce Willis, *The Adinkra Dictionary*, The Pyramid Complex, Washington, DC, 1998; Alfred Kofi Quarcoo, *The Language of Adinkra Symbols*, Sebewie Ventures (Publications), Legon, 1972.

CHAPTER 2

PAN-AFRICANISM, GHANA, AND THE POLITICS OF POSITIVE ACTION

When it became clear that the British colonial authorities were blocking Bill's entrance to Nigeria, he decided to change plans and head for the Gold Coast. He cut through some red tape, with the assistance of George Padmore, by sending support letters to Kwame Nkrumah from British M.P. Reginald Sorenson and Padmore himself. The letters were hand-delivered to Nkrumah by Arthur E. Morgan, a Quaker who had headed the Tennessee Valley Authority. Morgan had been invited to the Gold Coast as a consultant to the Volta River Project, an economic initiative to help utilize the vast natural resource in the north of the country. Since the Gold Coast had control of its own immigration by December of 1953, Bill soon had his visa.

"When the ship arrived in Accra," Bill recalls, "a British civil servant–impeccably dressed in white shorts, Boy Scout–white socks with a pipe stuck in one–presented me with a letter from Nkrumah's office welcoming me to the Gold Coast. Accra, the capital city, had no docking facilities. I was put into what was known as a 'mammy chair', swung over the side of the ship, and lowered into a huge canoe. The scene seemed out of some old adventure movie! We, the passengers for Accra, were rowed ashore by singing Black rowers, muscles rippling. When we got to shallow water, we were carried piggyback to dry land.

"The letter from Nkrumah apologized that he himself was not able to be there; he explained that a major West African conference was in progress. I was taken to the Seaview Hotel, where a room had been reserved for me, and the next thing I knew there was a car pulling up, with chauffeur saying 'You are to come with us.' I was driven to another car, and upon entering it, I saw Azikiwe, met Nkrumah, and was told that the three of us were going to a major rally for West African unity! Events, by that point, were moving at a rapid pace."[1]

In actuality, after that first momentous day, Bill lost a certain amount of contact with the very busy Nkrumah. It might have been, to a great extent, because of the agreement he had made to try to establish pacifist chapters–of War Resisters International or International Fellowship of Reconciliation–on the African continent. Some of his Quaker contacts, Walter Birmingham for example, offered him living quarters. Things might have turned out much differently if Bill had "thrown himself at the mercy of the courts" – and asked the CPP for lodgings.

Bill's own main objective was to work in support of the African liberation movements. There was also the question of finding a bread-and-butter job. Discovering that the Gold Coast was completely tied in with the British educational system, he soon learned that they looked down upon the U.S. approach and qualifications. A few weeks after he arrived, however, he was invited to go down to what was called New Year School, organized by the School for Adult Education by the University. There Bill met Efua Theodora Morgue, a Ghanaian teacher and poet whom he married some six months later. He also met some people who were interested in building up education in the eastern region, including some special kinds of practical education for young people.

Not finding any employment elsewhere, Bill got in touch with the States, particularly with colleagues at the American Committee on Africa, which he had helped to found. They agreed to give him a subsistence wage to travel to the eastern region and work on the educational project. Efua, in the meantime, was working as a teacher in Takoradi, which is in the extreme east. Together they set up a school, in an area called Tsito Awudome. It was to be a secondary school, which would have, as an experiment, an Antioch-style work-study project for teenagers. Two-thirds of the student's time would be spent on conventional studies, but during one-third of their time they would go to the government's health department, social service department, or works projects, learning through the experience of actual work. This was absolutely anathema to the British-trained people. They didn't want to have anything to do with it! Efua and Bill worked at this project for several years, but against great obstacles and great resistance by the government's educational system.

* * *

My own work as Multicultural Coordinator for New York City's Alternative High Schools and Programs had come to a close for the year as I left for Ghana in July of 1992. Arriving in Accra a day before Bill, I was met at the airport by Bill's eldest daughter, Esi Sutherland Addy, a dynamic woman who herself was in the education field. Esi at the time was Ghana's Deputy Minister in Charge of Higher Education, working directly with the Minister of Education and other top government officials. After my long plane ride, the VIP reception I received due to Esi's position was much appreciated. It was a relief to chat with Esi and other members of Bill's family, while Ghana protocol officials handled immigration and customs formalities. I was then driven to an elegantly appointed bungalow where Esi's husband, J.P. Addy, an official of the Volta River Authority, had arranged our stay.

The next day, Esi, and I went over our list of appointments and general schedule. In addition to her work in government, Esi had many contacts from her days as the founding chairperson of the management committee of the Dr. W.E.B. Du Bois Memorial Center for Pan-African Culture. The Center, set up in the former residence of the great

African American intellectual, contains many of his old books and research notes, and stands not only as an open conference center, but also as a living tribute to the Pan-African connection.

Most important for me, however, in the time we had before Bill's plane was due to arrive from Tanzania, was a visit we paid to the newly opened Kwame Nkrumah Memorial Park. At the dedication several weeks earlier, Namibian President Sam Nujoma and South African leader Oliver Tambo (both of whom Bill and I were later to meet with), gave strong testimonials on the importance of Nkrumah to the liberation of the continent. The erection of this monument in Accra was clear evidence of Nkrumah's restoration in his own country to his rightful position as Father of the Ghanaian nation.

My own knowledge of Nkrumah's significance came both from my extensive readings, as well as from anecdotes that Bill had shared with me years before, based upon his past personal experiences.

The significant literary and political figure from Trinidad, C.L.R. James, had been a friend and neighbor of Bill's in Manhattan during the 1940's, and their association had continued in Africa, the USA, and England, until the death of James in 1988. Arguably one of the greatest modern historians, James himself, at the time of Nkrumah's death in 1972, assessed Nkrumah's impact alongside of that of Lenin, Gandhi and Mao as one of the outstanding twentieth century figures attempting to "complete the emancipation of all underdeveloped peoples."[2] James, on the other hand, did not hesitate to criticize Nkrumah for what he considered serious blunders, especially Nkrumah's failure to recognize that democracy was not simply a matter of the rights of an opposition party, but in some way must involve the active participation of the population.

Bill repeatedly heard the story of how James introduced Nkrumah to George Padmore. After Nkrumah's university studies in the U.S., he planned to study law in London. James wrote a letter of introduction to Padmore, describing Nkrumah as a young African determined to "throw the Europeans out of Africa" but "not very bright!" James felt that Nkrumah was clear on issues of colonialism, but "talked nonsense" on issues of economics, needing Padmore to educate him as much as possible.[3]

Padmore's role as Nkrumah's mentor soon turned to one of colleague and advisor, especially as they planned together the Fifth Pan-African Congress, held in Manchester, England in 1945. Nkrumah's central role, along with the presence of Kenya's Jomo Kenyatta, Northern Rhodesia's Harry Nkumbula, and Peter Abrahams of South Africa, indicated that the torch of leadership was being passed from the Africans of the Diaspora to the Africans of the continent. It was not long after the conference–in 1947–that Nkrumah was called to the Gold Coast by the United Gold Coast Convention (UGCC), a body of middle-class Africans (doctors, lawyers, retired civil servants, and some traditional chiefs). Between 1947 and 1951, Kwame Nkrumah set in motion a people's movement for independence which went far beyond the original intention of the UGCC.

It is important to note that Nkrumah used several conclusions reached at the Fifth Pan-African Congress (PAC) as guidelines in leading the fight for freedom in the Gold Coast. First, the Congress declared that colonialism could only be eradicated through the concerted actions of the colonial peoples themselves. Secondly, it was clarified that the job of ending colonialism could not be done by a few intellectuals alone, but must be achieved through a mass movement and the creation of institutions responsive to the needs of the people. Finally, a principle was established that peaceful civil disobedience in the form of strikes and boycotts should be used in the struggle against colonialism. Violence, it was asserted, was not to be used unless circumstances made it the only viable option. The organizers of Fifth-PAC were clearly influenced by the successes of the Free India movement with which they had fraternal relations.

James followed events closely after the return of Nkrumah to the Gold Coast, and captured the spirit if not the details of the period. He claimed that Nkrumah discovered and unleashed immense latent power of the people and created organizations to harness this power. "To think that Nkrumah merely mobilized the people," James wrote, "is to misunderstand one of the great political achievements of our century." It was a crusade, a revivalist campaign.[4]

When Nkrumah began his work, the UGCC had barely thirteen branches where middle-class Blacks got together, talked and published a few documents.

The UGCC had been formed in the mid-1940s, calling for "legitimate and constitutional" means of ridding the Gold Coast of British control. As Nkrumah traveled ceaselessly in urban and rural areas, people joined by the thousands. A boycott of foreign goods opened 1948 with a new wave of direct action.

The conciliatory UGCC slogan of "Self-Government in the Shortest Time Possible" failed to capture the urgency of the moment. By 1949, Nkrumah had agreed to lead the Convention People's Party (CPP), initiated primarily by the youth within the UGCC, under the banner, "Self-Government Now." Nkrumah, who set up the *Accra Evening News* as a vehicle for communication and spreading information, was fined for contempt and several key activists and journalists were jailed. Maintaining their call for complete and immediate independence, however, the CPP initiated a campaign of Positive Action in January 1950.[5]

The Party organizers followed Nkrumah and set up village, city, and regional units. Schools were established for students and teachers expelled for political activities. The *Evening News* was besieged by news vendors, and 50,000 copies a day could have been sold in Accra, a town of 150,000 people, had the facilities to print that many been available. Although a large proportion of the population was illiterate, copies were passed from hand to hand. When the Party called for a rally, people came from far and near; though poverty-stricken, they were able to raise on the spot what were sometimes astonishing amounts of money. The freedom movement had become a way of existence, not something to be done in one's spare time. To Africans and people of African descent everywhere, James declared the name of Nkrumah had become a symbol of release from subordination to which they had been subjected for so many centuries.

Now, after forty years of change and transition, the name of Nkrumah was finally being restored to its full stature in the capitol of Accra. The creation of the Memorial Park, which I had just visited, felt like a triumphant honor after many years of vilification and neglect. Though Bill had missed the opening of the Park, his memories of the "old days"–from the time just following Nkrumah's election as "Leader of Government Business" under British authority in 1951 to the transition to full independence as re-named and re-claimed Ghana in 1957–were just waiting to be rekindled.

Bill arrived at the airport to a scene of much rejoicing; a family reunion of children and grandchildren was interspersed with the occasional "hello" and "good to see you back" from various travelers who recognized him. Once we got to the bungalow, we reviewed our list of people to meet, and began to form a plan of action which would both allow for discussion of the early days of Ghana's freedom struggle as well as bring us up-to-date on the contemporary issues facing Africa's first decolonized nation.

* * *

During the years following Bill's first arrival in the Gold Coast, the educational project that he and Efua were part of was facing more and more difficulty. On the other hand, things on the home front were a bit more productive. Efua and Bill had three children in this period: Esi was born in 1954; Ralph, named after Bill's conscientious-objector prison buddy, was born in 1955; Amowi was born in 1957. In addition, Dr. Marguerite Cartwright, a friend from the U.S., began to put Bill in touch with a Ghanaian she was close to–one of the "big three" of the CPP. In addition to Nkrumah and Kojo Botsio, Komla Agbeli Gbedema was one of the leaders of the independence organization and political party. Cartwright said that she could see how Bill, from her point of view, could have a very important role in working for Gbedema. As he prepared to become Ghana's first post-independence Finance Minister, he needed someone to be his private secretary. In her words, she said she was going to "knock their two heads together," and, according to Bill, that's exactly what she did! Bill worked for several years as Gbedema's right hand man.

Gbedema, unfortunately now deceased, first provided us with an "insiders" perspective on the nature of the struggles and events leading up to Ghana's independence. His association with Nkrumah went back to the late 1920s, when both attended Achimota, the most prestigious secondary school in the Gold Coast. They were personal friends, lived in the same dormitory, and Nkrumah apparently taught Gbedema–who was Ewe–the language of Nzima, from Nkrumah's region of the country. Though they parted company in 1930, Gbedema recalled their reunion in the late 1940s: "Someone mentioned that a fire brand named Nkrumah had come in from the United States. I wondered if this could be the same man. I went to a session of the Watson Commission, which had been set up by the British colonial government to investigate the violence that broke out at the Ex–Servicemen's March of 1948. Lo, it was he!"

Gbedema himself had an experience with the Watson Commission and with the demonstrations of 1948. In February of that year, an unarmed group of returned veterans staged a protest march on Christianbourg Castle, then the seat of colonial power. They had planned to simply present petitions stating their grievances: lack of jobs, minimal educational opportunities, and no chance to participate in the vital political and economic affairs of state. In the film documentary about the affair, which Gbedema loaned to us after our first dialogue session, the British Senior Police Officer, Major Imray, testified that he did indeed give the order to shoot upon the nonviolent group, once the ex-servicemen appeared ready to break through the police barricades. One of Imray's non-commissioned officers disobeyed his orders, not once, but twice. The Major seized one of his men's rifles and commenced firing himself! Imray killed three ex-servicemen, and wounded several others. This became the spark that caused riots and looting in Accra and several cities across the country.

On that particular day, Gbedema, who was working as a senior building contractor and lay preacher, was passing through the western section of Accra. As a witness to some of the looting, he gave testimony under oath to the Watson Commission on the cause of the riots. According to Gbedema, the looting was spontaneous and unorganized, and the people instinctively attacked the European stores. The colonial government tried to put the blame upon the African activists, but could not refute the evidence presented. The slogan, which grew out of this series of key incidents, was: "The Shooting was the Cause of the Looting."

Reclining with us at his home, in dark glasses and with a regal air, he reminisced about his preliminary involvement as a writer and organizer. He met with Nkrumah at the offices of the *Accra Evening News* and found that his old friend was sleeping on a grass mat in a corner of the press office. Inviting Nkrumah to become his houseguest, Gbedema was eventually convinced to become editor and treasurer of the newspaper and was one of two journalists imprisoned for writing "seditious articles." "In July 1949," Gbedema recalled, "soon after the inauguration of the CPP, the colonial government had wanted to get Nkrumah out of the way. He was the owner of the *Evening News* and therefore the manager of the paper. There was a matter in court that the paper had commented upon, for which he was allegedly in contempt of court. The court tried to use the technical legalities to charge and imprison him. The demonstration of the people around the court grounds prevented this; however, as the government thought there would be bigger trouble if they sent him to jail. Nkrumah's very presence stirred the whole of Accra. Thousands of people were milling around the court area, shouting. Some were uprooting young trees and shouting "Today be the day! Today be the day!" If the police had started attacking them, that would have been it.[6]

"The British judges fined Nkrumah three hundred pounds, which in those days was a lot of money, but could be found. They didn't send him to prison," Gbedema continued, "some well-wishers paid the fine so that he wouldn't have to go to jail.

"Two months later, I was–technically speaking–in the same position. Nkrumah was out of the country, and I was the manager-in-charge, controlling the paper. When I was served a summons on Friday, I was given six days to appear in court for being the man in charge when another article was published which was 'likely to cause alarm.' I went from my house, first to CPP headquarters, and then went to the courthouse at 9 p.m. In less then two hours after leaving my room, I was in prison. I was sentenced to six months hard labor, and later learned from the wardens that my cell was the cell that they had prepared for Nkrumah!"

In 1950, in the midst of the UGCC and CPP campaigns and repression, Nkrumah published the declarative pamphlet, *What I Mean By Positive Action*, in which he called for intensified nonviolent methods of struggle. "As regards the final stage of Positive Action, namely Nation-wide Non-violent Sit-down-at-home Strikes, Boycotts and Non-co-operation," Nkrumah wrote, "they will constitute the last resort." Nkrumah gave recognition to the successful nonviolent methods used in the struggle for the independence of India. Later, Nkrumah commented, "We had no guns, but even if we had, the circumstances were such that non–violent alternatives were open to us, and it was necessary to try them before resorting to other means."[7]

Gbedema confirmed the organizing philosophy of the time: "The Gandhian movement was our model. Some considered Positive Action a strategy or tactic, others a principle," Gbedema stated. "As for me, I had a Quaker teacher named Charles Deacon in the town of Achimota, who taught me that violence begets violence and in the process you may not achieve what you want."[8]

When the CPP launched Positive Action, scarcely six months after its own formation, the situation in the country was more than tense. January 1950 marked the beginning of a Trade Union Congress–initiated general strike, and the British authorities declared a state of emergency. This time, Nkrumah himself was jailed, along with most of the top CPP leadership, but their stature was only magnified. In fact, Nkrumah and Gbedema were called the Gandhi and Nehru of Africa. Several African parties, including the UGCC, were preparing electoral campaigns for a nation-wide constitutional and legislative vote, scheduled for February 1951. The CPP, though organizationally hampered by the massive arrests, continued to emphasize the grassroots. Positive Action on the local level was designed as confrontational direct action, aimed at mobilizing ordinary citizens in such a way that would draw sympathetic international attention.

Gbedema had just completed his prison sentence as Nkrumah was jailed. The British called for the elections to take place while Nkrumah was still in prison, providing Gbedema with a great opportunity and responsibility. Gbedema proved to be a gifted organizer, and he was always careful to recognize Nkrumah as the leader as he regrouped the CPP–first clandestinely, then publicly. A year passed before the state of emergency was lifted and public meetings were allowed; the first openly called CPP meeting drew 30,000 people! Gbedema claims that he introduced the "prisoner graduate cap"–similar to one worn by political prisoners in India–as a badge of honor for those fighting for freedom. Britain's parliamentary system ironically allowed Nkrumah to run for office while in prison, and he won an astounding victory. He was literally led from prison to the government offices, to become, as stated, Leader of Government Business.

The achievement of internal self-government through Positive Action seemed a phenomenal success for Gandhian strategy as we have defined it. The British government apparently conceded an irreversible step towards independence of the Gold Coast in a fraction of the time it had taken a comparable process to take place in India. However, what had really happened and how? We put a series of questions to Gbedema, to some of the younger generation of dialogue participants, and to ourselves. To what extent had the struggle really been nonviolent? What was the decisive factor in bringing about change? What was the role of the British government? Did external forces play a role? Was action done on a principled or pragmatic basis? In other words, had the strategy worked?

In Gbedema's view, it had worked–not perfectly, but in some key ways. "Positive Action," he reflected, "was a show of force–not violent, but cool action–to bring down the government down and get power. It did work, because it stopped the violence from escalating." On the other hand, he felt that the British officer who killed the ex-servicemen "opened the gate for independence"–the resulting riots caused the British to act more quickly than they would have otherwise. Gbedema also asserted that Positive Action worked because the British "had a conscience" and, under the scheme of internal self-government and international allegiance to the Commonwealth, the Gold Coast would still be a protectorate under the British crown. He quoted Queen Victoria, who apparently stated that she would "rather have the hearts of the people of the Gold Coast than their land."

Kwesi Botchway and Kojo Tsikata held views about the British that had some clear differences from those of their elder colleague. Botchway, an economist, and Ghana's Minister of Finance at the time of our meeting had grown up during the independence struggles. Tsikata, a youth who had taken Nkrumah's Pan-Africanist vision to heart and traveled throughout the continent, was among Ghana's top governmental leadership, serving as Member in Charge of Foreign Affairs and Security. Esi Sutherland Addy also added her commentary.

Regarding the British "good conscience" and the view that the British "handed" Ghana her independence, Dr. Botchway laughed: "People who say that just don't know their history. The struggle started before Nkrumah and went on until 1957. It's a hell of a thing to say that the colonists were tired and just wanted to give up. They shot people dead. No, it was not a case of a tired empire giving in. There was a bit of a weariness, yes, but it didn't stop them from fighting, first with repression and–when that didn't work–trying to steer people away from Nkrumah and nonviolence so that they could make their peace with a more reformist and conciliatory crowd. By the time the British realized that Nkrumah could not be defeated, it was too late to make a deal with the so-called moderates."[9]

Captain Tsikata thought that the British may have calculated that instead of taking a violent response to the demands for freedom, they could better contain and defuse the anti-colonial struggle in other, more devious ways. "Nkrumah was very successful in using mass nonviolent activities against colonial rule," he noted, "and in building up the Convention Peoples Party as a mass organization, a broadly-based mass organization, to spearhead the anti-colonial struggle. Our leaders had to manage to overcome the British attempt at containment. If you look at the struggle in Ghana, at every stage the British had tried to minimize the thrust of the anti-colonial push by Nkrumah. Nkrumah had to find a way to accept their limitations, but at the same time find a way around them. I don't think that the British would have given a second thought to suppressing Nkrumah violently," Tsikata concluded, "if they thought that it would pay off."[10]

Esi Sutherland Addy observed that the potential threat of violence accompanying nonviolent actions may cause the "establishment" to act. If there are 10,000 people, for example, coming down the street in protest, it is not because of what is written on their placards that the authorities will take note. "Ten thousand people," said Esi, "can actually come and hurt you!"[11]

C.L.R. James noted that, in the case of India, the British government proposed to send force to beat the movement down, but Nehru let it be known that if increased colonial force were used to try to prevent independence, India would leave the Commonwealth immediately. "The British government did not give or grant anything," James suggested, "They were helpless before the new nation."[12]

One clear agreement, we discovered, was that–at least on a pragmatic and short-term basis–Positive Action played a decisive and significant role. But even at the time, Nkrumah himself noted the risks of accepting an office that left the people of the Gold Coast "half slave and half free." Though a corner had been turned, the push for full independence continued until 1957, when Ghana would emerge as a new republic.

* * *

Bill was with Nkrumah and the CPP at the time when it was announced that Ghana would be granted full independence in 1957. Even at this time, however, the CPP found itself dependent to a great extent upon the British civil service. The British idea, which is classic, was they would do their best to control the minds of the "natives" and to hold on to as much economic dominance as possible. For Ghana and the CPP, like a number of other independence movements, the aura of independence was so heady that they went along with a lot of this, somehow thinking that they could turn it around after taking over the government.

Through his relationship with Gbedema, Bill suggested that a young African American preacher be invited to the independence celebrations. Rev. Martin Luther King, Jr. was already getting some national attention in the U.S. for his fine oratory skills and the campaigns in Montgomery, Alabama. In fact, Dr. King had recently gotten his picture on the cover of *Time* magazine. Other Blacks from the U.S.–including A. Philip Randolph and Adam Clayton Powell–were also in attendance, but King was young, impressionable, full of vitality. Bill and Dr. Robert Lee, an African American who gave up his dental practice in the U.S. to set up shop in Ghana, organized a dinner for King to meet Julius Nyerere, who was campaigning for the freedom of East African Tanganyika.

Bill noticed that Martin and Coretta King were visibly impressed when, on that fateful night in 1957, the British flag was lowered, and the flag of Ghana was raised. Nkrumah, dressed in traditional kente cloth, his fists waving in the air, tears streaming down his face, shouted over and over again: "Free At Last, Free At Last, Free At Last!" Six years later, when Martin closed his own speech on the steps of the Lincoln Memorial with a similar phrase, which he attributed to an old Negro spiritual, Bill couldn't help but wonder if those thunderous words in Washington D.C. had not come from King's memory of that historic evening in Ghana.

* * *

Between 1957 and 1960, during the early years of the Republic, the structure of a western parliamentary system was maintained. A traditional constitution and a capitalist-oriented industrialization, worked out under British supervision before their departure, was also a feature of this early period. With respect to Pan-Africanist internationalism, however, Nkrumah wasted little time in charting his independent course. His deep concern and support for liberation movements across the African continent was most significantly expressed with the convening of the All-African Peoples Conference (AAPC) barely a year after independence. "The independence of Ghana itself," Nkrumah had asserted, "is meaningless unless the whole of Africa is free."[13]

The convention brought together three hundred delegates from sixty-five organizations and parties. All but one of the eight African countries, which had recently obtained independence, sent governmental representatives. Padmore and Nkrumah made a dynamic team, articulating their proposals for African unity. The AAPC was attended by large delegations from Algeria (which was in the middle of its bloody war against the French colonists), from Egypt (which was undergoing massive changes under the leadership of Pan-Arab socialist Gamal Nasser), and from the recently formed Pan-African Freedom Movement of East and Central Africa (PAFMECA). Patrice Lumumba was a youthful representative of the new National Congolese Movement, brought to the conference in part because Bill informed a Belgian WRI friend, Jean Van Lierde, who helped arrange finances and logistics for Lumumba. Tom Mboya, then of the Kenyan Federation of Labor, was there representing the imprisoned Jomo Kenyatta; Mboya was chosen as the conference chairman. At Padmore's suggestion, Bill served as the hospitality officer for the continental gathering.

The underlying issues of the day presented themselves within the larger framework of the need for African unity and freedom. The prospects for non-alignment, and the appropriate course for independent development, was discussed amidst the backdrop of the growing East–West conflict. The Soviet Union and the People's Republic of China sent sizable contingents, symbolizing their interest in the region, and in sharp contrast to the one-member official U.S. "delegation." Strategic and tactical questions were also debated. On the one hand, the call to the conference stated clearly that the anti-colonial movements would use nonviolence as their principal strategy. Nkrumah's opening speech made mention of the successes of positive action in Ghana. On the other hand, the Algerians believed that nonviolence was out of date, and not relevant to their struggles against the seemingly intractable French. Conference Chairman Mboya noted that he "supported the large majority of delegates who felt strongly that violence as a policy could not work." In his view, however, the question was not whether it was wrong to use violence, but whether "nationalism can be expected to remain silent when provoked," as it had been in many cases throughout Africa.[14]

Over the following year, as French foreign policy continued to focus on its desperate attempt to maintain its colonial possessions, it was also bent on catching up militarily to its colleagues in NATO. By 1959, plans had been publicized for a French atomic test in the Sahara desert, at Reggan in Algeria. Bill was alerted about the test through a letter from Michael Randle and April Carter, two members of the direct action wing of the British anti-nuclear movement. He brought the matter to the attention of the CPP and received a favorable response to a proposal to set up an international team to protest the French action directly at the test site.

Coincidentally, official government business was requiring Gbedema as Finance Minister to travel to both Britain and the U.S. This afforded Bill the excellent opportunity to act as a liaison between the Ghanaian and British activists, and to introduce the idea to the direct actionists in the United States. Eventually four movements–the CPP, which rallied the African forces; the British activists, who aroused the British anti-nuclear forces; and the U.S. activists, who gained support from both the peace and civil rights groupings–all joined together. Gbedema already had a limited history of international peace activity, and had been a president of the World Federalists Association. British Campaign for Nuclear Disarmament (CND) leader Michael Scott joined Michael Randle and A.J. Muste in Accra, to set up the Sahara Protest Team.

The team was made up of eleven Ghanaians, two Africans from outside of Ghana, and six members from France, Britain, and the U.S. One team member was Dr. Ntsu Mokhehle from the southern African country of Lesotho, who was elected President of Lesotho in 1992. The Ghana Council for Nuclear Disarmament served as the official local sponsor, but it was clear that the CPP–led government was fully supportive. One interesting aspect of the Sahara Protest was the way in which movements that are generally opposed to governments in power joined with a new young government and enjoyed that kind of official backing. "It was so exciting," Bill recalls, "because we felt that this joining up of the European anti–nuclear forces, the African liberation forces, and the U.S. civil rights movements could help each group feed and reinforce the other. Both the civil rights struggle and the CND were on a high at that time; they were really strong, people's movements. Then, to be sponsored by a majority political party in government clearly marked a unique moment in progressive history."[15]

Gbedema, who was named Chairman of the Protest Team, recalled the reasons and implications of CPP support: "We were the strongest political base in Africa, the strongest political party in government apart from the northern African countries like Tunisia and Egypt. If we didn't do anything, the French would have taken advantage of our inactivity and continued with their bomb schedule. The central committee of the Party decided that we should have this front, not governmental but a political party front, where things could be done without the government being diplomatically implicated. So we organized our CPP members to carry on the campaign, and they went with the team into the desert. There is one chap here in Accra who is still nicknamed 'Sahara' today, four decades later!"

"Our main aim," Gbedema continued, "was to present the case that if bomb testing–nuclear bomb testing–was so good for Africa, why not do it in France?" They should not test their bombs here, we argued, even though the Sahara is sparsely populated. The winds carry poisonous gases. If the French thought that it was so safe, they could do it in France!"[16]

Calling it "the most significant in the series of direct-action civil-disobedience projects, in which radical non-pacifists have been involved," A.J. Muste described some of the issues from a non-governmental perspective, in his essay *Africa against the Bomb*. "Any sort of tie-in with a government obviously represents problems for almost any private 'cause,' and very real problems for a project of a radical, nonviolent character," Muste wrote. "It would be folly to assume that any government is truly devoted to nonviolence and its revolutionary implications.... On the other hand, I am satisfied that a project of the size of the present one could not have been set up without real support from persons in government. An immense propaganda job for the idea of nonviolence has been done among the masses and a considerable amount of intensive training in nonviolent philosophy and strategy has been given."[17]

The Sahara Protest Team caravaned through northern Ghana, stopping for support rallies at towns along the route. Crowds of people would meet the Team at each major center, cheering them along the way. From a political point of view, this indicated both good organization on the part of the CPP as well as at least a minimum of understanding that what the French were proposing to do was bad. According to Bill, "the plan was to get as close to the test site as possible, letting folks know about the French plans and preventing the testing through our physical presence."

Crossing the Upper Volta border, the Team was stopped at a French Control Post at Bittou. When the French neither arrested the Team nor let them pass, they maintained their presence in Bittou, handing out leaflets in French, English, Arabic, and Hawza. Once it was clear that the group was well received, evident by local offers of food and shelter, the French police surrounded them, confining them to a space of fifty diameters. The first Team eventually withdrew, to be followed shortly after by a second Team of reduced numbers. This smaller group, it was felt, might have a greater chance of complete passage.

Bill, a member of both teams, discussed how, after getting to know the African guards at the border post, the second team moved early one morning across the border between Ghana and Upper Volta. "The guards did not try to stop us physically," Bill remembered, "but they did alert their French superiors, who arrested us after we advanced about one mile into Upper Volta. We were put into jail, but we could hear the two-way radio crackling continually in the office even though our French was not good enough to understand what was being said.

"The next morning, we were all put into a large van and the amiable military officer in charge led the way in a small Land Rover. We did not know where they were taking us, but we drove on for several hours. Unfortunately, the officer's land rover skidded and turned over on the very sandy road. The team of seven of us was allowed out of our van to help put the overturned vehicle right and we continued on our way! Eventually, we reached a point near the opposite end of the border from which we came, and were dumped unceremoniously into Ghana."[18]

Another vehicular story from the Sahara Protest Teams concerned a moment of impasse on the Upper Volta side. Bayard Rustin, who was one of the U.S. representatives, said "Let's start up our motors and see what happens." As soon as they started the motors, the French paramilitary came and took their positions with their weapons at the ready, and the team members stopped the motors. Bayard noted that, for the first time, one could see how a motor vehicle could be used as a lethal weapon! Bayard and Bill also passed some of the less intense moments of waiting by singing and using "Negro spirituals" to get people enthused.

"As a member of the second team," Bill continued, "I gained a few insights into the British character, through observation of our friends Michael Randle and Michael Scott. One was that whenever we were in some sort of difficulty, one would invariably call out to the other: 'I say, let's have a spot of tea!' Randle was one of the most single-minded people I had ever come across. Once, when I was telling him of an occasion I had to converse with the famous French actress Simone Signoret, he looked puzzled for a moment and then exclaimed: 'Oh yes, now I remember her. She signed one of our petitions demanding nuclear disarmament!'"

Bill returned to Accra to discuss the next stages of the Sahara Protest with Gbedema, and was–admittedly–quite tired. "I thought that we had made our point, but the Sahara Protest Team's confrontations at the border had aroused so much international interest–with sympathy fasts, demonstrations and rallies being held in African countries and in other parts of the world–that Gbedema enthusiastically sent me back with a message urging another try."

"Once again the second team crossed the border–not at an official immigration post, but in the middle of the night led by a local guide along a path usually used by smugglers. We hid in the bush," Bill continued, now an expert at illegal border crossings, "and started our journey again by foot, on the main road to Upper Volta's capitol, Ouagadougou. We were very tired and had run out of water by this time. We decided to flag down a truck, which was one of the few vehicles we saw on the road through all this time. The driver stopped, and we climbed into the back. I noticed that he looked at us strangely, but we were too exhausted to notice anything else until he drove us directly into a large police station! The commandant came to the back of the bus and said: "Oh, Reverend Scott! Quel Courage!"

"Once again we were in jail. This time, we decided not to cooperate. So, in the morning, when we were ordered into the truck, we refused to go. Each of us was carried and dumped into the van, and in a few hours time, we found ourselves once more on the Ghana side of the border."

In early 1960, the French did explode several nuclear devices in the Sahara, but the Algerian war was intensifying and so was mainstream anti-nuclear sentiment. Eventually, the French decided to abandon African nuclear testing. Though they relocated their testing several years later to a site in the South Pacific, the immediate decision regarding African testing was seen as a victory for the Sahara Protest Project.

Discussions at this time between Michael Scott and Kwame Nkrumah led directly to the planning of a third significant international initiative, the Positive Action Conference of April 1960. Nkrumah agreed after the French explosions despite the massive protests, that a conference was important to discuss next steps. In the meantime, the Sharpeville Massacre had occurred in South Africa, and that was included as a significant part of the conference agenda.

When Nkrumah asked the international grouping of mainly pacifist advisors to see what they could "come up with," even the most experienced amongst them found it to be a formidable task. Veteran U.S. tacticians A.J. Muste and Ralph Abernathy worked long into the night with such figures as Madame Tomi Kora of Japan, Madame Asha Devi of India, Esther Peter and Pierre Martin of France, and Britain's Michael Randle. They proposed a center, a pacifist West Point, to train African revolutionaries in nonviolent strategy and tactics. Some African delegates were not at all happy with these overseas advisors moving behind the scenes.

"A xenophobic Liberian delegate," Bill recollected, "spit out more hate and violence than the most zealous of those engaged in armed struggle. On the other hand, Frantz

Fanon, who represented Algeria's National Liberation Front (FLN)–involved in the most intense armed conflict on the continent–spoke in a quiet and sober voice explaining his view of the regrettable necessity for armed struggle. Outside of the conference hall, Fanon described to the nonviolent advisors the attempts to attain Algerian independence by nonviolent means: 'We tried this method, but the French came into the Casbah, broke down door after door and slaughtered the head of each household in the center of the street. When they did that about thirty-five consecutive times, the people gave up on non-cooperation.

"Nkrumah was also under pressure from many Africans participants," Bill continued, "who resented his international advisors and considered them dangerously romantic. The action emphasis, which had attracted Nkrumah to the Gandhians, had no influential advocates among the African delegates, and George Padmore was no longer there to discuss the pros and cons of different methods of struggle. So the Positive Action Conference, which Nkrumah opened with a speech advocating a continuation of nonviolent positive action as the principal tactic, ended with only a passing reference to the original proposals.

"I think that there were two significant changes happening at this time. Nkrumah did feel that in the world scene, Ghana and his movement ought to be on the side of the anti-nuclear forces. But as far as the liberation struggles were concerned, they definitely were moving away from nonviolence. Nkrumah himself had written to me saying that we were going to set up this ideological school in Winneba, which would have a nonviolence wing to it. He had hoped that Michael Randle and I might play a role. As it turned out, there was no nonviolent wing at all. The center became a place for CPP education and training.

"This was also at the time when the Non-Aligned Movement was coming to the fore and Nkrumah felt that Ghana should be very much a leading part of that, along with Tito in Yugoslavia, Nasser in Egypt, and India. Nkrumah's anti-nuclear commitment continued, but his advisors shifted from the pacifist direct action advocates to British Members of Parliament, like Geoffrey Bing, and Canon John Collins, whose approach was more oriented towards world leaders influencing one another. In some ways Padmore, who was not a pacifist by any means, had played a crucial role in helping Nkrumah to put things in perspective. 'Kwame,' he'd chide Nkrumah, 'Just remember that if four hundred million Chinese decide one day to spit, Ghana will be drowned!' By the end of 1960, discussions about strategies and tactics had come full circle."

Nkrumah was undoubtedly the leading voice of Pan-Africanism on the continent, and had become the leading African voice on the world scene. The nonviolence advocacy so prominent in the 1958 All African Peoples Conference, in the 1959 Sahara Protest Teams, and in the planning for the 1960 Positive Action Conference were all but eliminated from the mainstream of political discourse. The Ghanaian government continued to provide support for the more conventional peace politicians, hosting the World without the Bomb Accra Assembly in 1961, but there was little space or time for the radical experimentation of the previous years. As Nkrumah's perspective began to shift, the distance between him and his previous advisors seemed to grow greater and greater.

* * *

As personal secretary to the Minister of Finance, travel was a constant feature of Bill's job with Komla Gbedema. One of his sharpest memories of this period was a 1958 trip to a World Bank meeting in the U.S. The Ghanaian delegation was at the United Nations Building in New York, and there were two African American professors from a university in Delaware who wanted Gbedema to give a speech at their college. They said that they would pick the group up at the UN and take them down by car.[19]

"We started off on the journey and we stopped just across the Hudson River at a Howard Johnson's for a bite to eat," Bill began, hoping to spark Gbedema's own memories of the period. "Several hours later, as we got nearer to our destination, one of the professors said, 'Now Minister Gbedema, here's a very interesting thing: at Howard Johnson's in New Jersey we were able to be served, but down here they won't serve you because you're Black.' He was just making conversation, but Gbedema took him very seriously. He said 'I don't believe it! Why don't we stop at Howard Johnson's right now.' The guys were really frightened because we were on Route 40 in Maryland and we knew that southern Maryland was supposed to be as racist as Georgia.

"At any rate, they couldn't show how uneasy they were, or maybe they did show it but they couldn't stop him. Gbedema went in and I went in with him, knowing full well what would happen–but it wasn't my job to take care of the U.S.'s dirty linen. He asked for orange juice, he was refused, and we came out again. We proceeded to the school, gave the talk, and when we came back to New York City, he was being received by the Mayor at City Hall. In the hallway, as usual, there was a group of reporters. Gbedema was talking openly to somebody about the incident, and some reporters picked it up and made a sensational story about it."

"Oh yes," Gbedema finally remembered, "Some of my friends told me that it served me right for ordering orange juice!"

"The next thing I know," Bill continued, "there is a call to our hotel suite in Waldorf Towers from E. Frederic Morrow. He was President Eisenhower's "African American" in the White House, and I knew him because he had been going out with my elder sister. Fred calls me and says, 'You know, the President has heard about the orange juice incident and he's quite disturbed about it. He'd like to invite the Finance Minister to breakfast.' I relay the invitation to Gbedema, and we have a little discussion about whether or not he should accept. Of course, being invited by the President of the United States was not insignificant, yet at the same time there is this idea that if Eisenhower was really going to deal with the problem, he'd have to open up a series of Howard Johnson's himself to take care of all the people who had experienced discrimination!

"Nevertheless, it was decided that we should go. We got on the train that night, so we'd arrive in D.C. in the morning, and I then realized how much of a showman Gbedema was. He had entered the train in his usual business suit, but when he came out of that Pullman the next morning; he was in the most gorgeous full-length kente cloth you've ever seen. All that Ghana colorful toga-type thing, which made him impressive for the photographers!"

When the delegation reached the White House, as soon as they got inside of the gate, someone touched Bill on the shoulder, saying, "Will you come with me please." So even though Bill was also discriminated against, he didn't get the Presidential treatment. They took Bill to Fred Morrow's office while Eisenhower had Gbedema to breakfast. An interesting side story to this meeting is that an aide to Eisenhower had asked the President, "What are we going to talk to this African guy about?" Somebody who was knowledgeable in the African Affairs section of the State Department had said, "Well, you know, there is this Volta River Project and he would be interested in that." This was really the beginning of significant American economic involvement in Ghana.

In the meantime, Bill caught hell from the U.S. State Department folks back in Accra, because they accused him of setting the whole thing up, bringing Gbedema into the civil rights struggles of the U.S. by plotting the incident. "The truth of the matter is," Bill admitted, "it wasn't all that much of a surprise, but at the same time, I did not plan it. By the same token, I surely wasn't going to advise Gbedema not to get involved."

Work for Gbedema back in Ghana was primarily filled with trivial details, not with adventures such as the "U.S. orange juice incident." On occasion, however, Bill and Gbedema recalled a discussion they had on philosophical and strategic matters. One set of questions, about the role of politics, power, and pacifism, came on a trip to a World Bank meeting in India. Bill had gotten a letter from Arlo Tatum of the War Resisters International as an introduction to the President of India at the time, Rajendra Prasad. Gbedema and Bill had been in Japan for a World Federalists Association meeting, and President Prasad also happened to be in Japan and offered to fly them to India in his presidential plane.

"On our way to New Delhi," Bill said, "the secretary to Prasad came to me on the plane, and told me that I would be received. When I was taken back to the compartment where the President was sitting, there were no chairs–it was a fairly empty space–and he sat cross-legged on a mat. He welcomed me warmly and then began to chat about the WRI, and said how much he regretted having to resign as an honorary WRI Vice-Chairperson. With a wry smile, Prasad said that he couldn't very well serve in the WRI post, and also be commander-in-chief of the Indian armed forces."

Gbedema reflected upon his own conflicts between a commitment to nonviolence and his top position in state affairs: "My pacifism, I believe, turned out to be quite relevant to my experiences in government. A pacifist is one who doesn't want to hurt the other person and is prepared to sit down and see if they can come together. When this is applied to nations, their leaders will be prepared to sit down and sort matters out. If you are in power, you are in the stronger position than the ordinary person is. Pacifism, in that case, would be good–if you can see the other person's point of view and see if there is another way besides confrontation or the use of force." On the other hand, Gbedema felt that a military force was necessary, and that certain undemocratic policing measures–such as preventive detention–were also necessary for the security of the state.

One of Nkrumah's most controversial policies of the early 1960s was the Preventive Detention Law. Under this law, those suspected of anti-government activity could be locked up without trial for indefinite periods. It was a law which contradicted most of Bill's political principles, and which he opposed in discussions with Gbedema and other political allies at the time. In 1960, Bill wrote a personal and confidential letter to Nkrumah in which he tried to outline his objections in a practical and concise fashion. "I asked him whether he really felt it was necessary to use a sledge hammer to kill a gnat," Bill noted, "since the country was so totally behind him." Bill expressed his feelings that it was wrong both in principle and strategically.

Several days after Bill sent along the note, Nkrumah's Secretary of Home Affairs, Krobo Edusi, called Bill aside and told him that he had heard that Bill had written a confidential letter to the President. "If it had been anybody else," he informed Bill, "they would have been deported immediately." Because of his years in close support of the CPP, Bill was simply told not to bother Nkrumah directly with such matters. By this time, however, Bill had already begun thinking about leaving government service and moving on.

* * *

By the end of 1959, in addition to Bill's troubles with Gbedema and the government, he and his wife were becoming more and more estranged. He decided to leave his job, and spent some time traveling and looking for alternative work. In this period, Bill had developed a friendship with Ehud Avriel, the Israeli Ambassador to Ghana. This was a time when many leaders in sub-Saharan Africa felt that a relationship with the Israeli government would be of mutual benefit. In 1961, Avriel invited Bill to work in Israel, at their Center for Asian-African Cooperation. Bill decided to accept the offer.[20]

"I then notified Erica Powell, who was Nkrumah's secretary," Bill recalled. "I said that I was going to be leaving Ghana and I'd like to pay my respects and say good-bye to the President. Normally speaking, a person would make such a request and maybe about five days later they'd say that he'd see you in two weeks. I put my request in at nine o'clock in the morning, and at about ten o'clock Erica Powell called back and said that Nkrumah would see me at noon. I was a bit surprised, but I went to see him and Nkrumah said, 'What's the matter? Why are you going away?'

"I told Nkrumah that since I had left Gbedema I hadn't been able to find a job, and that my marriage with Efua was breaking up and I felt that I ought to move on. I could see this noticeable expression of relief on his face and he relaxed and said 'Well, perhaps it might be a good idea for you to have this experience, and in view of our relations with Israel....'

"What I now think was happening," Bill analyzed, "was that Nkrumah knew at that time that he planned to ditch Gbedema. I'm sure that he thought that the rumor had gotten out, and that I was, in a sense, running. He really wanted to see what I knew. A short while after I left Ghana, Gbedema made a speech before Congress stating that 'the lights of liberty were going out all over Ghana,' and immediately thereafter fled the country.

"There may have been several reasons for the splits between Nkrumah and Gbedema," Bill continued, "but the final split was a long time coming. Nkrumah and Botsio had a socialist outlook, and Gbedema was the capitalist in the group. Nkrumah had not been comfortable with having Gbedema in the cabinet, but since Gbedema had done all of this early CPP work and was one of the three most powerful men in the country, it was very hard to get rid of him. I think that Nkrumah also wanted to take personal charge of the Volta River Project."

Sadly, Bill never had another direct contact with Nkrumah after that period. The years between 1962 and 1965 were difficult ones in Ghana, with increasing civil unrest. Charges of corruption against Nkrumah were largely unsubstantiated, though many of his old cronies in the government were indeed lining their pockets, and Nkrumah was responsible for keeping them in key positions. This caused greater and greater disillusionment among the general population about socialism, because they could see what was really happening. Nkrumah was doing a magnificent job for the Pan-African movement. The average Ghanaian, however, wanted him to focus more attention and resources on matters of domestic concern.

After the 1961 assassination of Congolese leader Patrice Lumumba–a murder that was originally planned by the U.S. Central Intelligence Agency (CIA)–Nkrumah's disillusionment with nonviolent strategies became solidified. It is also significant to note that Nkrumah's book *Neocolonialism: The Last Stage of Imperialism* angered many in the U.S. government, and was published just prior to the 1966 military coup which was to oust Nkrumah and send him into exile for the remainder of his life. At the time of the take-over, staged by members of the military and police, Nkrumah was on a visit to Vietnam and the People's Republic of China. The revolutionary Pan-African vision that he was ever intent on leading had gained him the admiration of people across the continent and globe. At home, however, the domestic crisis and his own lack of a strategic hold on the military caused his downfall from state power. Right-wing elements, with possible collusion of the U.S. government, were able to gain control.[21]

Nkrumah, who took residence in Guinea as co-President with Sékou Touré, also became more sure of the need for liberating armed struggle. His *Handbook for Revolutionary Warfare*, published in 1967, became Africa's "little black book"–a guide for the African guerrilla. It detailed the need for a military balance between liberated, enemy and contested zones. Developing a structure for an African High Command, it advocated the building of political-military organizations: an All-African Peoples Revolutionary Party and army. "Revolutionary warfare," he wrote, "is the logical, inevitable answer to the political, economic and social situation in Africa today. We do not have the luxury of an alternative.... People's armed struggle is the highest form of political action, the revolutionary catalyst in the neo–colonial situation."[22] Nkrumah died in 1972, heart-broken that he was never able to return to the country that he led to freedom.

* * *

In Ghana after 1966, a period of military rule began with almost immediate negotiations with the International Monetary Fund (IMF). With loans re-negotiated, basic goods imported, and a stable economic horizon, the ruling group conceded state power to a civilian government late in 1969. Less than three years later, however, another successful coup was staged, this time to fight corruption. The tumultuous 1970s, though, were barely a time for freedom of expression.[23]

The 1972 military coup was justified in the name of revolution. But the military government of General Acheampong was substantially worse than its predecessor. Corruption was at its height, throwing the country into its deepest economic crisis since independence. Progressive grassroots organizations faced widespread repression, confining much of the anti-government activity to academic efforts and small-scale initiatives. The Socialist Society of Ghana, co-founded by staunch Nkrumahist Captain Kojo Tsikata and law professor Aki Sawyer, sought to publicize the injustices of the Supreme Military Council. In 1975, Tsikata was arrested on subversion charges–attempting to overthrow the government–and sentenced to death. Later in the decade, the New Democratic Movement (NDM) was one of several attempts to continue to work for change. Kwesi Botchway, an NDM co-founder, explained: "It was clear that we were not going to get out there and propagandize, not just build a politburo in the city. We were a rigorous study group. We were going to build a mass political party, perhaps win an election."[24]

By 1979, the rank-and-file of the military, according to Botchway, "decided to execute the officer corps" along with their corrupt commanders. A charismatic Flight Lieutenant, John Jerry Rawlings, struggled among them not to carry out massive assassinations. A controlled coup, Rawlings argued, could get rid of the rotten officials and quickly hand the country back to civil leadership.

After the 1979 coup, power *was* handed over to a civilian government, after an Armed Forces Revolutionary Council supervised a free and democratic election. Tsikata, who had spent four years on death row, was released from prison. The NDM was able to organize freely. "We were pragmatic," noted Botchway. "We needed to form an alliance of all patriotic people who wanted to see the country develop, including capitalists. The real enemy was the world capitalist system, and we needed a social consensus behind national development. But the basic cutting edge would have to be formed through those classes who have a stake at radical social change–a disciplined, well-trained, well-educated group."

The June Fourth Movement (JFM) also played a distinct role in this period, taking its name from the date on which Rawlings staged the coup. Grounded in the student movement, the militants in the JFM believed that the anti-corruption morality of the young officers needed to be preserved, and that handing over power to a possibly corrupt civilian politician would not be in the country's best interests. When it became clear, just months after the coup, that Rawlings was set on implementing elections, they set forth their organizational plans, modeled themselves after Cuba's July 26 Movement, and asked Rawlings to become JFM's Chairman; Kojo Tsikata became a member of the central committee. The JFM brought together a wide and sometimes contradictory spectrum of left forces.

Under civilian control, the economic decay only worsened. The deficit had risen to almost $500 million; violent crimes in the urban areas increased. Historian Emmanuel Hansen, in his essay *The State and Popular Struggles in Ghana*, concluded: "The government appeared ineffectual. To many people it was not governing . . .. To the mass of people the government appeared to be not only unable but even more importantly, *unwilling* to do anything about the situation."[25]

On January 1, 1981, for the fourth time in Ghana's twenty-four year history, a successful military coup d'etat was staged. Jerry Rawlings, again at the lead, informed the population that "the military is not in to take over." Looking to transform the existing political and economic order, Rawlings declared the December 31 Revolution, pledging that from now on, nothing in government would be done "without the consent and authority of the people." A Provisional National Defense Council (PNDC) was set up, with Rawlings serving as Council Chairman (head of state), and leading civilian activists brought in from the progressive movements. During this period, an unprecedented level of worker's actions took place–in the streets and at the factory level. Although this experiment in people's power was ultimately unsuccessful, it represented a revival of the mass-based organizing, which was widespread during Nkrumah's days.

* * *

Captain Kojo Tsikata was one youthful soldier who took Nkrumah's strategy–and his commitment to Pan-African solidarity–quite seriously and quite literally. In the early 1960s, he became one of the youngest commissioned officers in Nkrumah's armed forces, earning the rank of captain. He was sent to Central Africa, to fight alongside Lumumba's colleagues against the counter–revolution-taking place in the Congo. He then traveled to southern Africa, fighting against the Portuguese with the burgeoning Popular Movement for the Liberation of Angola (MPLA). After the 1966 coup against Nkrumah, he remained in exile, but returned several years later to challenge the corrupt regime. Since that time, Tsikata has played a prominent role in Ghanaian political life.[26]

When Bill and I met with him, Captain Tsikata was the somber and thoughtful Ghanaian second-in-command, an intellectual who seemed to weigh the past with present needs. In charge of both internal security and foreign affairs, Tsikata balanced Marxism with Pan-Africanism and a forward-looking pragmatism. Speaking softly, carefully reviewing his continental perspectives and diplomatic responsibilities, he shared with us some of his concerns. "Looking at the liberation struggle in Africa," Tsikata began, "there have been two major strategies–one, violence, and on the other hand, nonviolence. In my view, you can't really say that one particular strategy is better than the other is, but it depends on the conditions and the circumstances. Of course, in all circumstances, one has got to combine both violent and nonviolent forms of struggle against colonial domination or racist domination."

Noting the Captain's unique personal history, we questioned him about the theories regarding the potentially liberating role of violence. He replied: "I myself subscribe, to a large extent, to the validity of Frantz Fanon's theory about the necessity of violence, but I'd like to say that I don't think that people arrive at that theory by glorifying or romanticizing violence as such. In the lives of our people, violence has been an aspect of domination. It has been camouflaged in certain respects, but I can't imagine anywhere in Africa–from the moment that the white man reached our soil–that domination has not taken a violent form, physically as well as psychologically. It would be a miracle for somebody to avoid any aspect of a violent reaction, while trying to overcome or struggle against something which is so violent in the first place."

As far as militarism itself was concerned, Tsikata's views seemed quite open-minded, given his role in the Ghanaian State. "This has been a very short period for the experiences of post-colonial Africa to speak concretely on the role of the military," he suggested. "It's very difficult to determine really what the military's role should be. However, I can say that now, many people try to see what they can do with this institution within the objectives that we set up for ourselves in Africa today. The military has been diverted into so many activities–both constructive and destructive. One hasn't really had a long stable period to develop any theory or any practice on the role of the military in Africa. We will find some definition in the years to come. I am sure about that. We must find some productive role for the military in the economic and social aspects of the life of a country."

The question of definitions led us to a more general discussion of the role of democracy, elections, and the changes taking place in Africa today. "There is a road we have to go on in order to find our own forms and our own concepts of democracy," Tsikata asserted, clearly critical of the hypocritical Western equation that implies that democracy and elections are synonyms. "Sometimes," he continued, "it is useful to go ahead with Western elections, because it is important to show the sham nature of things: important to expose it for people to see. The people," Tsikata concluded, "must discover within their own society the systems which will enable them to achieve democracy. We are all looking for systems that will enable ordinary people to have a say. That is the whole point of democracy: ordinary people will have a say in their own affairs."

* * *

It is, at best, difficult to define the philosophy of President Jerry John Rawlings, whose political populism and military might has enabled him to remain in power longer than any of Ghana's previous leaders. His 1981 decree, dramatically paraphrased since then by U.S. demonstrators against police violence, was: "So long as there is no justice, let there be no peace." This motto has set the context for a pragmatic approach towards governance.[27]

Dramatic is one word that fits Jerry Rawlings well. His enormous passion and energy seems to come from his anger at the injustices of past and present. Bill and I met him in a small living room area of Christianbourg Castle, where his office and residence is located. Our three-hour discussion was informal; Rawlings in his blue jeans, not wanting to be tape-recorded. As he jumped from topic to topic, his energy and interest in probing the problems of violence and non-violence seemed only to increase. Rawlings' booming voice negated Bill's usual auditory need to sit next to whomever he is talking with. "I should have been sitting on the other side of the room!" Bill remarked.

During discussions on strategies and tactics, Rawlings shared his recollections on biblical stories and childhood. "Christ himself was forced to do violence when he drove the money-changers from the temple," Rawlings reminded us. "You grow up in a situation where you're always told to turn the other cheek. I'm not a violent person . . . but you grow up in violence."[28]

"If I were to meet Christ, I would ask him: 'If you said to love your enemy, did you say that as a tactical ploy?' We have a saying amongst our people that's sad and foolish: 'the truth will endure.' But I want to tell my people that the truth will not be upheld on its own–you've got to fight for it.

"People like me," Rawlings continued, "are caught in a situation where we have two battles. After 1979, there were meetings between bankers from the U.S. and Ghana. After all the years of colonialism, and post-colonial inequalities, I had to make the effort to understand the U.S. bankers' point of view. Me, the victim! I wish that the bankers would have taken the time to understand *my* point of view. At the same time, in Ghana, I am criticized for persecuting rich people!"

By 1983, it was clear that there was a desperate need for foreign capital. This left the government with little choice but to negotiate with the IMF and the World Bank. Because they were able to negotiate an agreement to nationalize foreign trade, the PNDC argued that the IMF Economic Recovery Plan incorporated their own indigenous interests and needs. In the ten ensuing years, Ghana's IMF negotiations were considered among the "most favorable" throughout the African continent.

"The nature of the violence being done against us," commented Rawlings in regards to the neo-colonial legacy, "lies in the power of the English language.... It's not that they're unaware that taking away our indigenous languages is part of taking some of the spirituality away from us. For the Arabs, they fight their enemies on their own terms, using the oil weapon. In Africa, our weapon–through language–has been denied us as a means of self-defense. The minute that the gun was introduced into African societies–and it was *not* democratized–the Europeans began to take away the sustenance of logic that upheld our societies. From that time on, democracy was not going to be the issue anymore.

"Today, nonviolence is beautiful, providing that you have the time, the opportunity, and that you can push the right buttons. If you start firing at me, my singing in a high-pitched voice like Martin Luther King singing 'Amazing Grace' in the U.S. south won't stop your bullets. For nonviolence, there must be a common language of understanding.

"In 1979," Rawlings recalled, "during the moral revolution, I was simply talking about living our convictions. I was not introducing anything new to the people. When you treat a man like a dog, you should be shocked if he talks–you should expect him to bark! When the commanding soldiers were executed, the underdog felt good, if the persons responsible for society's problems were dead. Nevertheless, we were trying to make changes in the least violent way. The anger of the people was so great–just firing a few random shots would have been a relief. I could have done it–but innocents would die. One must be very careful with the weapon one chooses.

"You must use any means to make the people wake up–except the weapon of humiliation," the President commented. "If humiliation is used, you should be ready for the people to hate you. The most important and obvious ingredient in government is love. Love is great and can be a fine weapon, but hate can be an even more potent weapon, along with the fear of losing what one loves. The weapon of duty is important, but you can incite people with hate. Those were the conditions on the ground in 1979, available either for troublemakers or solution-finders.

"When you humiliate people, you press them. And when the time for justice comes–you can offer people the world, and they will slap you down . . . they want your blood! I have to explain to so-called educated men–lawyers–the heat of the moment, and the savagery of our time!

"People say that we should be God-fearing. I say that we should be God loving. The preachers should leave heaven alone and take on hell. Let them prove to the people that hell–our socioeconomic conditions–doesn't exist. They've indoctrinated our people to do well in their lives more from the fear of hell than from the love of god. Originally, I didn't want to join the air force, I wanted to become a priest."

In words not unfamiliar to many Christian pacifists, Rawlings reflected: "I've learned not to make the mistake of using the word 'enemy' too lightly. If that word is devalued, when a real enemy comes to shoot you in the back, you won't know. But I don't see how we could have achieved our liberation without de-mystifying the military. The military has always been the chief weapon in society–especially in times of unaccountable leaders. They will always need extra force to protect them."

The subject of accountability has been especially important to Rawlings, as Ghana again attempts to make the transition to non-military rule. In light of the new constitution, the extended freedoms of press and speech, as well as the open electoral process, the "organs of popular power" have given way to newly developed political parties. The People's Defense Committees (PDC), the CDRs, and smaller localized groups, hallmarks of the decentralization policies of the late 1980s, have taken on–at least temporarily–a diminished importance compared to the groupings vying for political and electoral power.

This new period, brought on both by IMF requirements and by a general desire for greater political dialogue, has had mixed consequences.[29] Marked by a flurry of accusations in the tabloids, it has been a challenge to separate critical analysis from rumor mongering yellow journalism. Though Rawlings replaced his military uniform with a civilian suit, to win the November 1992 elections by a substantial margin, rioting and demonstrations in certain provinces indicate a definite dissatisfaction among various sectors.

As Ghana enters the fourth republic, it should not be surprising that a return to the ideals of the independence movement has been a common theme. Seeking to escape the subtle shackles of neocolonialism, the Pan-African ethics of continental cooperation and self-reliance are heralded. President Rawlings' rhetoric over the last several years have echoed some of the perspectives of Kwame Nkrumah. Examining the impact of worldwide militarism, some positions would not have seemed inappropriate at the anti-nuclear Sahara Protest or Positive Action gatherings of three decades earlier.

"The total debt of developing countries," Rawlings explained at a talk on the proposed New International Economic Order, "would be wiped out by a fraction of the military expenditures of the superpowers. Hunger, poverty, and disease could be totally eliminated," he continued, "if the priority of peoples the world over were to address these deprivations instead of the huge outlays that the developing nations make on displaying military prowess. What is even worse is that even the poor developing world is deprived of limited resources by our countries being drawn into fratricidal wars with weapons of destruction that the merchants of war are hawking around the world."[30]

Addressing the 25th Anniversary of the Organization of African Unity, Rawlings reiterated the Pan-African theme: "In 1963, Dr. Kwame Nkrumah had the foresight to call for an African currency, an African Monetary zone, an African Central Bank, and indeed a common African citizenship." Recognizing that many considered these policies utopian, Rawlings noted, "because we refused to heed that call, we are poorer for it today–faced with economic stagnation, huge debts and an economic relationship with external capital that strangely makes us a net exporter of capital to the industrialized world.... Is there any wonder that our plans for less stringent conditionalities for external assistance, our call for fairer terms of trade and for an international conference on the debt have been largely ignored?"

Resurrecting Nkrumah's call for the formation of an African High Command, Rawlings emphasized the need for a militant, defiant, and revolutionary structure that can fight against "unacceptable inherited structures" that stand in the way of true self-determination and autonomy. "The experiences of many countries on the continent," he concluded, "show clearly that until the alienation between civilian and military is overcome, until we return to the wisdom of our own cultural traditions, in which...the military in effect is the people in arms, progress in stable nation–building is likely to elude us."[31]

* * *

The struggle for freedom and justice in Ghana foreshadowed what would happen in many parts of the continent. Nkrumah's Pan-African and socialist goals were broader and more far-reaching than those of some other leaders were, but the giant obstacles, which he faced in achieving those goals, have been the same everywhere in Africa. The inherited authoritarian colonial structure and capitalist economy, the ruthless interference of external forces represented by neocolonialism and Cold War pressures, and the internal weaknesses represented by ethnic violence and corruption all have been monumental problems.

Still, the people of Ghana did achieve political independence and Nkrumah was able to provide major support for liberation movements in the rest of Africa. The strategy of mass participation as a basis for struggle was a model for most other movements, although the nonviolent approach was accepted in only a few other countries. With hindsight it is possible to spot some weaknesses in the leadership as factors in the failure to achieve goals. These weaknesses included: a limited understanding of economic forces (which has been a problem for all political leaders generally); an under-estimation of the ruthlessness and manipulation by external forces; neglect of domestic concerns; and finally, too much impatience to get things done.

In our dialogues with our Ghanaian associates, Pan-Africanism has survived the provincialism that partially caused the overthrow of Nkrumah. Under the Rawlings government, Nkrumah's great contribution to the continent is recognized by his home country. His early contribution of the nonviolent strategy as an effective means of struggle is either questioned or accepted on a pragmatic level, and his later conclusion that armed struggle is necessary has become more widely embraced theoretically, despite the fact that revolutionary action–armed or otherwise–plays little role in Africa's day-to-day affairs. A real understanding of revolutionary nonviolence is as little understood in Ghana as it is in the rest of the world.

It is interesting to note how Nkrumah's devotion to Pan-Africanism and acceptance of nonviolence as a strategy led him, through the Sahara Protest, the Sharpeville Massacre, and other events to greater international concerns. He came to view himself as a player on the world scene, which was why he was visiting Vietnam and China at the time of his overthrow. Bill wondered if Nkrumah ever yearned for those pre-independence days when he was still living in his small house outside of Accra. When Bill visited his home at that time, two pictures were prominently displayed on the wall. The photographs were of two men not often seen together: Marcus Garvey and Mohandas Gandhi.

Nkrumah's devotion to Garvey's life-long Pan-Africanist concerns, and his use of Gandhi's methods in the independence struggle, helped bring to Ghana a self-respect and a sense of the need for people's power which remains, in part, to this very day. It is possible that the worldwide respect, which has come to Ghana through Nkrumah's vision and legacy has enabled that country to avoid the worst of the horrible violence that has been raging in other parts of the continent.

NOTES

1. Interview/dialogue with Bill Sutherland, September 14, 1993, Brooklyn, New York.
2. C.L.R. James, "Kwame Nkrumah: Founder of African Emancipation," *Black World*, July 1972; reprinted in *At the Rendezvous of Victory*, Allison and Busby, London, 1984, p. 185.
3. C.L.R. James, "George Padmore: Black Marxist Revolutionary," *At the Rendezvous of Victory*, Allison and Busby, London, 1984, p. 258, from a talk given in North London, 1976.
4. C.L.R. James, *Nkrumah and the Ghana Revolution*, Allison and Busby, London, 1977.
5. Kwame Nkrumah, *Ghana: The Autobiography of Kwame Nkrumah*, Thomas Nelson and Sons, Ltd., London, 1957.
6. Interview/dialogue between the authors and K.A. Gbedema, Accra, July 14, 1992.

7. Kwame Nkrumah, "What I Mean By Positive Action," in *Revolutionary Path*, Panaf Books, London, 1973; from a pamphlet published in Ghana in 1949.
8. Interview/dialogue between the authors and K.A. Gbedema, Accra, July 14, 1992.
9. Interview/dialogue between the authors and Dr. Kwesi Botchway, Accra, July 19, 1992.
10. Interview/dialogue between the authors and Captain Kojo Tsikata, Accra, July 19, 1992.
11. Interview/dialogue between the authors and Esi Sutherland-Addy, Accra, July 19, 1992.
12. C.L.R. James, *Nkrumah and the Ghana Revolution*, Allison and Busby, London, 1977.
13. Kwame Nkrumah, "Speech of Welcome to Representatives of Independent African States," in *Revolutionary Path*, Panaf Books, London, 1973; from the opening of the All African People's Conference. April 15, 1958.
14. Tom Mboya, *Freedom and After*, Little, Brown and Company, Boston, 1963, p.43. Another interesting reflection on Mboya's role and the varying perspectives on violence at the AAPC can be found in George Houser's *No One Can Stop the Rain*, Pilgrim Press, New York, 1989.
15. Interview/dialogue with Bill Sutherland, September 14, 1993, Brooklyn, New York.
16. Interview/dialogue between the authors and K.A. Gbedema, Accra, July 17, 1992.
17. A.J. Muste, "Africa Against the Bomb," *Liberation*, January 1960; reprinted in Nat Hentoff's (ed.) *The Essays of A.J. Muste*, Clarion, New York 1967.
18. Interview/dialogue with Bill Sutherland, September 14, 1993, Brooklyn, New York.
19. Interview/dialogue with Bill Sutherland, September 22, 1993, Brooklyn, New York.
20. Interview/dialogue with Bill Sutherland, September 22, 1993, Brooklyn, New York.
21. Kwame Nkrumah, *Neocolonialism: The Last Stage of Imperialism*, International, New York, 1965.
22. Kwame Nkrumah, *Handbook of Revolutionary Warfare*, Panaf Books, London, 1967.

23. Eboe Hutchful, *The IMF and Ghana,* Institute for African Alternatives/Zed Books, London, 1987.
24. Interview/dialogue between the authors and Dr. Kwesi Botchway, Accra, July 17, 1992.
25. Emmanuel Hansen, "The State and Popular Struggles in Ghana, 1982-1986," *Popular Struggles for Democracy in Africa,* Peter Anyang' Nyong'o, ed., United Nations University/Zed Books, London, 1987.
26. Interview/dialogue between the authors and Captain Kojo Tsikata, Accra, July 19, 1992.
27. Jerry John Rawlings, "Resisting Injustice," in *A Revolutionary Journey,* Information Services Department/ Ghana Publishing Corporation, Accra, 1982, transcribed from the national broadcast to the nation, December 31, 1981.
28. Interview/dialogue between the authors and President Jerry John Rawlings, Accra, July 18, 1992.
29. A variety of sources have looked at the role of the IMF/WB in Ghana, including the recent "Gender and Adjustment: Pictures from Ghana" by Lynne Brydon and Karen Legge, appearing in Gloria T. Emeagwali, *Women Pay the Price: Structural Adjustment in Africa and the Caribbean,* Africa World Press, Trenton, 1995. See also Kwame Ninsin's "Ghana Under the PNDC: Delinking or Structural Adjustment," in Azzam Mahjoub (ed.), *Adjustment or Delinking?,* United Nations University/Zed Books, London, 1990.
30. Jerry John Rawlings, "The Need for a Just and Equitable International Economic Order," in *Towards A Greater Tomorrow,* Information Services Department, Accra, 1989, from a speech to the Diplomatic Corps, January 8, 1988.
31. Jerry John Rawlings, "Make Real the Ideal of an African High Command," in *Towards A Greater Tomorrow,* Information Services Department, Accra, 1989, from a speech on the occasion of the twenty-fifth anniversary of the founding of the O.A.U., Addis Ababa, May 25, 1988.

CHAPTER 3

MWALIMU, TANZANIA, AND THE MEANINGS OF FREEDOM

"There's no place like home–That's why I left!' And that's why hundreds of Blacks are fleeing America and thousands more are about to do so."[1]

So reads the cover promotional tag-line of Ernest Dunbar's *The Black Expatriates,* a 1968 book on the Pan-Africanist inclinations of U.S. Blacks, written in the midst of the growing Black Power movements and featuring a chapter on none other than Bill Sutherland. Though the quote didn't exactly reflect Bill's experiences and perspectives, it is an interesting projection of the mood of the times–a period when Bill's next home, Tanzania, was well situated to play host to many African Americans searching for their roots. His house became a haven for many of the expatriates, travelers, and exiles, in the new center of the Pan-African movement.

While Bill was working in Israel, he was invited to the 1961 founding conference of the World Peace Brigade (WPB), in Beirut, Lebanon. The WPB, a predecessor of Peace Brigades International, was set up to practice a Gandhian approach at the international level and to bring the lessons of the Indian movement, the Sahara Protest Team, and other initiatives into an ongoing organization. A.J. Muste, Michael Scott, and Indian leader J.P. Narayan were chosen as the three co-chairs of WPB. At about the same time, Northern Rhodesia's Kenneth Kaunda and Tanganyika's Julius Nyerere, both of whom had signed on as patrons of WPB, were the leading forces behind the Pan-African Freedom Movement for East and Central Africa (PAFMECA). Shortly after the 1961 Beirut gathering, a WPB team was invited to a conference of PAFMECA. Michael Scott, Bayard Rustin, a delegate from India, and Bill were selected as the representatives to the PAFMECA proceedings, held in Addis Ababa, Ethiopia. After briefing Martin Buber and the Israelis of the WPB initiatives, Bill "set sail" once again–literally, down the Red Sea–to re-connect with the African liberation movements.

Nelson Mandela had just come out of South Africa for a short period, and PAFMECA became PAFMECSA, including southern Africa (and including both the ANC and PAC). Kaunda, who was especially interested in nonviolence and the use of direct action tactics, invited the WPB to become an international support apparatus for the freedom struggle in Northern Rhodesia/Zambia and for his United National Independence Party (UNIP). Nyerere's Tanganyika African National Union (TANU) offered, in turn, that Dar-es-Salaam be the headquarters of WPB in Africa. Dar was already the center for PAFMECSA, which was headed by Kenyan activist Mbiyu Koinange, whose father, Chief Koinange, was co-leader with Jomo Kenyatta of the Kenyan independence movement.

"I had known Mbiyu for a long time," Bill recalls, "since we had met in London and I had been with him in Accra when he was representative for East Africa at the Accra African Affairs Center, after the All Africa People's Conference. We all knew each other very well, we decided to put the forces of UNIP, TANU, PAFMECSA, and WPB together into what we called Africa Freedom Action (AFA). We set up AFA specifically to support the movement for independence in Zambia.[2]

"Independence was kind of working it's way southward. Tanganyika had become independent in 1961. As we moved down south, we were moving into the more and more difficult areas– Zambia, Malawi, and Zimbabwe (which were then Northern Rhodesia, Nyasaland, and Southern Rhodesia). It was a logical moment to go down the continent; everybody in PAFMECSA agreed that it was the way to go."

The World Peace Brigade, working through AFA, had a special role due to Kaunda's special interests. They were to organize a march on Northern Rhodesia, along the same lines as the Sahara Protest. The plan was to use the resources and leadership of each of the organizations involved, to coordinate a truly mass action. WPB was to be the training group for the participants.

"We were going to be the nonviolent technicians, so to speak, the people to organize and train others how to be effective in the march," notes Bill. "That was the role that was seen for us, and it became clear that Kaunda, on principle, and Nyerere, on personality, leaned towards us. Most of the rest of the PAFMECSA leadership at that time did not have such a strong interest in direct action. Of course, mainland Tanganyika had achieved independence primarily through nonviolent means and, along with Ghana, posed an alternative to the drive towards armed struggle that occurred after 1960. Even with the Sharpeville Massacre and the Algerian war, UNIP and TANU still leaned towards nonviolent action, and TANU was very cooperative in assisting the Peace Brigade. They gave us a house to live in, they gave us access to transportation, and–like Ghana–they immediately provided a home for the various liberation movements of countries not yet free.

"All of these parties and individuals from the international movements were able to come together for a mass rally at Mbeya, near the Tanganyikan border of Zambia. And it wasn't too long after that, before the march to Zambia was to take place, that the British did an about-face and said that they would allow for an election which would provide for majority rule. One of the police officers of Northern Rhodesia who was British told us years later that the rally and planned march were taken very seriously by the British government. They were preparing ways to deal with us when we would attempt to come across the border. Even though the march was never held, AFA was definitely an element in forcing the British to make an agreement with UNIP which would allow for a majority-rule election."

By the time Zambia became independent, Bill was already working for the Tanganyikan government. When the march was called off and Kaunda decided to run for President, the U.S. and European pacifist movement, which had been financially supporting the WPB office, decided to turn it's attention to other "hot spots." In 1962, Julius Nyerere, who had become Tanganyikan Prime Minister at the time of independence eighteen months earlier, left government to focus on TANU Party activities and turned the Prime Minister position over to Rashidi Kawawa. Bill had become a staff member in Kawawa's office, dealing primarily with the needs of refugees. After serious political conflicts in neighboring Rwanda, there had been a great influx of refugee Watutsi from the north. He was also selected to be a member of the Tanganyikan delegation to Geneva that negotiated a United Nations High Commission for Refugees participation in East Africa.

"It was very interesting," Bill recollects, "that Bayard Rustin came over to close out the WPB operation when it became clear that we were not going to march. He went straight to Nyerere when it was a question of whether I would be employed by the government. Nyerere told him that he wanted me to stay on; he said that I'd been writing observations which were analytical and critical and he liked it and thought it would be good for me to stay." Already, Bill was beginning to host various activists from the liberation movements, though the refugee job involved much cross-country and international travel.

"Once, during the Spring of 1963," Bill remembers, "I saw an article in one of the major U.S. magazines that was carried overseas about the August civil rights March on Washington, D.C. I said that I thought the African movements should give some outward expression of support to the civil rights march, and the TANU officials agreed. Originally, I was supposed to get over to the U.S. in time to give the message of greetings to the March, and being part of the UN turned out to be one way of getting me over there. Unfortunately, the delegation didn't get to leave until after the March on Washington, but I was still able to fulfill one role, as an advisor on the U.S. Black movement to the African liberation groups.

"It was at this time that I had a lot to do with Prince Sadruddin Aga Khan of the world Ismaili community, who eventually became the UN High Commissioner on Refugees. He and I became really good friends and, in fact, we were having lunch at the UN Building in New York later that year, along with Bayard Rustin, when we heard that President Kennedy had been shot. Nobody believed it at first, but then, about twenty minutes later, the rumor was confirmed and the whole dining room emptied out. We had all been set to have a big party that evening, including a member of the Nigerian delegation to the UN who, it turns out, was a family relative of mine. But, of course, all affairs were off.

"The next day, I ran into Ehud Avriel, the Israeli ambassador to Ghana who had been my old benefactor. ' You know, we are just completely nonplussed by this country,' he said to me. 'It's one thing for a head of state to be assassinated–that's kind of like the risks you take, it's an occupational hazard. But here, you see the murdered head of state and the murderer shot on television. This country and it's violence!' It really overwhelmed him.

"At the end of the 1963 UN General Assembly, I returned to Africa via Kenya, which was having its independence celebrations. I was a little pissed-off at Tom Mboya because they hadn't officially invited me, but I decided that I was going to go anyway. I went to Nairobi and there was a party that was being held for invitees and delegates by the City Council, which was essentially an all-white body at that time. I put on my Ghana robe and costume and I thought that they wouldn't dare do anything–they didn't know who I was–and I went right in. Once inside, a dear friend, Caroline Plaskett Barrow, comes up to me with her husband Earl Barrow, who was then the Prime Minister of Barbados. While I'm talking to them, Mboya comes along and Caroline says to him: 'Oh, Tom, this is so wonderful, that you should invite Bill and me to this wonderful occasion.' Mboya replies: 'Oh, yes, I'm so glad that I invited you both.' From then on, I had 'invitee' status. I guess that that was the first independence celebration that I crashed!"

When Bill got back to Dar-es-Salaam in early 1964, he began a series of temporary positions, where he would essentially work himself out of jobs. "What the Tanzanians would do," as he describes it, "is put me in a position until there was a Tanganyikan qualified for it, and then they would move me on." Thus, he moved from the refugee officer position to a job working on the tenth anniversary celebrations of TANU. *Saba Saba* Day, the seventh day of the seventh month, came and went in July of 1964 with Bill in charge of foreign entertainment, taking care of U.S. folk singer Odetta, a Chinese acrobatic troupe, and others. He was then put on staff of the Ministry of Information, editing a public relations journal for the country. Next, he became editor of the nation's civil service magazine.

In a less formal capacity, Bill continued to serve as a bridge between the movements in the U.S. and the African liberation movement leaders. Maintaining contact with his colleagues in the War Resisters League, he learned of the early anti-Vietnam war activities. Once again deciding to put together a solidarity greeting, Bill coordinated signatures from leaders of TANU, UNIP, the ANC, SWAPO of Namibia, and FRELIMO of Mozambique, on a statement against the war in Vietnam. In 1965, he flew to New York, just as Student Nonviolent Coordinating Committee activist Bob Moses was getting ready to leave for Africa on a journey to increase his own Pan-African connections. Bill took Moses' place on the podium as a speaker at the first mass Fifth Avenue Peace Parade in New York, and delivered the African's message of support.

"I was really very thrilled," recalls Bill, "and impressed with the growth of both the civil rights and anti-Vietnam war movements. When I went to Africa in 1953, I really thought that everybody would be knuckling under to McCarthy and that there would be a dead period in the U.S. I was very happy to be proven wrong about that. I had some mixed feelings and partly a desire to be back in the U.S. and involved again. On the other hand, I was firm in the position that we were all in a global struggle, and that we would each choose our own battlegrounds. I had chosen Africa, and wanted to stick with that choice. I didn't feel dis-associated from the U.S. in any significant sense, and what impressed me so was the mass nature of these movements. I had, from my old days, been used to being one of only a dozen people on a picket line.

"Through this period in Tanzania, I got to see Nyerere less and less, because that's what happens when people become presidents of countries!" Nyerere had gone back into government after a ten-month period of working for the Party. "I was keeping in touch with various people within the government and TANU hierarchy. I would, of course, meet up with Nyerere on occasion, but mainly I would put my comments in writing and send them along. I particularly remember one time when I was very disturbed about government bureaucracy, and wrote about how the bureaucrats were really the killers of the dream. Joan Wicken, Nyerere's long-time personal secretary, wrote back saying that she realized how frustrating it was not to receive any replies, but that I should be assured that the letters were being read by the President, that he valued them, and that they were being appreciated. In the meantime, I had to deal with my own discomforts about being a government bureaucrat in many of these situations, trying to fit in and to help humanize the operations."

Bill reflected more generally on the role of individuals–particularly African Americans–attempting to play a role in newly independent African countries and governments. "When you go into a country where America's foreign policy has definitely rubbed the leaders and the people the wrong way, naturally you have a very rough, tough row to hoe if you're becoming politically active. One would have to remain in a country for a good length of time and have the people get to know you fairly well, because of the problems often caused by 'outsiders.' "

Discussing this dynamic thirty years ago with Ernest Dunbar, Bill noted that a feeling was particularly strong among certain groups in Africa that "America was going to use it's Afro-Americans as a possible 'fifth column': use their color to get in and gain access. This related, for example, to American policy in the Congo, to which most Africans objected. If you're an American government employee and you're an Afro-American, it's your job to interpret the American point of view on your government's actions in the

Congo. As a Black person who is also a U.S. official, what is one going to say about the racial situation in the U.S.? Are you going to point toward the 'positive' things at a time when there are riots or there are Selmas?

"In 1966, on the Fourth of July celebration, an Afro-American group that was in Tanzania decided to boycott the traditional party given at the U.S. Embassy because they felt that there was nothing to celebrate. It was to celebrate "independence"–and they weren't independent. There was an Afro-American official here who had to develop a diplomatic 'illness' because he was in a fix and didn't know what to do. He didn't know whether to join the Embassy crowd or to stay away with his friends."

These contradictions took some interesting turns for an African American working not for the U.S., but for the African "host" government. As in his experiences traveling with the Ghanaian delegation in the racially segregated U.S. south, Bill's early years in Tanzania included some events which required his own political clarity and independence.

"When I came to Tanzania at first," he recounted, "there was an accusation of an American plot here; that America was plotting against Tanzania. At that time, they had American officials going around to the houses where Americans were living, alerting them. One came to me and handed me a mimeographed paper saying that there were going to be anti-American riots and demonstrations and that I absolutely shouldn't go downtown. This was part of the Embassy plan for safeguarding American nationals.

"As far as I was concerned, my first reaction to him was simply to tell him that I was sure he had many other people to handle and that he should sort of pass by my house. I didn't say anything to him because he wasn't the responsible party. However, I did get to some of the Embassy people I knew, and asked them what the hell was going on. They said, 'Well, after all, we've had experience with these things in Asia and so we wanted to be sure you were all right.' So I said to my American Embassy friends, 'If you were really concerned about me, then what you should do is to contact your 'embassies' in Mississippi and Georgia and Alabama. That's where I'm really in danger!'

"You know, I have attended meetings and I have gone with no hesitation into the middle of Dar-es-Salaam at the height of anti-American disturbances. The thing is, I'm in more relative danger in the United States than I would be here."

* * *

Julius Kambarage Nyerere was born in 1922 in the village of Butiama in northern Tanzania, the son of the Chief of Uzanaki. A secondary school teacher by occupation, he went to university at Edinburgh, Scotland before returning to Tanganyika and, in 1954, became the first President of the newly-formed TANU. When Tanganyika became independent in 1961, Nyerere negotiated in two years time a union with neighboring Zanzibar, and the United Republic of Tanzania was born. Architect of the Arusha Declaration establishing the policies of socialism and self-reliance (*Ujamaa na Kujitegemea*), he led the formation of frontline states in solidarity with the southern African nations still under colonial rule. A past President of the Organization of African Unity (OAU), he stepped down as Tanzanian President in 1985, subsequently becoming Chairman of the South Commission. Nyerere is affectionately called Mwalimu, the Swahili word for teacher.[3]

Despite Bill's forty-year history with Mwalimu, and his thirty-plus-year residency in Tanzania, the two only meet on occasion, every few years. When we requested a visit through Joan Wicken, still Nyerere's assistant in the Dar office of the South Commission, it became clear that traveling to Butiama would be the easiest way to arrange a meeting. Traveling north on Air Tanzania, past the slopes of Mount Kilamanjaro, we discussed our overview of questions for the master statesman. Though holding no official government posts, a certain level of protocol still exists around Mwalimu, which became clear as the Regional Commissioner of the Mara Region met us in nearby Musoma. Informed that we would meet with Nyerere at his house the following morning, we prepared our notes at quiet accommodations near Lake Victoria. Our drive to Butiama, through the rural province, underscored Nyerere's own preference to get "back to the roots"–to his own ancestral homeland, to the farming environment that makes up most of Tanzania, and to simpler social surroundings than the noisy and dusty Dar.

Bill began our discussions, of which the following is an excerpt:

BS: One early story in our relationship that I wanted to recall is of your coming to Ghana during the independence celebrations. Dr. Bob Lee and I had arranged for a dinner between you and Martin Luther King.

JKN: Yes, that was my first time to meet King.[4]

BS: You were coming between 1958–61 to Ghana on various visits with regard to the African liberation movements and I recalled one time just before the independence of Tanganyika you came and you spent some time with Efua and me. We got into this hot debate about preventive detention and we talked so long you kept Kwame Nkrumah waiting for about 15 minutes! We were so engrossed we didn't realize how the time was going. Then, in 1962, of course, was when TANU invited the World Peace Brigade to set up headquarters for the Africa Freedom Action, to support Kaunda in the struggle for independence in Northern Rhodesia.

JKN: I even had the idea that we should march to Mozambique! That is the period when I was outside government. It was immediately after independence and I had resigned from government.

BS: Yes, then you were in a period of relative freedom.

JKN: Yes, a little...actually quite a lot of freedom, because at that time I had not been too much entangled in the bureaucracy. I had been Chief Minister and Prime Minister for a couple of years perhaps. But Tanganyika had been independent for only a couple of weeks before I had resigned. So I had not been too much involved in the government, I still had that feeling of freedom.

It was very difficult to get people to believe it, but I never wanted to be administrator at all–I wanted the independence of the country. The real achievement, I saw, the real cement of the country, was the Party. It had built the unity of the people, it had achieved the independence from colonialism, and it was quite clear to me that if I continued in government–and I had no interest in government at all–the Party, which I saw as more important than government for the people, would disintegrate. The cadres we had built wanted to join government; they all wanted to join the government!

I recall one meeting in a district called Njombe in the south. They were saying to me, "Mwalimu, what is our future?" And I tried to explain to them, "Well, the future is the Party. What do you mean *our* future?" Frankly, as I explained this to them, it sounded to myself rather unconvincing coming from a person in government. Fortunately I was not myself interested in government at that time. I had to get out and organize.

But it was not smooth; my getting out was not smooth. It was misunderstood. The British bureaucracy (which we still had) thought I was being pushed out of the Party. And some of the Party members themselves who did not know what was happening (because I had not told them) thought that I was rather disgusted–which was not true. So it took a long time before I could convince people. They thought that I was fighting for my political life!

Unfortunately, it did not last long because in nine months' time I was back in government as President of the Republic. I got stuck. I got stuck in government, and couldn't get out! Once I had done it a second time there was no way in which I could say I am getting out, so I got stuck in government for twenty-three years.

BS: I remember in the history of India, that Gandhi had said to the Congress Party: "Don't take power, go back to the village republics." That's what he wanted to do. And these people said, "Are you joking? After all, we've been through, all these sacrifices, we're not going to get any of the benefits?" So it never worked.

Now, the question that we're raising, and I know it's not the first time we've talked about it, is beyond the justification for the independence of countries in Africa, there is the independence and the dignity of ordinary African people. And the conditions we're in now, for so many of them–for millions of them–are horrible and terrible times. If you could reflect on how we have come to the independence of so many African states, and the strategies used for the governing of them...even today, can you think once more about whether, within Africa itself, there has to be any kind of new look at how independence is achieved? More importantly, with the conditions as they are at present and the work you have been doing all your life on self-reliance and the dignity of peoples, are there new roads–politically, economically, socially–that we must consider for the present and the future?

JKN: The answer is, of course, yes. All living things have to have a new look all the time. This is the meaning of life. If things are living, they have to change. This is normal for all living things, including living societies. Some of the pressures of change are internal, some are external–but such is life. This is true of countries also.

These countries became independent, and their leaders had a vision of the future. Some articulated it, Kwame was one of the most articulate of our leaders, and he articulated the future of our peoples and our continent. I did articulate, to some extent. And never in life can you achieve your articulation. It is easier to formulate an objective than to achieve it.

I wrote the Arusha Declaration myself! It's very easy. I read it today and I say, "Boy, I didn't know, that was something!" So we have not been able to achieve what we sought as the ideal of independence. The British used to say "You people can't become independent because you don't have this, you don't have that, you don't have the other thing." I'd say this is rubbish. I myself used to say, as a polemic: We wanted to be independent because we are people. Full stop. You can't put conditionalities on our independence. We simply want to be independent. Full stop! We want to be independent in our own country. It does not matter how we live.

Kwame put it differently. Naturally, we didn't simply want to be independent, we wanted more. But we wanted that independence as an instrument of the more. I used to use the Swahili saying. It sounds better in Swahili, you can't really translate it: "A guinea hen does not lay eggs in captivity. It has to be free." It can't thrive under conditions of unfreedom. This fellow is talking to us about thriving: "You have not thrived and therefore don't become independent." This was absurd to me. We could not thrive until we became independent.

So we had this vision of what we wanted to achieve. And we have not achieved it. But this is quite normal and therefore we go through the process. Some of these failures were completely normal because obviously the objectives were idealistic. This was to be expected. Of course, there was also a lot of stupidity, because then things began to go wrong very rapidly after independence.

Kwame was removed. I never agreed with Kwame one hundred percent. When I was in Ghana recently they asked if they should publish those letters I used to exchange with Kwame. I said, "Why don't you wait until I die!" We exchanged some rough letters because we disagreed on the way towards African unity. We agreed about African unity, but we did not agree about how. And Kwame did not last long. Ghana became independent in 1957 and eight years later he was gone, removed. Kwame is given as an example of one of those Africans who did not want to leave power. But he was President of Ghana for only eight years. That's all, eight years–the normal term for American presidents, even two hundred years after the independence of the country. And here was a young country, and this fellow had been head of state for only eight years.

Things then began going wrong in Africa. The military took over everywhere, and it was not the military who were articulating the ambitions for Africa at all. The political leaders, people like Kwame, they didn't have a chance! Actually, of all of them, I had a better time than most. I lasted. So things naturally went wrong, again, from that point of view. The history of the continent that was expected to take place after independence actually did not take place. We had too much interference. I mean, it would have happened in any case, but I have to talk about history as it is. And history as it was, Africa again was not allowed to develop in freedom because the Cold War took over and we had these externally supported dictatorships everywhere over the continent. And so we ran into trouble. We did not develop. I naturally resent some of the implications I get about the "wrong things" that are happening on the continent of Africa. We were never allowed a chance!

I resented it. I got that letter from U.S. President Ford in 1975 after Angola became independent. Here was this President of the United States writing to all of us saying he can't accept the idea that the MPLA should take over the government of Angola. This is a letter to us! To him, the MPLA was Russia. So that country has been in trouble ever since. But it's not the only one that was subjected to the Cold War. One side of the Cold War or the other supported ALL the dictators of Africa.

So, we are starting again. Again, with a tremendous trumpeting from the outside. Again not allowing the continent to evolve, to evolve itself. This is a very difficult time in which we are living, for the small nations. I was saying earlier, before we started this discussion, that I'm going to the Nonaligned Summit. How many leaders there are going to open their mouths about what is happening now with the world? Who is going to say "Why are you continuing to do this on Iraq? We thought that war was over. Why are you destroying that country? We thought that war was over. That war had a limited purpose–free Kuwait. So why are you killing the people of Iraq?" Who is going to say this? It's very difficult now.

This is what is happening on this continent–tremendous pressure from the outside. There is no period in history when any continent, when any peoples, were subjected to this kind of thing. Once again you see what is happening in Africa: so-called democracy and the manuals of democracy, the manuals of all the governments which are "blessed" by the West. The manual has been prepared in Paris, written in Washington, and all of these countries have to act in accordance with that manual.

We of the older generation, for us it is "*A Luta Continua*"–it is really "The Struggle is Continuing." The younger generation, they feel that we have let them down–and they have a right to think that way. In a sense, it is true; perhaps we could have resisted more. But we succumbed, we thought we had won, and we did not continue the liberation of our people because we thought we had arrived. I think that sense of arrival is true even now. I fear that with the so-called democratization, the new generation will feel "We have arrived." And again another round of disappointment will come.

So, I am not too happy. We cannot say the continent is free. The continent as a continent is not free. We did not simply want to put up a flag, we wanted our people to feel free–and on their own continent, that sense of freedom is not there. It's absurd. It's not necessary to blame outsiders all the time for these things because, again, we can resist. At the very least, we could resist the pressures that reduce the degree that our people can determine their own affairs. That is not happening now.

BS: Now you tried, and other people have tried to do something different for your countries. Here you had written about and set the plans for Ujamaa. Jerry Rawlings and his people were trying to do something else politically, rather than just trying to take over what they inherited. The question is what really happened there? We used to have some discussions: if you didn't accept the economics of the north, should you have accepted the political structures of the north? And when I say north, I'm not talking about the East or the West–whether it's communist or capitalist, it doesn't matter.

Basil Davidson has written a book called *The Black Man's Burden* and he has subtitled it "The Curse of the Nation–State." His position, which I think you should be very familiar with, is that within the African traditions there is something to build on which is not taken over from outside of the continent, that there are things in the African tradition to build on. As I recall, Ujamaa was based on the idea of building on a traditional familyhood. Yet opposed to that is the nation-state, with its bureaucracy. I wrote you a letter once, calling bureaucracy "the killer of the dream." The center interfered with the concept of Ujamaa.

This is a question not only for Tanzania, but also for the rest of the continent: do you think that there could have been other approaches that would not have resulted in what I would call structural violence? You have talked about this many times yourself, the fact that peace is not just the absence of tension, it's the presence of justice. Do you think now that indeed, on the African continent, there needs to be another look at the structure of the nation-state, with the built-in repressions that there are, in order for the people to benefit? I've often wondered whether you have felt that Ujamaa had ever really been tried. Has it ever really been tried?

JKN: I was not seeing Ujamaa outside of the nation-state. I've questioned many, many, many things from Europe, but I've not questioned the nation-state. I cannot think, how do I think in terms of *not* the nation-state? I don't accept the states in Africa because I think they are all artificial nations. We could have had more normal, more viable, more reasonable nations, but I was not thinking outside of the nation-state at all. My questioning did not reach the nation-state. My questioning focused upon the borders. And although I question the African borders, nevertheless I did say in Accra in '64 that we had to accept the borders as we inherited them from colonialism because if we begin to disentangle the borders–as Somalia was trying to do, as Morocco was trying to do–you run into trouble. You say you want all the ethnic groups to put the state on the basis of heterogeneity, and you run into trouble.

Therefore, what I was questioning was not the nation-state. I've never questioned the nation-state. I know the problems of the nation-state; I don't know the answer! I know the problems of the bureaucracies, I became a bureaucrat! I told Samora Machel of Mozambique once, "Samora, at one time I was leading the people of Tanzania–now I lead their bureaucracy!"

When you lead a bureaucracy, you almost inevitably lose touch with the people. So I know the problems of bureaucracy, but I don't know the answers. If I discover it–because I do worry about this problem–if I get the answer I will tell my friends, "This is the answer." I don't know the answer to the nation-state problem at all.

There is a movement in the world that is quite good I think, questioning the powers of the nation-state. But at present the relationship of peoples in the world is through the nation-state, the defense of the nation-state, etc. Why doesn't the international community move? Inevitably we are globalizing relations, why don't we globalize governments also? But the big powers don't want to globalize government because they want both. They want to be able to control the world and not be controlled by it. To globalize the world means to democratize it, and to democratize it means you give up powers to others.

So it's easier for the bigger powers to globalize, but to keep the national power (because they have the national power), to be able to use it to impose on others. At that level one can say the nation-state is a problem–not simply the problem of an individual in a country. It's a user of power against the individual; it's a wielder of power against society. At the international level, it prevents greater linkage between people because it's not an instrument of integration.

For Ujamaa, I was thinking of using an existing African system to build upon–I did believe that you don't have to absorb things from outside. Society is a living thing, you can grow, you can develop, you can use ideas from the outside, but you have to have a base because you are a people. Being a people, you have your own base and on the basis of that base you continue developing yourself. If you are building society in terms of equality–even from a purely Marxist point of view (and I was not a Marxist)–all basic societies (what they call primitive societies) build upon the individual, but an individual *in* society. And I said, why don't you begin from there? In the modern world you are thinking in terms of a big society, but where the central communities are strong and some people have destroyed them, we are trying to build them–or we still have them. So why don't we build Ujamaa on the basis of the attitudes which we already have here?

We have not achieved all we wanted to achieve, perhaps a lot less, but again there is a question of societies being allowed to develop. The modern world is very different from societies that were allowed to develop before.

So again, how much were we allowed to develop? Don't blame me for continually going back to what the outside has done to this continent. Societies develop–they make their own mistakes and they develop. Of course they fight, they have armies–and you can't think of societies in Europe without armies. But that was the instrument which established the state. In fact, it is incredible that the unarmed societies survived. The ones with the guns came and said, "What you have is no good. We are going to liberate you." And they began to "liberate" us from our own culture! And this was not yesterday–it was more than 400 years ago. So in liberating, us they imposed colonialism on us–this was the way they liberated us. For them the way to stop oppression within our societies was to dominate us.

Societies have to develop; they have to have room to develop themselves. Today societies that have not reached the position of being on top have very little room to develop–especially these fragile societies of Africa. They are very fragile. We have to develop in the present atmosphere; we cannot invent. That's where I come back to what you said. The nation-state is a given. I don't know how we could question the nation-state. To the extent that we have to accept the world as it is the nation-state is there. What I say to Africa is: Do you have to have Tanzania as your nation-state? Shouldn't we build bigger, more viable nation–states?

BS: Part of the problem seems to be that the center has not been happy with the development at the grassroots. The center would feel threatened by the grassroots development which was happening under Ujamaa and would attempt to crush it. I hear clearly that you always thought of development within the nation-state structure; but even within that structure, the built-in bureaucracy, anxious to hold on to its own power, was always a counter–force....

JKN: I don't think this is a valid criticism of these countries at all. These are countries that started without a bureaucracy. We have much more of a bureaucracy today, of course, in Tanzania than we did at the time of Ujamaa because we really didn't have very much. The attempt at that point would be to develop power at the center. The attempt in these young nations, which are really not nations at all, but impositions–African nations were lucky if they became independent with some power at the center. So the power at the center was not something to spit at–this is what you wanted because otherwise you are not going to have a nation. The colonial power was able to say that there is a Tanganyika because the British governor was there, with all of his authority, and that was how they were able to control this country. Now you come and you want to build us into a community. You don't have the machinery. So the building of the machinery–which is what we call the bureaucracy–is part of the nation building. It wasn't there. And let me go back and perhaps remove the idealism from my resignation. What we really had was the Party as a cementing force, which really built the nation.

MM: But what of the balance between the need for the development of a center in order to develop a national culture and the over-bureaucratization or abuses that will stifle the grassroots? How to mediate between those two needs? I am thinking not just of the past, but now on into the future. You have mentioned the South Commission not being hampered by being just a governmental body but people-to-people, community-to-community.

JKN: Well I think that there are many of these countries–not many, but several (and I include Tanzania among them)–where the center is now strong, quite strong. They can afford to democratize. But it is important to have a strong center, otherwise you just disintegrate. There is no democracy without discipline. So Tanzania has built its mechanism, it's government. I don't know what's going to happen now. We are going to have a multiparty system, and we can afford to further democratize. Now whether that is going to happen I don't know, because if it becomes chaotic you go right into tyranny. It must be democracy and it must be disciplined democracy. Discipline should be self-imposed, but there are no countries where discipline is self-imposed. There are laws and the people in the community will have to obey those laws. If you don't obey the laws then you run into trouble. So we have democracy and it has to be defended by law. Sounds almost like a contradiction in terms, but you have to do that. This country is strong, we have built it, and perhaps we have succeeded in a sense because we have consolidated what we inherited from colonialism.

My differences with Kwame were that Kwame thought there was somehow a shortcut, and I was saying that there was no shortcut. This is what we have inherited, and we'll have to proceed within the limitations that that inheritance has imposed upon us. Kwame thought that somehow you could say, "Let there be a United States of Africa" and it would happen. I kept saying, "Kwame, it's a slow process." He had tremendous contempt for a large number of the leaders of Africa and I said, "Fine, but they are there. What are you going to do with them? They don't believe as you do–as you and I do–in the need for the unity of Africa. BUT WHAT DO YOU DO? THEY ARE THERE, AND WE HAVE TO PROCEED ALONG WITH EVERYBODY!" And I said to him in so many words that we're not going to have an African Napoleon, who is going to conquer the continent and put it under one flag. It is not possible.

At the OAU Conference in 1963, I was actually trying to defend Kwame. I was the last to speak and Kwame had said this charter has not gone far enough because he thought we would leave Addis with a United States of Africa. I told him that this was absurd; that it can't happen. This is what we have been able to achieve. No builder, after putting the foundation down, complains that the building is not yet finished. You have to go on building and building until you finish, but he was impatient because he saw the stupidity of the others.

But here we are. I think this country has achieved much–sometimes I think we are too complacent. But the truth is we are still as fragile as most countries in Africa. But we have done something. I live in the village and people in the villages are very free. I really don't see the bureaucracy here. We have constraints here but the people can't say that it is a bureaucracy that is causing the problems.

BS: But they could complain about the sale of their cotton and other products and the prices determined by the parastatals....

JKN: They do.

BS: Another question we have. Do the methods of achieving independence in the different countries have anything to do with what happens afterward? The question of ends and means? For example, I was mentioning that the African states in the Lusaka Manifesto 1969 said that you all would try to achieve freedom in South Africa by peaceful means. Obviously, you said that because you felt that was the best way to achieve this objective, had it been possible. However, you also made it clear that you would support the liberation movements in their armed struggle if there were no alternative. Many of the liberation movements ignored the latter statement. Do you feel that there is any connection between the methods to achieve independence and what happens afterwards?

JKN: It all depends. Certainly, there are some countries that go through a long armed struggle for independence. Other countries achieved independence, as we did, without a long struggle and without armed resistance. We achieved independence through political mobilization in a relatively short period, and other countries have suffered long and with much bloodshed. It must affect the condition of the people somehow.

It should also determine the kind of government at the end of the day. Governments would inevitably look more militarized if armed struggle had been a decisive factor. In Tanzania, we were the most civilian of governments because we did not engage in armed struggle. I've always made it clear what I felt in the drafting of the Lusaka

Manifesto. People kept on saying "it's fine for you since you achieved independence without bloodshed" and I said, "Yes, but I didn't want bloodshed for nothing, because it was possible for us without it."

For me, the nonviolence of our movement was not philosophical at all. That's why we had–in the case of Mozambique, in the case of the Portuguese, but also eventually Zimbabwe and South Africa–we had to support the armed struggle. It seemed to be the only way out because the Portuguese said, "We don't have colonies, Mozambique *is* Portugal." So the only way you could shake those fellows off was by armed struggle. Rhodesia's Ian Smith was saying the same thing. Smith was saying, "Not in one thousand years, not in my lifetime." So the only way we could shake this man was through armed struggle.

The nationalists did not always like my ideas. My own idea about taking power was that nothing succeeds like success, but also nothing fails like failure. Those who would win would be those who showed early success. I kept saying that we had to be selective. Some wanted us to take on the whole of southern Africa. I said you can't–we don't have the means to take on the whole of southern Africa. We had to tackle the problems of southern Africa piece by piece. It seemed to me that the Portuguese were the weakest of the group. I said, "Let's take on the Portuguese and win." When you win, the morale of the African freedom fighters will go up and the morale of their opponents throughout southern Africa will go down. I said that that's what we should do–demonstrate success–which we did.

BS: We found in our travels that people were very, very much concerned about the violence-taking place in their societies. They were saying that there has to be some way to avoid the increase of this culture of violence....

JKN: True, that is a point I did not make. Correct. When you have a society that goes through, as you say, almost a culture of violence and for such a long time–well, you inherit some of it.

BS: If you look at South Africa, for example: the mass action that they engaged in has been their most effective means throughout their history. The armed struggle was really a more dramatic form of propaganda.

JKN: That is true. In that sense, though, in all of our other liberation movements in southern Africa, it was the other way around. The ANC and the others were better organized politically than they were militarily. With Mozambique's FRELIMO and Angola's MPLA, they had the guns but they had very little political organization in the country. It was really like that. After all, the ANC is more than 70 years old. FRELIMO consisted mainly of those who remained in the bush; the Party and those with arms were almost identical because the Portuguese did not allow any political activity in the country. But in South Africa, the violence in the country must be blamed on the apartheid regime rather than on the method of liberation. Of course, those who were criticizing me were saying that I was deliberately delaying the armed struggle in South Africa.

BS: What people often say is that the only thing the colonizers will understand is force, and I say "Yes, they understand it a damn-sight better than we do *and* they have the means, so we must invent something else. We always say we believe we are revolutionaries first, and we are seeking nonviolent alternatives. But revolution is the key.

JKN: Gandhi was philosophically opposed to violence completely. So was Martin Luther King. And that is the clan to which you belong.

As a Christian, I read the Bible, and it says, "Thou Shalt Not Kill." There is no exception there, it just says "Thou Shalt Not Kill"–full stop. As a Christian, I should come to that conclusion–but I couldn't come to that conclusion at all. I have not been able to come to that conclusion. My opposition to violence is the unnecessary use of violence. As to the violence of oppression, we are dealing with states and states wield power. So sometimes you have to use violence against the violence of the state.

I find myself in that position in Tanzania. I have opposed violence. I have said don't use violence for nothing, because we can achieve our own independence without the use of violence. At least let's try and see. If we fail, of course, that's a different thing–but we succeeded. Then I was misunderstood because I was discouraging violence in Tanzania during the Mau Mau in Kenya. While I was discouraging violence in Tanzania during that period of tremendous violence in Kenya, I was associated with Gandhi and I said, "No, I don't take the position of Gandhi." I don't call myself a violent person, but I'm not opposed to violence philosophically.

BS: One of the problems we are raising in South Africa is this: if one uses nonviolence only as a tactic, then you take away a weapon. Part of the power of the nonviolent approach, however, is the spiritual force. So those who use it simply as a tactic and then say it failed because they use a little violence over here and a little nonviolence over there are making a mistake. We say–at the very least–that each campaign must have a consistency. In armed struggle, you wouldn't take a man's rifle away from him. In nonviolence, the rifle is a belief in spiritual power.

Could we pursue one other point a bit further? You said that you and Nkrumah had one objective, but you differed on how to achieve it. When you thought about a united Africa, did you think that the present nation-states would merge?

JKN: When I clashed with Kwame, it was when we were very close to a federation of East African states and Kwame was completely opposed to the idea. He said that regionalization–that's what he called it–was Balkanization on a larger scale. I said, "Look, Kwame, this is absurd." I thought that historically there were grounds for different groupings of countries trying to come together. West Africans at one time–under the British–had a common currency. Basically, the French had two huge colonies–French Equatorial Africa and French West Africa. I thought it was possible to move towards unity by putting those areas together. But even that didn't happen. I thought that these groups could come together naturally, within the OAU. Then there could be the propaganda, an incentive, and the push for greater unity.

Kwame thought that we all could just sit down together and come out as a United States of Africa. I really think that Kwame was perhaps over-influenced by the way that the U.S. and the Soviet Union came together. You know the way the thirteen colonies came together, drafted a charter, and then declared the United States of America? I never thought it would work this way, because these African countries had become independent and the mistake was evident in East Africa. If we wanted to come together, we should have come together *before* independence, because if you wait until after independence it cannot be done. With four presidents, four flags, four national anthems, four seats at the UN–ahh! It's extremely difficult.

BS: And I don't think there was anyone else besides you who stated that they were willing to delay their own independence....

JKN: I did, and I ran into trouble with my own party. I said it's so dangerous if we want a united East Africa for Tanganyika to become independent before the others. We should delay our own independence and wait for all the four countries to become independent together, and we come out of colonialism as a single country. Well, ideals are one thing, but achievement–we ended up with only Tanganyika and Zanzibar coming together.

BS: Didn't you note, about the preamble of the OAU, that it says "We the heads of state"–it doesn't even say "We the People?"

JKN: No, what I said was that the UN Charter has it better: it says "We the People of the world," whereas the OAU Charter says "We the heads of state."

BS: Did you not, at a certain time, just shake your head and say that there must be a devil in Africa?

JKN: I said that there *is* a devil in Africa. I went to Addis and it was an incredible meeting. Here is this continent of young nations coming from colonialism and so forth and the debate is awful, and really what provoked me was the French-speaking counties you know. With all of their French culture, training in rationalization–you can't really argue with those fellows. And I discovered some of these fellows have their visas–THEIR VISAS–signed by the French ambassadors in their own countries! And I said, "Oh, but I thought you were fighting for freedom?"

I had given up PAFMECA. PAFMECA was 1962, and in '63 the North African and the West African countries had divided themselves between the Casablanca group and the Monrovian group, the radicals and the conservatives–really absurd! So I welcomed the idea that we could all be together, rather than have a continent divided along ideological lines. After the OAU was established in 1963, I allowed PAFMECA to die out. I'm still quietly complaining, because PAFMECA was a movement of the people. It was an organization of the liberation movements, and therefore could *be* a movement of the people. "We the heads of state!" When I hear the African heads of state talking like a bunch of colonials sent by France, of course I get livid! That's why I said there is a devil in Africa, and that devil is still around. We're still fighting that blessed devil!

BS: Thirty years ago, when you were late for your appointment with Nkrumah, you told me that if I were not in favor of preventive detention, I was going to be against you. You said the reason for that is that all of these "liberal" countries can afford to have so much freedom because they have powerful armies and powerful police, and when the security of the state is really at risk they can clamp down. You suggested that we also had to have some mechanism to control those types of situations. Given our experiences over the years, and given the abuse of these laws which has taken place, do you still feel the same way about preventive detention?

JKN: Yes–the quick answer is yes. Once you've accepted the nation–state, you accept the consequences–including armies, including security services bureaucracy, police, and the lot. As to abuse, well, the army can be misused. Many of the armies on the continent are used against their own people instead of fighting external enemies. The army was always intended to fight an external enemy, but African armies are often used to fight the people *within* the country. There are misuses of these instruments of state. It is true–it is true everywhere. There are differences of scale, but the scale depends upon the sense of security of the nation. And every nation under the sun, when they feel that the security of the state is threatened, invoke all these methods everywhere.

In Tanzania, I had the responsibility of building these instruments of state

During a time in my Presidency, people were actually tortured. I was furious, I said we cannot allow this. There is no way we can allow this. There was pressure on me not to have the security boys tried, and I said they jolly well have got to go to court. And they all went to court. First of all, I got the Minister and the Regional Commissioners who were involved out of office. I had to get the Minister of State for Security out of office as well. I said these officials have to be tried, and they were tried and were locked up. I think one or two of them were convicted of murder. I had stopped allowing capital punishment, so we locked them up for life.

I don't want to be misunderstood on this. I do accept the rule of law and the courts. Usually we have to go through the courts. All I'm saying is that no nation has found that when the security of the nation is threatened, the court system is enough. No nation under the sun! When they feel the security of the state is threatened, they lock people up. In the case of a young nation, you know that the mechanism of the law and courts cannot handle it. So, you build a mechanism that can handle it. Sometimes it is misused, and when it is misused you should have a system which is able to say that it was not the intention that it be misused. You must also have a mechanism to protect the citizens.

BS: All I'm saying is that fatherhood belongs to God. Brotherhood belongs to mankind! That's how I would put it.

JKN: Fine, but we do have governments, and governments do wield power. I don't know how you get out of this. What I dislike is when nations are stopped from evolving naturally. The stunting of the economic, social, and political growth of the continent of Africa is what I don't like. Nations do grow, and there are thinking people in these nations, and in the course of history there is development. People don't stop, people have ideas. Nations evolve, but nations must evolve in freedom because there is no other way you can evolve except in freedom. Sometimes you speak of freedom as anarchism, but really there is no way you can have freedom without organization–and organization sometimes means restraints, means laws, means "don'ts."

I believe in freedom because I can't think and develop without freedom. This must be true of every human being.

BS: Ok. Let individuals develop, and let the nations be secondary.

JKN: It cannot be. I'm telling you, Bill, if the blessed Lord had wanted a planet for myself, He would have done it. He could have made a planet for every single individual but He never did it. He put us in community, and we jolly well have to live as part of it. Of course, I'm an individual and I respect my own individuality. But I am an individual *and* a member of a community. And the community has conditions. All the commandments–Thou Shalt Not–are about community. Now there is an anarchism that is called democracy, but rejects the community. But I don't accept that, I don't accept anarchism.

I wish that we had had a chance to develop Ujamaa because I don't believe we have failed in Ujamaa. I believe it is in the spirit...individuals, yes–but individuals in the community. Individuals, yes–because I myself am an extremely assertive individual. Nobody can doubt my own commitment to my own individualism, but I am still an individual within the community.

BS: I agree! I believe, though, in my personal opinion, that the stopping of Ujamaa here, for example, was more because of the state bureaucracy at the center than because of anything else.

JKN: Ujamaa can still come to the fore...and it will! Bernard Shaw, who was an atheist, once noted that somebody was saying Christianity had failed. And he was saying that you cannot say Christianity has failed: where has it been tried? Ujamaa has yet to be really tried.

* * *

In his 1968 essay collection, *Uhuru na Ujamaa/Freedom and Socialism,*[5] Julius Nyerere outlined his visions of village communalism as well as early musings on the meaning of freedom. Though some countries in Africa had achieved "nominal independence," he wrote, they have "no real freedom to determine their own policies–either domestic or external–because they are held in thrall." Asserting that "the struggle for freedom must go on," he commented on the methods needed in achieving freedom: "Our preference, and that of every true African patriot, has always been for peaceful methods of struggle. We abhor the sufferings, the terror, and the shear waste, which are involved in violent upheavals, and believe that peaceful progress is worth some sacrifice in terms of time. But when the door is slammed shut, and bolted, then the struggle must take other forms; we cannot surrender." Ultimately, he concluded, "legal independence is not enough."

It's noteworthy that, despite over two decades of changes in world politics, Mwalimu's perspective–and the relevance of his remarks–remain unchanged. Unsurprisingly, his words still hold significance for Pan-Africanists and activists worldwide, as recently evidenced by the 1995 re-publishing of his essay "Capitalism or Socialism: The Rational Choice" by the U.S.–based New Afrikan group, Spear and Shield Publications.[6] More than simply a rhetorical speech, the paper is an analytic presentation on the implications of economic independence and freedom. As with his more recent work with the South Commission, he helps to summarize the conditions and options of the entire "under-developed" countries.

"Third World capitalism," he noted, has "no choice except to cooperate with external capitalism, as a very junior partner. Otherwise, it would be strangled at birth. You cannot develop capitalism in our countries without foreign capitalists, their money, and their management enterprise. And these foreign capitalists will invest in Third World countries only if, when, and to the extent that they are convinced that to do so would be more profitable to them than any other investment. Development through capitalism, therefore, means that we Third World nations have to meet conditions laid down by others."

On the other hand, he accepts that "to argue that capitalism is incompatible with the aspirations of the Third World does not mean that the alternative of socialism is an easy one, nor that success under it is automatic. But socialism *can* be compatible with our aspirations; by adopting socialist policies, it is possible for us to maintain our independence and develop towards human dignity for all our people.... None of this means that the great inequalities within the society, or the exploitation of groups, or even the seizure of power and privilege by a small minority, is automatically ruled out in a society that opts for socialism.... [But] the vital point is the meeting of people's needs, not the making of profit....

"It cannot be denied," he concluded, "that many difficulties face a Third World country which chooses the socialist alternative of development. Not least among these are it's own past, the dynamism of capitalist initiative techniques, and the gambler instinct which every human being seems to possess, so that we all hope we shall be among the privileged not the exploited. But I believe that we can choose the socialist path, and that by so doing we can develop ourselves in freedom, and towards those conditions which allow dignity and self respect for every one of our citizens."

Freedom for the South, according to this formula, is equated with development in general and socialist development in particular. Yet the unbridled hopes for an Africanist alternative in Tanzania were to meet with disappointments at least equal to its capitalist and communist neighbors. Though Ujamaa and the Arusha Declaration were the hope of all progressives, and Tanzania became the center for revolutionaries from all over the world, Ujamaa in practice–as Bill and Mwalimu discussed–was never given a full chance.

In practice, Ujamaa was to draw upon three aspects of traditional African culture: respect, common property, and an obligation to work. Loosely defining the family structure to carry out those three aspects, and maintaining flexibility as to how local communities may implement the policy, Nyerere suggested that community members must recognize the rights of others, must be responsible to the basic necessity needs of others, and must share in the community's work load. The complexities and demands of modern living made Ujamaa, in some ways, nonoperational.

Studying the reaction to Ujamaa among Tanzania's peasantry, political scientist Goran Hyden suggested that material conditions were not appropriate for the types of changes hoped for by the leadership. In *Beyond Ujamaa in Tanzania: Underdevelopment and an Uncaptured Peasantry*, Hyden wrote that "the real problem of Ujamaa [was] that the material base of the peasant mode was far too narrow for a rapid socialist transformation." Though neither uninterested in or incapable of change, the problem–Hyden surmises–is that the peasants were "unwilling, and usually unable, to achieve [change] at a pace and to an extent that other social classes demanded of them. Socialist transformation is as taxing on the peasants as capitalist development."[7]

As we have noted, Bill's own interpretation of the failures of Ujamaa place greater responsibility on the high-level government officials, who did not want to lose any of their new-found power. "It began in the Ruvuma Region," he recalled, "where a group of people had become really enthusiastic about the concept of Ujamaa, and were successful at spreading the word. They were one of the most promising of all the Ujamaa local projects, and the people at the center of government were becoming afraid of them. When the local activists felt that they had encountered one after another bureaucratic roadblock, they decided to incorporate–which was the only way to effectively spread out under Tanzanian law. The bureaucrats immediately accused the locals of being capitalists, and bounced them out! This dynamic was repeated time and time again–in Bukopa, in Tonga, and throughout the country."

In any interpretation, it is clear that the far-reaching ideas of Ujamaa never developed beyond the initial stages. The visions of the past–despite lofty ideals and the good intentions of some–have failed to create an improved lot for the common people at present. Discussing the forty-year post-independence period in Africa with Mwalimu, however, one is hard pressed to criticize the *content* of those early visions. Material forces, bureaucratic practices, or the very nature of nations themselves may all have contributed to the failures of development. What is needed, Mwalimu suggests, is not a re-writing of the idealistic freedom plans made in more hopeful times. What is needed, indeed, is a recommitment to making those plans work. It is necessary to devise a mechanism for implementing those plans in a more realistic way. The imperative is to forge a unity–in practice–of the concepts of freedom and development, and one that is meaningful and useful to all people.

The challenging words of the South Commission's final report remind us of the problems and the tasks ahead:

"Were all humanity a single nation-state," it reads, "the present North-South divide would make it an unviable, semi-feudal entity, split by internal conflicts. Its small part is advanced, prosperous, powerful; its much bigger part is underdeveloped, poor, and powerless. A nation so divided within itself would be recognized as unstable. A world so divided should likewise be recognized as inherently unstable....

"Development necessarily implies political freedom, for individuals as for nations....The people's interests and desires can only be known when they are free."[8]

NOTES

1. Ernest Dunbar, *The Black Expatriates*, E.P. Dutton, New York, 1968.

2. Interview/dialogue with Bill Sutherland, October 14, 1993, Brooklyn, New York.
3. ---, *Nyerere: 1961-1985...Passing on the Tongs,* Tanzania Standard (Newspapers) Ltd., 1986. *Though the above provides a useful, condensed overview, a better assessment of Nyerere can be found in Colin Legum and Geoffrey Mmari (eds.), Mwalimu: The Influence of Nyerere, Africa World Press, Trenton, 1995.*
4. Interview/dialogue between the authors and Mwalimu Julius K. Nyerere, Butiama, August 13, 1992.
5. Julius K. Nyerere, *Uhuru Na Ujamaa: Freedom and Socialism,* Oxford University Press, Nairobi, 1968. *Other important selections of Mwalimu's speeches and writings can be found in Uhuru Na Umoja: Freedom and Unity, Oxford, Nairobi, 1966 and Uhuru Na Maendeleo: Freedom and Development, Oxford, Nairobi, 1973.*
6. Julius K. Nyerere, "Capitalism or Socialism: The Rational Choice," *Crossroad* (Vol. 2, No. 3), Spear and Shield Publications, Chicago, 1989, reprinted in pamphlet form, 1995. *In addition to publishing an occasional booklet, Spear and Shield (1340 West Irving Park Road, Suite 108, Chicago, IL 60613) primarily produces the regular journal Crossroad, focusing on issues relating to the New Afrikan Independence Movement and to New Afrikan political prisoners/prisoners of war.*
7. Goran Hyden, *Beyond Ujamaa in Tanzania: Underdevelopment and an Uncaptured Peasantry,* University of California Press, Berkeley, 1980.
8. South Commission, *Final Report,* London: Oxford University Press, 1990.

CHAPTER 4

KENNETH KAUNDA, ZAMBIA, AND THE RIDDLES OF VIOLENCE AND NONVIOLENCE

More than most nationalist leaders, Dr. Kenneth Kaunda of Zambia has long been outspoken on issues relating to nonviolence. An early advocate, along with Nyerere, of the nonviolent direct action strategy of Africa Freedom Action and the World Peace Brigade, Kaunda reviewed his political choices on the eve of Zambia's independence. Having spent 1959 and 1960 in jail, after the banning of the Zambian liberation movements, Kaunda founded the United National Independence Party (UNIP) after his release at the end of 1960. While much of southern Africa was turning towards armed struggle, Kaunda's UNIP won a resounding electoral victory, as the colonial Northern Rhodesians were peacefully removed from power in 1964.

In the years just prior to independence, the rally of the combined forces of UNIP, WPB, and PAFMECA took place at Mbeya in northern Tanganyika, just before the British did their about-face on the issue of allowing for majority elections. Bill Sutherland, as one of the rally organizers, worked closely with Kaunda and remembered the striking challenges that Kaunda raised for himself and for the nonviolent activists. "It wasn't too long after the rally," Bill recalled, "that Kaunda came to us said: 'Look, it's quite clear now that we're going to have an election which will provide for majority rule, and the end of British control. I have been with you all this time. I have been nonviolent in principle and I've appreciated and wanted to thank you for all you have done. But I have decided that I am going to be a politician, and to go into government.'"[1]

Kaunda knew that he was the head of his party, and he thought that his party would win. "But," Bill noted, "he said: 'I'm going to have problems as a possible head of state. How, as a person who is a believer in nonviolence, am I going to be able to defend the country against the South Africans and the southern Rhodesians and all of these people who are coming in with their spies and attempting to destabilize us from the south? What am I going to do in the north, when we've got a greedy opportunist named Moishe Tshombe–who, from the Congo, is serving as a pawn of the imperialists, sending in goons to mess things up?' Kaunda put it to us directly: 'I'd like you to be burning the midnight oil to explain to me how I'm going to do this.' And we had a long session, far into the night, but the upshot of it was that nobody had a clear and definable answer. We were not really able to respond to Kaunda."

At this point, the WPB's role was basically finished. The UNIP people went back to Zambia to prepare for the elections, and WPB remained in Dar-es-Salaam. By 1964, Kaunda had become President. One part of the more mainstream peace movement did stay active in Central Africa, monitoring the election and after. The Quakers were still quite active, and Lyle Tatum and George Loft spent time in Lusaka, Zambia's capital, and all around the country, trying to influence the leadership in the direction of pacifism. The more direct action types, however, began to focus attention on the struggles in southern Africa.

Bill remembered that, when Zambia held its official independence celebrations in 1964, he was seated at one event next to Loft, and Kenneth came out in a general's uniform! "Loft actually had tears in his eyes, saying 'Ah, we have lost him . . . we have lost him.' His reaction," Bill notes, "reflected a kind of attitude among some pacifists who thought that–through personal association and conversation–they could significantly influence fundamental social change. There was a failure to recognize the more systemic pressures that are always present, which modify what one can reasonably expect from a head of state."

* * *

Kaunda's challenging questions stayed with him throughout his many years as President of Zambia, as did the further challenge of having both advocates of pacifism and armed struggle doubt his strategic commitments. In a sense, Kaunda's attempts to "play in the cracks"–to find a common point between the seemingly contradictory strategies of violence and nonviolence–mirrored our own concerns and questions. Responding to what he called the riddle of violence, he explored these issues in a series of essays published in 1980. He framed his fundamental question as: Can justice and freedom be *maintained* through nonviolent action?

To open *The Riddle of Violence*, Kaunda noted that, in his early days before independence, Gandhi had been his ideal. Gandhi, in his words, had "brought perfection to all qualities. I was struggling," he wrote, "to develop self discipline, austerity, a oneness with the people, a holiness that was not stuffy, sanctity with a sense of humor, and practical wisdom.... So it was according to the principles of nonviolence on the Gandhi model that the final stages of the freedom struggle in Zambia were conducted. The doctrine became the official policy of UNIP, and apart from a few regrettable lapses, it was honored by the masses, whose discipline in the face of grave provocation was remarkable."[2]

Kaunda recounted the work of Africa Freedom Action and Peace Brigade, and told a story of his conversations with Indian leader J.P. Narayan. Narayan suggested that Kaunda not take the presidential position, but rather, like Gandhi, stay out of the politician's arena to influence politics on a broader scale. After what Kaunda describes as a "couple of sleepless nights," he decided that Narayan's suggestions were not for him–indeed, that in order to serve the masses of Zambia, he must go into government. His writings reflect his initial conflict with what he sees as an unnecessary either-or choice–"between an uncompromising stand on the issue of nonviolence, and pushing ahead with a political career that must lead me occasionally to do things at odds with my convictions."

This either-or thinking, Kaunda asserted, would "rob political life of its idealists without affecting the need for politicians as such." Furthermore, an either-or absolutist perspective on the issues of nonviolence and violence are similarly uncalled-for. "Let me not overstate," he wrote, "the degree of antithesis between the strategies of nonviolence and those of armed struggle. It does not always follow that the way of nonviolence is more perilous. There may be times when it is the only sane course of action. Nor is armed struggle always the guarantor of national security. Far from it. But any leader must have the freedom to discriminate. For violence and nonviolence, far from being absolute alternatives, are complementary in practice. As a tactic, the effectiveness of nonviolence is enhanced when it stands out in sharp relief against a backdrop of imminent or actual violence. It has been said that nonviolence needs violence in the same way that stars need the night sky to show them off."

Describing the difficulties in making transitions from grassroots movement into national government, Kaunda elucidated upon his predicament: "The only strict principles are in textbooks. History, as well as experience, shows that the younger the nation, the nearer the surface are the roots of violence." In his position as a leader of government, he felt especially pressed to understand and act upon the often hidden or more subtle violence embedded in the status quo. Quoting a philosophical principle that "he who affirms the state affirms violence," Kaunda noted that all but a few "saints"–who have moved themselves to remote wildernesses–play some role in affirming the state.

In a 1981 personal letter to Kaunda shortly following the publication of the *Riddle* essays, Bill reminded him that, despite a general misimpression that Gandhi was a saint in politics, in fact the Mahatma described himself as a politician trying to live a saintly life. Rather than break with the Indian National Congress, as Kaunda implied, the Congress leadership broke with Gandhi at the time of independence, when he suggested that they *not* take power at the national level, but concentrate instead on grassroots power through the establishment of local political and economic entities, the village republics.

Kaunda's critiques of the nonviolence movement centered on the premise that it is unfair and unrealistic to suggest that everybody become a saint. In addition, while attempting individual sainthood, the absolutist sometimes fails to distinguish between individualized and institutional violence. "A thoroughgoing pacifism," he asserts, "encourages blanket judgments about political regimes, ruling out the marginal moral distinctions that are the raw stuff of statesmanship." Those pacifists who argue that any victory through violence is sterile because of the means used, may become dupes of totalitarianism, "because a strong despotic power very often does not need to use force to intimidate a weaker one, whereas free nations mobilizing to resist such aggression have to marshal their military resources, and thus infer the pacifist's wrath."

One citation made along these lines recalled a 1936 argument, when Hitler occupied the Rhineland without firing a shot. The anger of some European pacifists was not directed at the Nazis for territorial aggression, but at Churchill and others who argued that the Germans should be stopped by force before it became too late. Of course, this argument focuses only on the most conservative of pacifists, omitting the many nonviolent revolutionaries who were among the first to protest against the growing Nazism and fascist movements in Europe. The radical direct action wing of the U.S. pacifist movement, which included Bill Sutherland among many others, made clear that their conscientious objector positions during World War Two grew, in part, out of their understanding that Nazism and fascism were the logical extension of the racism and imperialism within the so-called democracies. Kaunda did acknowledge that Gandhi's whole political life had been centered upon a struggle against imperialism and for national independence, but suggested that Gandhi was an exception in the Indian and pacifist movements. Kaunda concluded that "in most conflicts it is necessary to take sides, because neutrality is a vote for the aggressor."

Bill's challenge to Kaunda emphasized that Gandhi and some of his more politically savvy proteges, such as J.P. Narayan, were calling for strong leadership–not neutrality or political abstinence–but leadership in a radical direction. "Putting real decision-making power in the hands of the people at the village level," Bill wrote, "would have been a significant gamble–betting that if you 'take care of the pennies, the dollars will take care of themselves.'" He admitted that Kaunda's 1962 questions about nonviolent national defense had stumped the direct action group that had advised him up till the point of independence, but Bill arrived at significantly different conclusions. "It was at that time," Bill remembered, "that I began to realize that there may be something fundamentally contradictory between true democracy and the modern nation-state." Bill's 1981 letter chided Kaunda that most African leaders had chosen to accept the Western model of the modern nation-state, only challenging colonialism, occasionally making mild critiques of neocolonialism. "Perhaps it is time," Bill wrote, "to be very political in the deepest sense of the word, and discover another system of political organization besides the nation-state?"

There can be little doubt that, as President of Zambia, some of Kaunda's most notable achievements were in his support for the African anti-colonial and liberation movements. South Africa's ANC headquarters were long based in Lusaka, and the struggle for the freedom of Zimbabwe–formerly southern Rhodesia–was in part waged from Zambian soil. The Zambian people suffered economic deprivation and actual military attacks because of their support for the southern Africa liberation movements. In lending political and material support as host to these armed struggles, Kaunda often stated: "we have run out of alternatives."

Unwilling to simply discard his beliefs in the power of nonviolence, however, he qualified and explained his support in a tactical context. "I am not suggesting," he wrote, "that the tactics of violence and those of nonviolence are indistinguishable. Nor do I think that since whatever revolutionary action we take must harm somebody, it doesn't matter if we do harm indiscriminately. I seek only to dispel the illusion of innocence." Innocence, Kaunda implied, is the dangerous position that extremists on both sides of the armed struggle/nonviolence debate evoke to justify their positions.

Kaunda outlined "war myths" and "peace myths"–inaccuracies generated by both sides to serve their half of the debate. Among the war myths cited are the tendency to idealize revolution and give it a flavor of romance and drama, the idea that certain forms of authority are legitimate and just, and the "last resort" theory that all else has been tried. In addition, he criticized the terminology of war used to suggest that it is something inevitable–"sent by the Gods"–which has no human agents, only human victims. War does not "break out" like a storm, he asserted, nor do nations "drift" into war, as a stumbling individual may drift into an unfamiliar neighborhood.

Peace myths, on the other hand, include the assertion that wars never solve anything, and leave behind more problems than they solve. Another myth identifies war as the "disease" of one particular political system, be it capitalism, communism, nationalism, or colonialism. Finally, Kaunda found it troubling that nonviolence is often posited as an alternative policy to war.

"Nonviolence," Kaunda argued, "is not a policy at all. It is the refusal to accept one specific policy, force, as a solution to certain problems." Once that refusal takes place, using whatever tactics, the key question of what to do next–to build a nation or create a just society–is forever raised. In his view, on a practical level, nonviolence has most strikingly been used "as an expression of moral outrage and a personal declaration of intent, but does not offer the raw stuff of political policies."

"My understanding of both Gandhi and Martin Luther King," Bill countered, "is that they were very aware of the inevitability of violence accompanying basic social change. The objective is to discover a method of struggle that would break the cycle of violence and repression. Both Gandhi and King were convinced that the spiritual power released by the 'soul force' of the oppressed in nonviolent direct action could break this cycle." While understanding and agreeing with Kaunda's assessment of rigid absolutists on both sides–such as the Zimbabweans who wanted to carry on the armed struggle regardless of the conditions of the people at the grassroots level, or those pacifists who would have nothing to do with people engaged in the guerrilla war–Bill struggled to remind Kaunda of a middle ground that could be taken. "I hope that you will give recognition to those who have worked with you," Bill argued, "and who still believe in nonviolence as an experiment in a way of struggle against the number one violence of our time–institutional violence as exemplified by the South African apartheid regime–without breaking our identification with the oppressed who see armed struggle as the only answer."

Kaunda's position, though qualified, had some parallels with Bill's closing concerns. "I personally would wish to see total nuclear disarmament," Kaunda wrote. "Nothing less can prevent the terrifying possibilities against which we are always being warned. But I must protest," he continued, "against the arrogant assumption that those powers which already form the nuclear club have the right to freeze its membership on the grounds that they can be trusted with nuclear weapons whereas the people of, say, Zambia or Switzerland or Iceland could not." The question of war within Africa–amongst and between Africans–seemed most tragic to this co-founder and twice chairman of the Organization of African Unity. "*Almost* any price is worth paying," suggested Kaunda, "to avoid the risk of Africa's ultimate war. Almost any price–except one. We will never, never rest until Africa is wiped clean of the foul stain of apartheid."

Summarizing his written comments on the riddles and challenges faced as a statesman, Kaunda stated: "I have found that the demands of political realism have led me to modify my pacifist convictions." His simple reply to his nonviolent critics: "Have you tried running a country on the basis of pacifist principles without qualification or modification, or do you know anyone who has?"

* * *

Kaunda's own years in government, spanning three decades as head of state, were filled with ups and downs. After twenty-seven years of one-party rule, Zambia became one of the first African nations to participate in a smooth, peaceful, and quick transfer of power. The 1991 election saw UNIP and Kaunda soundly defeated, with eighty-one percent of the popular vote going to the Movement for Multiparty Democracy and its leader Frederick Chiluba. Widespread dissatisfaction with the founding father of modern Zambia may have had something to do with a general desire for change, but was probably more based in frustrations due to the bleak economic situation. At the time of the election, Zambia's treasury was bankrupt, and its external debt was over seven billion dollars. Though rumors of corruption abounded, and Kaunda's arrangements with the IMF and World Bank had long been open to criticism through the 1970s and early 1980s, there can be little doubt that a substantial part of Zambia's economic woes were due to a freezing of international aid and cooperation that came about after Kaunda sought–in 1987 and 1990–to sever ties with the IMF austerity programs that constituted an economic recolonization.[3]

When Bill and I met with Kaunda some months after the election, he had had a chance to reflect on his years in public service. Living modestly outside of Lusaka, keeping one foot in and one out of the daily political discourse, he was beginning to set up a non-governmental agency, the Kaunda Institute for Peace and Democracy. We began by discussing the conditions throughout Africa since independence, and the role that differing strategic plans played in the shaping of modern societies.

"Bill and Matt–Welcome to Zambia!" Kaunda exclaimed, "the questions you raise are obviously extremely important. In trying to analyze these problems," Kaunda suggested, "one needs to understand the background conditions in as much depth as is humanly possible. The life of a nation does not begin just with independence–there is much activity before independence. That period before independence creates for us the source of some answers to the questions you raise. If we try to ignore that part of history of the nation, we are not doing justice.[4]

"We are looking at a very disturbed history. We have first the slave trade, and the slave trade destabilized the continent of Africa, but it helped to build the economy of the

West. The slave trade came, and after that came colonization. Colonization destabilized the continent further, because countries were divided not according to nationality but according to the whims of the colonizing power. That meant that for countries like Zambia you have four nationalities. You have in one corner of Zambia–near Zimbabwe–some ethnic groups that are in both countries. The same applies to Zambia and Mozambique, similarly between Tanzania and Zambia, also between Zaire and Zambia, as well as Namibia and Zambia. That obviously is very destabilizing."

We discussed how the divide-and-rule policy set one tribe against another, creating a divided continent. The Portuguese rule in Angola and Mozambique, for example, set the stage for the struggle between capitalism and communism. This created still more problems and divisions, and people fighting one another. These problems, of course, are not only problems for Africa but also for Asia and Latin America. "The northern attitude towards the people of the South," Kaunda noted, "is that we either dominate you or destabilize you."

Since these problems and this history are the common thread throughout the continent, we pondered the ways in which Zambia had specifically dealt with them. I asked Dr. Kaunda about the conflicts he faced during Zambia's early post–independence days. "What methods did you use," I asked, "to deal with the rapid changes going on, especially given your particular ideological concerns?"

"We followed a policy of nonalignment," Kaunda answered, "recognizing that there is no love in each side saying we are right all the time. There was no love in taking sides between East and West, fighting and killing each other as they tried to involve us by proxy. One wants us to kill so communism will succeed. The other wants us to kill so capitalism will succeed. And in the process ...it is the grassroots common person who suffers. It is like the old saying, that when two elephants fight, it is the grass that suffers! Now what is the role of the nonaligned nation under these conditions? Of course, I can only speak for Zambia. When we attained our independence, we had to educate our people; we had to provide health, security, and a generally good atmosphere for economic and political development.

"You can't develop these things without manpower which is well trained for the job. In our situation, that calls for education. We are proud of our achievements in that field. It is important to know that just before independence, we had only one hundred university graduates. We had only twelve hundred secondary school graduates. That is what the British achieved in all of their seventy years here! We had no roads to speak of, to cover the large area of our country, and no communication systems. Indeed, the British ran the whole civil service. Commerce and industry was in foreign hands. We had nothing. The army was under the British, the police were run by the British, the prisons were run by the British. Even the church was under foreign clergy.

"As the East-West confrontation was with us, we tried to stay nonaligned, because how could we have permanent enemies? We would rather have permanent friends than permanent enemies! With the West wanting us to hate the East, and the East wanting us to hate the West, how could we live like that? We said no. Each side wanted to adopt a holier-than-thou attitude. We wanted to be able to say 'You are right here' or 'You are wrong there.' When the U.S. bombed Vietnam, trying to bomb an idea, we were able to say 'Please don't behave like this, bombing children with napalm bombs.' When the Soviet Union invaded Czechoslovakia, we were able to say 'Look, we can't accept that.' When they invaded Afghanistan, we reserved the right to say that they were wrong. Our nonaligned position made us suspect on both sides, but we were acting according to our national conscience.

"With regard to our economic policy, we now have free education and free health services, because our people are poor. At this point in time, I do not regret that we gave these free services to our people. Even today, with our multi-party system, those who are in power benefited from the policies which we established through UNIP. In a way, we were born with a silver spoon in our mouths–a copper spoon, so to speak–because of our natural resources of copper. After independence, we used that money to bring educational facilities to our people, to bring health facilities to our people. The result is that instead of twelve hundred secondary school graduates before independence, we have over one million today. We have thousands of university graduates; some trained locally, others outside. In a short space of time–thirty years–we have been able to do all that. So we thank God for our economic possibilities that helped us to formulate our early policies."

Bill raised again the issue of neocolonialism and economic independence. The IMF policies that Kaunda had once embraced clearly limited Zambia's economic policies. What was his current analysis of the situation, now that the pressures of the Presidency were off his back?

"What we sell to the west, Kaunda responded, shaking his head from side to side, we are forced to sell at giveaway prices. But what we buy from there–the tractors, the lorries, the airplanes, what have you–we must buy paying through the nose. We are only a small economy, we have a little industry, but really we only produce copper. And when we try to sell this in the developed markets of the West, we face protective tariffs that work against us. You have heard of the great billion-dollar debt that Zambia has. If you were to analyze that in terms of what it's all about, you will discover that it is heavily weighted against us not because we bought so much. It has come from high interest rates. We need to borrow, but we borrow under their conditions, not under ours. And we pay through the nose again. Commercial bankers are even worse. So we find ourselves in a tight corner. Everything is weighted against us. When we talk about the debt of a nation, it means that the common person is also adversely affected. In the end it is the entire nation suffering, because of harsh conditions that we must live under."

Surrounded by his guitars and African sculptures in a small, oval-shaped living room, Kaunda's reflections indicated his continued passionate engagement in Zambian political life, though a somewhat strained relaxation appeared evident in his state of forced retirement. I asked about his visions for the future, and his plans outside of government.

"The reason why I have chosen to create the Kaunda Institute for Peace and Democracy," Kaunda responded, "is that I want to contribute to peace and the development of man, to democratic methods in the most modern terms. So many mitigating factors have destroyed the common man's chances in the developing world. One factor is the autocratic leadership in many countries. They do not accept that the voice of the people must be there all the time and is paramount. Some have come to power through military coups. Some have come to power through other means. But I am convinced that the people's participation at every stage is key. Once this is frustrated by methods of cheating, we are in serious trouble. We see leaders who want power at any cost.

"Our traditions are relevant. I would hope that the Institute would do research and gather information so that different concepts of democracy can be discussed. We would like to invite many scholars from all over the world to work on these questions of democracy and peace. There is no perfect system yet, because how can we call what our former masters left here as democracy. After all, in London they have street children in the twentieth century. How can we look on the American system as pure democracy when you have street children in New York? These are very pertinent questions–most disturbing.

"I am a student of nonviolence. That's why I want to know why billions of British pounds and American dollars must be spent on developing dangerous weapons to wipe out the whole world at one blow, while poverty is so evident in those very countries? Why was there so much poverty in the USSR after so many years of communism? The Soviet Union had so many natural resources. Why was so much of the wealth of the country spent on dangerous weapons? I am arguing that so much money spent on these weapons as against spending it on removal of street children from the street is sinful. We are committing sin, all of us. So the subject of democracy must be studied very seriously by scholars from East, West, North, and South."

Kaunda continued the review of his new organization: "We will also be examining some questions of method in the Institute for Peace and Development. We will have a peace studies program in global terms, and there will be study of democracy. That will be linked to research on the modern history of Zambia. Then there will be, of course, one work area looking at poverty because peace is not necessarily the absence of war. It is also the struggle against poverty. Finally, there will be cooperation with other non-governmental organizations, which will play an important part. I'm also interested in organic farming and we hope to invite specialists who may be able to help us design a plan to organize an organic farming campaign. In addition, we want to look at environmental problems and protection. There will be a plan for big business to support the Institute, in terms of financing projects. We will also invite private enterprise to come from the outside to give expertise in running various industrial and commercial projects.

"When it comes to what methods we should use, I think that for the moment we recognize that the main reasons for establishing the Institute–peace and democracy–is to work out methods for advancing the struggle. We have really not worked out all of our objectives as of yet."

Bill brought us back to the ongoing problems faced by the common people, even after these years of struggle and lofty ideals. "You yourself said," Bill noted to Kaunda, "that we can't always blame outside forces. Within the continent itself, we have the responsibility of our own societies. We are not carbon copies–we are human beings who have the right of choice. Yet within our societies, we have seen, time and time again, massive corruption, along with those on the outside who might wish to exploit us. Why," Bill asked, "do you think that this has happened? What can be done about it?"

"A lot has gone wrong," Kaunda suggested, "because of something I call the animal in man. Animalism is a very destructive disease. Getting power leads to many disastrous consequences, leads to military coups, and leads to rigging elections. Rigging elections is just as bad as military coups because you are cheating God's people. The challenge therefore is can we find a system, which works under this democratic umbrella that is participatory? At the moment, our democracies are not participatory. Can we make the system work to really fulfill our desires? Unless we discover how to make people active politically in-between general elections, domination by New York and London will continue and so will crime. And crime will overtake us. Instead of building an army to deal with East-West confrontation–instead of building armies to fight international wars–we will be building armies to kill our own people. Then the people will become angry, and you can build any number of armies, but they will become ungovernable.

"I am coming to your question, Bill," Kaunda smiled. "The answer certainly lies in spiritualizing–if there is such a term–human life. I am sure that we must eventually come to a classless society. Everything that I have mentioned before in describing the different aspects of society must be for the service of the people. So this is a very exciting subject, but also a very complex one."

As we began to conclude our discussions, Kaunda told us that he believed we must look to the root causes of the cycle of violence arising in our societies. Echoing our own perspectives, but seemingly contradicting some of his own earlier writings, Kaunda asserted that "nonviolence is the best form that man has worked out for peaceful change. Whether we can improve on that I don't know. But in principle, it's difficult to beat nonviolence. I want to look upon nonviolence not only as a way to achieve our objectives, but also as a way of life. If we are going to deal with life, then our structures–political, economic, social and cultural, scientific and ideological, even defense and security–all of our structures must be reorganized. Take politics, for example. At the moment, most politicians want power for its own sake. Is it possible to find a way of reorienting our society, to change it so that our basic political thoughts are aimed, instead, at service?

"We should think of nonviolence not only as a way of getting what we want, but as a way of life. To do that, we must look at all the areas of human endeavor. How do you make life economically nonviolent, socially and culturally nonviolent, scientifically nonviolent, and as a matter of faith nonviolent."

From the way Kaunda was describing the situation, the problem was, at its base, a spiritual problem. Underneath the economic and political issues, if there is going to be a nonviolent society there has to be a change in people's spiritual sense–both in terms of the leadership as well as the people. We noted that while Nkrumah said that the nations of Africa had to be allowed to make their own mistakes, within a nation people must be allowed to make some of their own mistakes without being repressed. Bill recalled the questions that Kaunda had raised years earlier to the Peace Brigade group, trying to define the role of a nonviolent politician about to take power. Thirty years later, Bill reminded Kaunda that they didn't have any clear directions for him, and that–in his letter some ten-plus years ago–Bill had only greater clarity of the problems we face. The questions of how to run and defend a nation nonviolently had been left unanswered.

"Even now there isn't any answer for that," Kaunda responded. "We didn't have the answer then and we don't have it now, thirty years hence. Some people think that I talk too much about God, and a politician shouldn't do that. But the spiritual side of life is as important as the physical side of life. These are two sides of one coin–if you pay attention to only one, the other side suffers. You can't live by bread alone, but no one can live without bread. This is the complexity of life. In trying to carry out my duties as president, I said to myself: 'God made man in his own image–love thy neighbor as thyself–do unto others as you would be done by.'

"We, in Central and Southern Africa, did believe in nonviolence as a way of life. We learned nonviolent methods from the independence struggles of West Africa, as well as from Gandhi both in India and what he did in South Africa. Our struggle, like the struggle in India, led to emergencies that Gandhi also had to face. Now, if I was forced to choose–and, of course, none of us had any power to choose our adversaries at all–I would choose the British as the one to have power over us. Why? Because I would be able to go to their country and campaign against their own government. But that was not the case with Mozambique, where the Portuguese were in power, or in South Africa under the apartheid regime. The liberation movements of southern Africa were fighting against regimes that banned everything, including nonviolent protest. They should not blame themselves. In the end, it was the apartheid government that forced them to engage in armed struggle."

At this point, Bill interjected a note of protest. The implication that the Gandhi or King movements were able to exist only because of the "civilized nature" of the British culture or American way of life seemed a serious misreading of history. "The British killed more Indians during the Amritsar Massacre following World War One," Bill reminded us, "then those who died at Sharpeville. Many of those Rhodesians who carried out the atrocities and secret executions in the struggle over Zimbabwe were of recent British ancestry. As for the U.S. South, the history of barbarity and monstrous brutality in repressing Black resistance tends to be forgotten in the context of reforms made in the 1960s and 1970s: limited victories of the struggle, both violent and nonviolent."

Given Kaunda's consistent emphasis on Christianity, I asked him for his opinion on the structure of the nation-state itself and whether the worship of the state hadn't become more powerful than religion. "What do you have to say," I questioned, "about the repressive instruments used by so many states, such as preventive detention?"

"Let me talk about our situation here," Kaunda continued. "We maintained the State of Emergency in the beginning, up to this last year when our colleagues came into power. The Movement for Multi-Party Democracy (MMD) abolished it. They campaigned against it very strongly during the elections. Now I had a very easy conscience about the Emergency Act. We got it when the British introduced it; we maintained it when we were being attacked from the Angolan side, from the Mozambican side, from the Rhodesian side. All around us there were forces against us at work. I maintained that the State of Emergency Act would never be used against Zambians, rather it would be used to protect Zambians. My colleagues who are now in power argued against that last year. I still maintain that the State of Emergency was used to protect Zambian society. We had been destabilized because of the liberation wars. With the exception of Tanzania, Malawi, and Zaire, we were in a state of war on all of our borders. There were effective efforts to undermine our own party.

"Of course, as with all methods of struggle, one must be very careful and considered. Whatever method is used by one group of people against another can easily be turned around and used by the second group against the first. Take mass action, for example. There is a question of mass action turning into riots. Is it good to strike against a government which is truly a government of the people–in fact to strike against one's self? Well, we allowed the opposition to carry on strikes and sometimes they turned into riots. Now, there have been more strikes in eight months under the MMD than we had in all the time we were in power."

Concluding our dialogue, Kaunda repeated that this is a most exciting period in world history. "It is crucial to analyze our situation correctly," he said, "and nothing is more important than spiritualizing our endeavors. If we do that, we will bring about a new society: not today or tomorrow–but it will surely come."

* * *

In this chapter, we have had glimpses of Kenneth Kaunda as a young freedom fighter, as a mature statesman, and as "the lion in winter." As the only African leader to become a head of state who adopted Gandhian nonviolence in principle, his story is central to our review of struggles to establish societies based on justice and peace. The young freedom fighter was able to lead his people to independence through essentially nonviolent means. The statesman Kaunda felt compelled to modify his position on nonviolence in order to govern a nation-state and to help fellow Africans achieve freedom, especially in apartheid South Africa. In our dialogue with "the lion" in his winter of discontent, we found him seeking to become relevant once again through the marriage of his original religious nonviolent beliefs to all aspects of society.

The tremendous contributions and sacrifices of the Zambian people under Kaunda's leadership, to both their own freedom and to the freedom of others, is implicit throughout this chapter. Despite these contributions, however, the limitations of the leadership of Kaunda, indeed even of his concept of leadership itself, comes into focus. He seems to have lacked understanding of the broad areas of Gandhian political action (in maintaining a peaceful society) beyond the electoral politics and governance of a modern nation-state. He was also not very innovative in dealing with the economic aspects of society. Like his fellow African heads of state, he tried unsuccessfully to reform an inherited authoritarian capitalist-oriented colonial structure in the face of ruthless manipulation by the external political and economic forces that dominated the world during the Cold War period. It was also true that there were times when Kaunda's practice of leadership ran counter to his philosophy of democratic control, although he certainly accepted the election which removed him from power.

The magnificence of Kaunda's contribution to the discussion of the problems raised in our dialogues is that he spoke from the experience of power and responsibility rather than an armchair theoretician, or an activist who is not faced with difficult decisions affecting millions of people. He raised questions of establishing and maintaining a just and free society, and of defending that society–questions that have not yet been answered anywhere. The fact that he himself continues to seek for answers within the context of his principles is a measure of the man.

NOTES

1. Interview/dialogue with Bill Sutherland, October 14, 1993, Brooklyn, New York.
2. Kenneth Kaunda, *The Riddle of Violence,* Harper and Row, San Francisco, 1980
3. Fergus Macpherson, *Kenneth Kaunda of Zambia: The Times and the Man,* Oxford University Press, Nairobi, 1974.
4. Interview/dialogue between the authors and Dr. Kenneth Kaunda, Lusaka, August 7, 1992.

CHAPTER 5

NATIONAL LIBERATION AND THE STRUGGLES AGAINST COLONIALISM IN SOUTHERN AFRICA

Unable to break the intransigence of the white settlers in southern Africa, the liberation forces were convinced that they could not succeed without armed rebellion. Half a world away, the example of the Vietnamese resistance to U.S. imperialism demonstrated that a people's war could be waged successfully against superior military power. For many anti-colonialists, armed struggle seemed the only way to achieve liberation.

As Dar-es-Salaam had grown to be the center of the Pan-Africanist movement, migration to Tanzania of southern African political figures, military leaders, soldiers, and civilians greatly increased. It should be of little surprise that Bill Sutherland served as host and guide to many of the newcomers. Without putting his own nonviolence aside, Bill's commitment to people's freedom as the fundamental goal enabled him to respectfully dialogue and work with those who disagreed with his nonviolent approach. Though actively engaged in waging armed struggle, the freedom fighters of Mozambique, Angola, Zimbabwe, and Namibia were

Bill's friends, allies, and colleagues. Holding in common a commitment to liberation and unity, these friendships–and dialogues–remain to this day.

"I first met the father of the Mozambican nation–Eduardo Mondlane–soon after I came to Dar," recalled Bill. "I had a good, true personal relationship with this founder of the Front For The Liberation Of Mozambique (FRELIMO). Eduardo was a very unusual and outstanding person, who got his university education at Fort Hare, went to the U.S. for further education, became a professor in the U.S., and married Janet, a white American woman–but then felt that he had to come back to his country and work for their freedom against the Portuguese.[1]

"With his U.S. background and interests, it was very easy for me to relate to him and talk to him. After FRELIMO was formed, I spoke of the importance of trying to achieve independence through nonviolent means and he would kid me about it, saying: 'You nonviolent people can't do anything for us at this point, but after we become independent you can come on down and help us!' I, in turn, brought up the example of the Algerian FLN. There was a time when they were losing their battles against the French on the military front, but were winning from the point of view of propaganda and world opinion. When the French attempted a very vicious provocation–throwing bombs into the Casbah to get the FLN 'terrorists' to react violently–the strong discipline within the FLN enabled them to resist these provocations and keep their people under control. The FLN did not–at that time–respond violently, and the French suffered a major setback.

"Later, after Mondlane had had a chance to speak directly to the Algerians, he came back to me and said: 'You know, you're right. They told me about the Red Hand–the French version of the CIA–and the violent provocations.' Even if the struggle was to primarily be an armed one, Mondlane suggested, it might be beneficial to have some training of people in nonviolent techniques.

"Mondlane informed me that he was putting the idea of training in nonviolence before his executive committee. I waited and waited, and finally he told me that the executive committee didn't buy the idea at all. FRELIMO's executive was composed of some pretty strong Marxist-Leninists, who thought that this idea was off the wall.

"Once, when he and I were sitting on my porch, he shared that some in FRELIMO felt he wasn't radical enough. ' I realize as we come closer and closer to independence, some will consider that I've done my job and should be swept aside. They want to bring in what they consider to be a realistic, radical program.' Though Mondlane had himself gone to the Soviet Union for assistance–after the U.S. had flatly refused to give any support to the anti–colonial efforts–he was by no means a dyed-in-the-wool Marxist-Leninist. Perhaps he was considered too bourgeois by some.

"Eduardo, we should note, was killed by a parcel bomb in the house of Betty King, who was a colleague and recruit of his wife Janet. King had a house on the beach, and in the years before independence, Mondlane would use it as a retreat, to get some writing done. It was there that he opened this package, and was sadly blown to bits."

Following Mondlane's death, one of his proteges–a young military leader named Samora Machel–became president of FRELIMO. The central role of the guerrilla fighter was highlighted, but FRELIMO's intensive health, education, and political participation programs–carried out even in the bush amongst combatants–became a special feature of FRELIMO's approach. Writing about the daily sacrifice and commitment of the guerrillas, Machel argued that every task was for the benefit of the people. "For one day to pass without fighting," he wrote, "is the same for one day to pass without eating.... Revolution is the best school for the oppressed people, the best university of all times, the best instrument for destroying colonialism and serving the people. We want our people," Samora proclaimed, "to really be the ones who govern their country in the future."[2]

After winning independence in 1974, FRELIMO was faced with the difficult task of transforming itself from a guerrilla army into a broad–based political party. In recreating the widespread social programs that had been modeled during the armed struggle, they relied upon mass organizations to mobilize and get input from the people of Mozambique. The strongest of these, the Organization of Mozambican Women (OMM), served to involve women in all levels of civil, economic, and political society.[3] Symbolic of their desire to continue the process of liberation for all Mozambicans, FRELIMO, and the OMM developed projects in literacy, agriculture, vocational training, and empowerment for peoples in rural and urban areas.

A fortunate participant in an OMM-sponsored trip ten years following independence, I was able to witness first-hand some of these national programs. Despite economic hardships and an infrastructure that the Portuguese viciously destroyed before leaving power, the popular slogan "The Struggle Continues" permeated all aspects of Mozambican life and work. At that time, problems had already surfaced with the Rhodesian-founded RENAMO– or "armed bandits" as FRELIMO called them. The bandits would steal food, burn buses, and terrorize people even remotely connected with FRELIMO, as they made their way around the country fighting Mozambique's growing army. Funded by the apartheid regime and U.S. CIA and mercenaries, the bandits cast a scary shadow on a country otherwise filled with hope at the prospects of true liberation. The people's resilience was aptly described in the phrase used to title Stephanie Urdang's excellent book on the OMM: *And Still They Dance*.[4]

Returning to Mozambique with Bill Sutherland, eight years following my first visit, I prepared myself for the shock of a country that had been ravaged by civil war. RENAMO's attacks had increased, with a growing amount of the country affected by them. It was clear that, lacking any coherent political program, RENAMO's main goal was destabilization, and they were successful at redirecting a large percentage of FRELIMO's social programs towards basic mechanisms for survival.[5]

The U.S. and Western Europe–often represented by the IMF, World Bank, and, in some cases, religious aid organizations–had at least partially succeeded in stopping Mozambique's experiment with socialism. And the peace accords which Mozambique had signed with the apartheid regime just months before my prior visit had proven futile: South African incursions on Mozambican soil continued, and President Samora Machel had been killed in a mysterious plane crash on South African soil.

As FRELIMO was being forced to negotiate with RENAMO, Bill and I became doubly aware of the ways in which negotiations–rather than being a tool of peace–can truly be used as a tool of war and injustice. Wanting to be sensitive to the many changes Mozambique had been forced to endure, we posed questions for dialogue that took into account the role that outsiders had played in their decades-long wars. We were honored to engage in discussions with one of the country's founding mothers: Graça Machel, widow of Samora.

A striking example of an indomitable spirit is the figure of Graça, who has now become an international spokesperson for human–and especially children's–rights. Speaking with us at her home in Mozambique's capital of Maputo, Madame Machel was both personally charming and passionate in her commitment to make her country and region a more peaceful and just place for future generations. Looking out over her city through wall-to-wall windows, Madame Machel stood tall and poised. The former Mozambican Minister of Education, Graça exuded a certain pride, confidence, and grace. For more than ten minutes, she gave us a brilliant analysis of the struggle in Southern Africa, displaying an excellent facility in a language not her own. As she searched for a word to express a particularly subtle concept, she looked at us anxiously. "My English is a bit broken, but I think that you can understand what I am saying?"[6]

"Oh yes, very well," we laughed. She looked puzzled for a moment, and then joined in our laughter. Quickly our discussion turned to her central theme and question: How can we break the cycle of violence?

"I caution people–I am, you see, a mother–that the biggest crime that apartheid has done to us is to criminalize our children. They have taken children of eight or nine years old, and turned them into killers. The most precious thing we have is our children–and they're not children any more. We have to wonder what human values are left in them, and how to rebuild those values. How to get them to regain respect for life? There are hundreds of thousands of children who have been affected by war, so it is not a small task."

Bill shared with Machel his own history with Mondlane, and the early days of FRELIMO. "What are your thoughts about the early move towards armed struggle in Mozambique?" Bill questioned. "How has this affected Mozambican society today?"

"All of our leaders," Graça replied, "before they decided for armed struggle, had tried negotiations first. All of them. In Mozambique, before Mondlane decided on initiating the armed struggle, he first tried negotiations with the colonial powers. He went to Portugal, he wrote to Portugal; he used the UN because he had been working with the UN before. He knew very well the machinery within the UN and he tried, with support of leaders like Julius Nyerere and others, to convince Portugal to accept the independence of Mozambique through a peaceful process of negotiations. But the Portuguese refused. FRELIMO was formed in 1962, but it was only in 1964 that the armed struggle had to be launched. Even after the creation of the Front, there was two years of continued attempts at negotiations and a peace process, which was denied by the colonial power.

"Of course," Graça continued, "what happened after a lot of time, after lots of sacrifices, lives of people lost, only then were the colonists forced to accept negotiations. That's why any armed struggle has got to end with negotiations. We come back to the beginning. After those pauses of having to organize armed struggle, having people killed, having infrastructures destroyed, after this then we shall have to come back to the beginning and start with negotiations. What we could have done if they had accepted it in the first place!"

Bill quickly agreed: "On the question of negotiations, we understand that they can't happen until the negotiators are on equal footing. We appreciate that." Bill remembered, however, a story of some indigenous nonviolent resistance to RENAMO. "What of the example of Manuel Antonio," he asked, "the traditional mystic healer who was able to galvanize people in a non-military fashion? Of course, I understand that this is just one side of a many-faceted approach to resistance."

"Most of the time, people just don't know these stories and examples," Machel responded. "They do show that the people are able to accept challenges and still take action. I really hope that after some years of cease fire, we will have many such changes for the better."

Thinking of all the hopes and visions for a new society that we had discussed with leaders throughout the continent, I asked Madame Machel about her own thoughts on the future. "What, concretely, are your hopes for the future?" I questioned. "In these times of war and violence, is there time and space to dream?"

"We will always keep on dreaming as long as we are alive!" she asserted. "In the case of Mozambique, after cease-fire we should continue to work for a real tranquility. Now there are many, many pockets of violence within the society–not only military forces and other armed forces of government, or RENAMO forces, but other violent elements. The first thing is to create a basis for consoling the whole country, but then there should be a process of demilitarization. This is so important: to be able to live in an atmosphere of tolerance without always using violence against one another. Not only at a military level, but also civilian violence must be dealt with. We need to learn how to live in harmony, in tolerance, in dialogue, in community–talking with each other without using violence.

"I would also expect," Graça continued, "to go back to some of the methods used immediately after independence: to organize institutions which would allow everyone–whether in rural or urban areas, working, in schools, in hospitals, wherever they are–to be in a place where they can make their voices heard. People need to feel that they are participating in decision-making. That does not mean only to be in Parliament; you can be at work in a hospital and you can have a voice in how your hospital is run. You can be in a school, as a student or a teacher or a headmaster, but there must be a collective way of how to hear and to listen, on how to run the school. In a village, you need to cultivate, but you also need to find ways of how problems of all villages are being solved. People need to be able to talk, to communicate, and to give their points of view, to be part of the decisions that are being made about their lives. In order to have the big nations working properly, you need the small cells.

"In the first years of independence in this country, that was the reality. You could go to villages everywhere and find small councils where people, elected by the village, would sit together and decide how they wanted the village to be run. In schools, you would find those participating deciding how the classroom has to behave and how to work better. These things were happening in Mozambique, and I dream that we should be able to do this again, improving the methods of organization, improving also the channels of communication from bottom to top and top to bottom."

"There are now some preparations going on," explained Mrs. Machel, "regarding how to reeducate the children. I think on the one hand that it is important to give an alternative for survival to those people who have been affected by the war: how to work, how to live. You know that most of them went to RENAMO or to the government armed forces when they were very young. Most of them did not have any profession, they were in the military for five to six years; and now–in a disarmed situation–they have to work for themselves. But the only thing that they know how to do is to kill–for any reason. So they have to learn how to go to the fields, to cultivate land as a source of life, how to build roads, how to fish, or how to work in factories, for example. We must retrain and reorient society. Our solutions must lie in the willingness of the people to get involved in alternatives which we can put into place."

"In addition," Graça Machel concluded, "it happens that Mozambique has become impoverished, but it is in fact not poor. No. The first wealth of this country is our people, ourselves. We have already shown in our history that when we know exactly what our goal is we are able to organize ourselves––we are able to do what needs to be done. One of the priorities after cease-fire is how to organize people to rebuild our self–confidence, our self–esteem. We need to be able to define at a different level what the priorities are, and especially to struggle against hunger. We want to be able to go back to our fields to produce maize, cassava, whatever. It is a question of dignity: to live from what we ourselves produce."

Mozambican Prime Minister Pascal Mocumbi also had strong thoughts on what had to be done. Bill first asked him what his hopes were for his country's future.

"My vision," he began, "is first that we will establish stability, beginning in the family. In the last ten years, people have had to keep moving, out of fear of random attacks.... Secondly, we must establish stability with our neighbors–to pacify the region. Finally, we must develop all our resources–human, material, and economic–for the benefit of the people."[7]

Though not a man with a military background, Dr. Mocumbi–a physician–spoke of the need for a small, strategic army. "We must limit the military institutions to the necessity of defending sovereignty. The military should be productive and play a role in the economy. The methods in the fight against the terrorists were–in a way–to defend our very lives. Until after 1990, we couldn't even identify a national leader of RENAMO, with certain political aims. When they attacked a village, they killed indiscriminately–FRELIMO and RENAMO supporters together. When we fought against Portuguese colonialism, we always made distinctions between military and non-military targets, and even within the Portuguese military we tried to separate those soldiers who were on an offensive against us and those who might be won over to support us.

"People often said that Mozambique became free because of the revolutionary officer's revolt in Portugal, but–in fact–some of those officers had previously been in touch with FRELIMO. So, FRELIMO played a role in the changes that took place in Portugal; we had influenced the mentality within the Portuguese military."

I was interested in knowing what the Prime Minister thought about any alternative to armed struggle in the fight for Mozambican freedom.

"You will not find in any document of FRELIMO the words 'armed struggle'," Mocumbi commented. "We said that we would fight by all means for our liberation. I attended the first FRELIMO conference, as a Mozambican student, and I can tell you that these words were deliberate. We wanted to reach our objectives through peaceful means."

In recounting the early-armed campaigns that took place in 1964, Mocumbi discussed how FRELIMO's orientation was not to be antagonistic. "We decided," he pointed out, "to write a message to the Portuguese people: that FRELIMO was not formed to fight against the Portuguese people, but to fight against colonialism. We perceived the Portuguese people as being denied their own rights by a fascist regime.

"Today, in southern Africa, we have to conceive of an environment where our countries have more and more confidence in themselves, where the state and the regions have the mechanisms of preventing conflict. The armies should have a limited dimension. But we should not forget that the process of nation building is still on, and there are still factors that may hamper national unity–factors that may degenerate into violence. One needs ways for the state to maintain its integrity. The army, along with civil service and political parties, should be an instant for forging national unity, for forging our nationality.

"One of the main post-cease-fire challenges," Mocumbi concluded, "is how we Mozambicans can reconcile amongst ourselves. We have to adopt a new attitude, and lead in the process of change. We must educate ourselves in reconciliation, so that the soul of Mozambique is restored."

* * *

Many of the problems faced by the new Mozambique came as a result of its determination to assist movements for freedom by the people in neighboring countries. The atrocities committed by the Rhodesian–founded RENAMO previously mentioned were just a part of the suffering endured by Mozambicans in order to help the Zimbabwean African National Union (ZANU), led by the astute Robert Mugabe. The war for independence in Zimbabwe had its most significant moments in the years following Mozambique's and Angola's independence. Fighting not just against a vicious version of European colonialism, the struggle for freedom was aimed at the entrenched white settlers who had claimed the land as their own, calling it Rhodesia.

When the settler regime was defeated in 1980, FRELIMO leaders were the principal advisors to Mugabe in the negotiations for majority government. On the basis of their own experiences, they warned ZANU not to have a hard line regarding the role of the white population. The exodus of the Portuguese from Mozambique had meant not only the sabotage of many industrial installations and large farms, but also meant the removal of technical expertise which some sympathetic Portuguese were ready to contribute to the new country, had they felt welcome. They also told ZANU not to be romantic in thinking that they were a Marxist vanguard party, because ZANU was a coalition of both Marxist and nationalist elements. The negotiations called for a ten-year interim period in which certain advantages to the white minority population were to be maintained.[8] It was a gamble: would the Black majority be able to slowly wrest economic and political control from the whites during this period, or would the white minority co–opt a segment of the Black population to join in exploiting their own people? The outside world did not appreciate that these compromises had been worked out after careful analysis amongst the leadership of both ZANU and FRELIMO, recognizing the experiences of the previous years and struggling for a new approach towards meaningful and lasting social change.

Prime Minister Mugabe was the first freedom movement leader to respond positively to our request for a dialogue. Unfortunately, however, he was not available when we arrived in Zimbabwe's capital, Harare, in July of 1992; a terrible drought had taken place at that time which demanded his presence in other parts of the country. However, Nathan Shamuyarira, then Foreign Minister and currently Minister of Industry and Commerce, was happy to receive us. Nathan was a close personal friend of Bill's who had been in exile in Dar, and worked there as a professor of political science at the university. He had been personally called back to the struggle by Mugabe, and had spent a number of years with ZANU in Mozambique. Before our discussions even began, Shamuyarira warned us that he "didn't go for all this non-violence business!"[9]

But as with Machel and Mocumbi, Minister Shamuyarira emphasized the early non-military attempts that had been made by ZANU and other liberation groups. With leaders jailed and shot, and with the Rhodesian regime "setting the dogs on our people," it was determined that nonviolent methods could not succeed. "In fighting the colonial regime led by Ian Smith," Shamuyarira recounted, "our people focused on the system, and on the armed elements of that system. We focused our attacks on the army, on the police, and on the intelligence services which we knew were hunting us down. Our people concentrated on attacking those forces–we never attacked soft targets. We never attacked children, hospitals, or schools. We never attacked Europeans in general, although they were the rulers at that time. There was never an attack as people went to cinema, or to any peaceful activity. There were only attacks–using land mines or using the AK-rifle–aimed at the armed forces of the Smith regime. We knew that this would bolster the morale of our people, and it would also demoralize the Smith regime.

"An attack on their morale was a very important part of the armed struggle. After each armed conflict, we followed up with propaganda materials, by radio and by leaflets, saying why the action had been taken, and why it was appropriate to use this type of method. Each military action had to be explained very fully, not only to the guerrillas and to our movement, but also to the enemy population so that our supporters within Zimbabwe could understand and our enemies–the white regime at that time–would understand why the action had been taken. It took a lot of discipline to get the guerrillas to reach such a high level of organization–so that they would not pick soft targets. FRELIMO did similar work in Mozambique. The local white Portuguese were only drafted and were not really part of the government authorities. This same approach was also used in Namibia."

I observed that the strategy of nonviolence–and any truly revolutionary strategy, in fact–requires a great deal of discipline and training. "How would you compare the various methods of struggle?" I asked.

"If you had to use the nonviolent method," Shamuyarira responded, "the requirements of discipline are even harder and more pressured, because there are people who will not be able to reply back with AK-rifles, as we were doing. They must maintain a very high moral plane, to sustain their own efforts and to wait for the public opinion to crystallize in their favor, even behind the enemy lines. There are not many people who can have the patience to wait for that, so the requirements of discipline are much higher in that situation. But discipline is important in both situations."

In further discussions on the role of nonviolence, Shamuyarira continued: "I'm reminded of the statement by Mahatma Gandhi of India to a friend of mine, a political scientist in India. This friend responded to a question that I had asked him: 'In the case of colonial Africa, what would Gandhi have said?' My friend suggested that Gandhi's message was very clear on nonviolence: he said it was better to die on your feet than to live on your knees. In other words, you should rather die fighting, than to live as a slave. You should not allow yourself to live under colonialism. It was correct that people were prepared to die fighting colonialism. Of course, the way he did it in India was different from the way it was done in other countries because the situation in India was very different. The India Act of 1935 had accepted the independence of India as a conclusion of British colonial policy. When Gandhi arrived in India in 1947 at the end of the war, Britain had been weakened by the war and the question of independence had already been considered. It was, therefore, easier to use nonviolence to mobilize opinion in India and to mobilize public opinion in Britain against their own government.

"On the other hand, ZANU did not take up the ideas of any one philosopher. We borrowed from many philosophies, and many sets of ideas. Frantz Fanon's ideas, for example, were not really accepted within ZANU. No one felt that we cleansed ourselves by adopting violence. The aspect of Fanon's philosophy that did appeal to our people was the aspect of improving or trying to change society so that those who are last–the poor–can be first. We believed in supporting the wretched of the earth."

Bill replied to Shamuyarira regarding his rendering of Indian history. "Gandhi, in fact, arrived back in India in the 1920's," Bill noted. "Gandhi had used nonviolence for decades before the independence of India. Independence is rarely gained simply because of the relative weakness of the colonial power. It is gained because of the determined freedom efforts of the colonized. But, I would like to move our discussions to the post-independence era. What have been the major problems faced in attempting to improve the lives of the ordinary Zimbabwean?"

"After colonization and independence," Shamuyarira suggested, "the social conditions of the African people in general have not improved to the extent we wanted them to. Three main factors ought to be noted here. One is climatic change, which has brought drought to southern Africa and has reduced crop production in many areas. In southern Africa, we had median rainfall of twenty-five to thirty-five inches a year; it has now dropped to fifteen or twenty inches. In 1992, we only had eleven inches and other countries in the region had even less.

"The second factor hindering our efforts involves our dependence upon the global market, and our 'inheritance' of the crops of the colonists. We are still dependent on selling our produce to the imperialists. If America has a recession, we feel it here too. In this process of unequal buying and selling, African countries are now in debt. The debt is so big that there is no possibility of our being able to pay it. In some countries, the interest rate alone is thirty percent to thirty-six percent of the total budget. Many countries cannot pay the interest rate, let alone the capital. The IMF and World Bank, those monitoring and enforcing this debt, have largely taken control of our colonies, through their lending and borrowing systems. They continue the impoverishment of the African states.

"The third factor," Shamuyarira continued, "is the collapse of the Soviet Union. That had more strategic value in Africa than in the Americas or in Europe. We feel that Africa is no longer strategically important to the West, because the Russians are not waiting next door to take us over! This was the Western theory all those years: that Russia would take over. Because of all these factors, the social condition within African states is not as good as we had thought it would be. Education and health care has improved greatly in our country, and in other countries. But we have not made the strides that we had hoped for. One cannot deny that there have been mistakes made within African states, which have contributed to these social conditions. But I think the major reasons are the ones I've given."

Since so many Western critiques of post-independence Zimbabwe have centered around the issues of governmental corruption and abuses of power, I asked Minister

Shamuyarira for his perspectives: "What is the meaning and role of democracy and nationalism in Zimbabwe today? What about the allegations of political repression?"

"Regarding authoritarian measures inherited from the colonialists," Shamuyarira responded, "People are not perfect! Although colonialism had ended, we still had thieves and petty criminals, and we had opposition groups–some of them constructive but most of them not constructive–wanting to overthrow the government by force. That's why we've had so many military coups in different parts of Africa. In that type of situation, the rulers found themselves in a position where they needed the colonial laws in order to remain in power, because they had usurped power without the will of the majority. This is why there is a strong movement in Africa today to return to the democratic principles and democratic procedures. If you don't have them, you are bound to rely on the weapons of control which colonial regimes had. It is true that many African governments found these repressive structures necessary to use. The only way to replace them is to democratize the political situation, so that you don't have to regard everybody who speaks against you or who writes against you as an enemy.

"People should be entitled to their own political views. This is the new thrust in Africa today, which is having a beneficial effect. Here in Zimbabwe, we hated the colonialism and the racism of Ian Smith, but we did not hate Smith himself as a person, or hate individual whites. That is why, more than fifteen years after independence, Ian Smith is still living and working here. Smith is still extremely racist and critical of the government, and he used to–before independence–make obnoxious pronouncements that there would never be a Black government here in his lifetime. But, given our commitment to political freedom, Smith is allowed to make these criticisms. I think that regimes, which took power by force or that then kept power by force will find it very difficult to continue ruling in the new Africa today. The colonial weapons of control are discredited in the eyes of the people."

Bill then noted that ZANU has spoken out against capitalism and in favor of socialist alternatives. "What about the role of the nation-state?" Bill asked. "Are these

European-created and boundaried entities still useful in providing for the common people?"

"As far as the structure of the state is concerned," Nathan replied, "I think you need different states that should be held together by a minimum of social orders. It is only within that kind of nation-state that people can live in peace. Otherwise, you have anarchy that destroys the basis of that peace. There was a commentator the other day on British television who said that they would discuss nationalism in Europe, ethnicity in Asia and tribalism in Africa–but they are all the same thing, the same phenomenon!

"My general point is that decentralization needs to be controlled. Otherwise, if you follow it logically, it will lead to total disintegration of society. We will get the kind of society that philosopher Rousseau wanted: a society of the city-states, which are very small, so that everyone will know everyone else. That kind of egalitarian utopianism will create more problems than it will solve. At this time, we'll make more progress by recognizing the nation–states that are there, trying to organize them in as democratic a fashion as possible.

"Capitalism, on the other hand, allows–by its nature–those who have power to grab what they have, and those without to be exploited. It's a system of survival of the fittest. There is not enough space for everybody. Although it has been modified in many states–such as Sweden and Norway–essentially it's a doctrine that will produce inequality in society. If you have a nation–state built on the basis of capitalism," Shamuyarira concluded, "then you are likely to run into a lot of trouble."

As we prepared to leave Zimbabwe, we wondered whether ZANU had won the gamble regarding white minority privilege versus Black majority power. Had the promise of freedom for the common people been met?

* * *

Traveling on to Namibia, we considered a pattern regarding armed struggle in southern Africa. As we prepared to visit the country most recently freed by use of a prolonged people's war, we wondered how militancy, militarism, and the issue of compromise with the colonial powers interacted, as freedom spread throughout the continent. The 1980s were not a time when most progressive movements around the world were winning victories. We dialogued with leaders of Namibia's South West African Peoples Organization (SWAPO) on what strategies were most effective in relatively reactionary times.

For Bill, beginning a dialogue with Namibian President Sam Nujoma was like rekindling a discussion between old friends. When TANU agreed in 1962 to provide space in Dar for a nonviolent training center, the idea was quickly transformed after Zambia achieved its independence. The building, which Bill ran and lived in, became a place where housing and sustenance could be provided for different movements in exile. By 1963, it was primarily a hostel for SWAPO leaders, who came to work and plan. Now, Bill and I came to meet him for an informal lunch at the Presidential Palace!

Nujoma and Bill had met several years prior to 1963, at the Positive Action Conference in Ghana. The Sharpeville Massacre had just occurred, and Oliver Tambo of the ANC left South Africa. Stopping in Dar, the ANC group found Nujoma and proceeded to Accra. "I came out in March of 1960, following my arrest in December of 1959,"[10] recalled Nujoma. A nonviolent demonstration on December 10th–International Human Rights Day–left several killed and fifty wounded in Namibia's capital of Windhoek. Nujoma was charged with incitement to riot, even though it was the police who caused the fighting. "Verwoerd, the South West African Minister for Native Affairs, initiated a policy that there must be a buffer strip between the Black and white residential areas. And our people were being removed from their homes and relocated."

Throughout the early 1960s, Nujoma–along with veteran activist Mburumba Kerina, Peter Katjavivi, and British Gandhian Michael Scott–petitioned the United Nations to grant sovereignty to Namibia, which had been annexed by the South African regime as South West Africa. When the UN's International Court of Justice threw out a petition on the matter introduced by Liberia and Ethiopia, saying that these countries had no real interest in the case, the

Namibians launched a campaign of armed struggle–in 1966. After thirty years of struggle, in March of 1989, Namibia was finally granted independence.

"Militarily we were very strong," noted Nujoma, who had led SWAPO in exile for all those thirty years. "South Africa tried all along to create the impression that we never had forces inside the country–but who, then, were they fighting against? We fought side by side with the Angolan National Army and the Cuban internationalist forces. After their defeat, with the backing of UN peacekeeping forces, the implementation of independence was able to take place." During the years in exile, the diplomatic work at the UN had been built up alongside of the armed struggle, such that the UN was now on record for an end to the occupation of Namibia.

"Since independence," continued Nujoma, "the integration of our guerrilla forces into the population has not been too difficult. We have initiated a training program for former guerrilla fighters, including the citizens who stayed in the country under the development brigades. We are training them in subjects such as carpentry, bridge–making, agriculture, animal husbandry, so that they become skilled workers. And the government, through the Ministry of Trade and Industry, has given them some resources in order for them to create their own light industries. It's one way for us to eliminate unemployment, which we inherited from apartheid South Africa. We have also now begun building our own vocational training, under the Ministry of Labor and Manpower Development. So all of these are aimed at creating a nucleus of skilled workers.

"Of course," Nujoma continued, "we also have established our own Namibian National Defense Force, which is at the present moment comprised of over 7,000 men and women. Slowly, we are also now building up the Air Force wing and the Maritime wing, because we have a long coast. As a matter of fact, our patrol boats have seized seven Spanish boats, which had been illegally fishing in Namibian waters." Bill noted that one attempt on the part of the colonizers and their allies was to drain the sea of fish before Namibia gained their freedom!

"They are making billions and billions of dollars off of our fish," Nujoma agreed, "without benefiting the Namibian population. Of course, under apartheid, individual whites–particularly the members of the Nationalist Party–were getting licenses and were then contracting people in Spain, or Germany, or France, or Italy, to do the fishing for them. And the money would just sail out on a boat! That's how the money would go out of Namibia, whereas our people are still suffering from poverty. Our first act, as a matter of fact, was the extension of a 200-mile national protection zone for Namibia, under the Law of the Sea.

"Since independence, we have created many democratic institutions, under the supervision of the United Nations. We have a system of multi-party democracy–we don't have a one-party state here. That was a decision of the Namibian people at the elections–that they wanted a multi-party system–and my government is determined that this system be maintained so long as the Namibian people want it. We have also adopted a system of free market economy. And there has been a real process of reconciliation here."

I asked President Nujoma to describe the whys and hows of Namibia's decision to develop strong reconciliation policies. "What," I wondered, "were the basic motivations and goals of reconciliation here?"

"We have taken over this country from the ashes of war," Nujoma answered. "There was racial tension, racial hatred, created by decades of the apartheid regime. So, we *had* to adopt a policy of national reconciliation. By this, we mean to look forward and not to look backward to a history that is negative. We have to carry on with positive efforts: economic reconstruction and nation building. We are a multi-racial society in this country; our nation really emerges from different ethnic groupings, as it also has happened in other African countries. And that includes the tribes of Europe, such as the German and the English and the Boer. That is who we are. We have to exercise patience, tolerance, and the entertaining of other peoples' views. We are cementing our unity; even those whom we fought against now accept reconciliation in this country. We have all accepted this policy of national reconciliation.

"We have learned, finally, during our long struggle, that you must never impose a policy on the people. Let the people themselves participate. What we do here is consult and participate. I don't want to create an impression that everything goes well here. We still have problems of land reform, because much of the land is still owned by the whites who just seized it from the indigenous people. We've had a Land Reform and Land Question Conference, which involved all of the ethnic groupings. We said, 'Here is the problem we have; how do we solve it?' We have tens of thousands of landless people, and this cannot be allowed because it is precisely why we rose up to arms, to solve the land question. After a weeks debate in which everybody participated, we agreed that the question must be resolved by dialogue. We have appointed a Committee of Experts to recommend its findings to the Cabinet and to the National Assembly, to adopt a law. But by involving everybody in the process of dialogue, we learned never to force a policy upon the people without inviting participation.

"We still have many problems," Nujoma admitted. "But as I have already pointed out, we have embarked upon a crash program of training, in order to supply employment and education to our people. Because if the people are not trained, then they cannot participate and contribute effectively to our economic reconstruction and nation–building. Education to us is the main priority. Our highest budget goes to the Ministry of Education and Culture. We pay great importance to the training and educating of our people."

President Nujoma's optimism was shared by most of the Namibians with whom we spoke. It seemed that while few people expected immediate and drastic economic reform, a belief in the process of positive change was generally shared. Had people developed low expectations, given the previous experiences of other southern African liberation movements? Or was the answer, in part, due to the relative strengths of the diverse aspects of struggle that had been developed on the road to independence? Foreign Minister Theo Ben-Gurirab offered his suggestions, highlighting the foundations of SWAPO and their approaches towards liberation.

"From the beginning," the Foreign Minister began, "with inspiration from the ANC's Freedom Charter, we talked about the common humanity of all people. We talked about the land, but we also talked about the people who worked the land. In the early days, we looked for leadership to all those who made contributions in our common struggle–indeed, to leadership provided by none other than Mahatma Gandhi in South Africa. If one studies our struggle from decades past through today, you will see not only a knack for organization, an identification of goals, but also a patience to mobilize people for those goals.[11]

"Now one is not born with political wisdom. It's the struggle itself that teaches you to learn tactics and strategies, to have a proclivity for identifying goals. It's the struggle itself that teaches you. We set out when we realized the demonstrations were not enough, and as we realized that the contract labor system was brutal. Apartheid practices and law were brutal. We had not quite linked these manifestations of apartheid to the larger questions of colonialism that meant land, that meant the need for people to be given an opportunity to express the right to self-determination, that meant liberation, that meant getting rid of colonial domination. Certainly we were not thinking at that time about the fact that the system which we were fighting against here was the same system in Botswanaland and in Southern Rhodesia, Northern Rhodesia, Angola, and even South Africa, India, and elsewhere in the world. It was during the evolution of the struggle–when we met Bill in the early '60s in Dar! We were not really quite able–beyond reporting to you about the suffering–to explain the extent of our suffering.

"But there is no escaping the challenge, once you have identified the problem. Having analyzed it and understood the problem–it's dimensions–the one thing that is indispensable is organization. Whether you couch it in terms of a party or a mass organization, you need to be organized to build the movement. We realized that the demonstrations were necessary, but they were not sufficient to remove oppression.

"We sat down there in Dar-es-Salaam, and in the ensuing years we had to slowly but systematically go through the steps that we would need to take. It was decided that there were three main fronts on which we must simultaneously wage the struggle. The political front, the first front of national resistance, must be continued. The heritage we inherited–of those who stood up and fought against the Germans–that struggle must continue. This national resistance is a people's struggle to get rid of foreign domination and exploitation. That we call the first front.

"The second front was the international front: diplomatic solidarity, support that we needed from friends that we knew through other friends. On the basis of these two fronts, we launched the third front: the armed struggle. And we decided we must carry out these fronts simultaneously, which required careful organization."

Ben-Gurirab's years in exile were spent primarily in the U.S.–learning from the diversity of the struggles in the States, as he promoted the Namibian cause. "After I completed my studies," he recalled, "I started serving as SWAPO Chief Representative to the UN–from 1972 until 1986. During those years, starting with the early 1960s, you had so many activists and leaders. But two of them, to make a point, presented a contrast. Malcolm X spoke to my heart as a young man. He made my blood boil, as he was able to do with literally anybody who cared to listen to him. You also had Martin Luther King, Jr. For a time, I too fell victim to the distinct disinformation that these two men stood for different goals.

"They perhaps differed in methods, but in terms of final goals that they were talking about, they came to the same thing. Malcolm always felt strongly about organization and goals. I met him briefly as he was talking on these issues, just before he was killed. I learned later, in a book written by King, that he and his aides–so many of whom are personal friends of mine now–used to sit down and have brainstorm sessions on what to avoid and how to organize for and achieve your goals. We learned from both of them that goals must be clearly articulated, strategies carefully thought out, and tactics used at any given stage must be appropriate and also clearly articulated. Policies, which are used to mobilize the masses of people, should be clearly defined. However great or small the problem, you cannot achieve your goals without organization.

"In SWAPO, having identified three separate but related fronts, we understood that national resistance politics, diplomacy and negotiation, and the armed struggle were not contradictory. Rather, our tactics were complementary and our strategy was that they must always be carried out concurrently. That was the basis for our organization."

A brief discussion with Professor Mburumba Kerina revealed a similar understanding of the fluidity of tactics. "These forces," he suggested, "actually operated hand-in-glove. One might ask the question: Is it possible for a country that has gone through this kind of process of violence to end up with a multi-party democracy? How can guys who were on opposite sides of the gun one day sit on opposite sides of a Constituent Assembly the next, formulating a democratic constitution? Did God intervene to create this kind of chemistry? Eventually we realized that if we did not respond positively to one another–if we did not really become men and women to face the future–then we would never have a chance at peace."[12]

Kerina remembered an incident from the early 1960s, before the armed struggle was initiated. A cartoon in a South African newspaper showed him and Michael Scott standing together, Scott dressed as a priest and Kerina in barefoot with a club in his hand. The caption suggested that Scott would try to go to the UN in an appeal for a civilized understanding, but if that didn't work, there was always the African with the stick in the background! The struggle, Kerina indicated, was to get beyond these racist images.

In the mid–1970s, one group of Western pacifists did break through some of the divisive disinformation to organize a creative solidarity campaign called Operation Namibia. Though clearly offering nonviolent direct action as an alternative to the mounting military violence, they targeted their critiques at the illegal South African occupation and supported the political work of SWAPO. Initiated by the U.S.–based Movement For A New Society, and planned at the 1975 War Resisters International Triennial in Holland, a Books For A Free Namibia sail boat was launched to deliver material aid in defiance of the racist regime. "Launching a peace offensive," wrote activist Martin Priar in WIN Magazine, "is like undertaking guerrilla warfare; it is a decision to achieve a realignment of power by non-negotiated means. As such, it represents a conclusion that the existing power relationship is intolerable, and that the changes deemed necessary cannot be brought about by dialogue but only by actions which tend to destabilize and restructure the relationship."[13]

After three decades of integrated tactics with a clearly defined strategy, it appears that the post-independence dialogues were able to bear real fruit. Although Professor Kerina initiated the South West African National Union (SWANU)–a liberation organization which had key differences with SWAPO–his assessment of the positive nature of change matched Ben-Gurirab's and Nujoma's positivism.

"Fortunately, we negotiated, we discussed, and the process of negotiation itself provided a sort of clinical process for us," noted Kerina. "We began to transform ourselves from those weary soldiers into full human beings. For the first time, we began to see the humanity that we had been deprived of: to see its face and look at it eye-to-eye."

Some analysts have suggested that Namibia's situation was greatly influenced by it's having a relatively small population spread out over a relatively large area of land. Others have noted that Namibian freedom fighters had a particularly internationalist perspective–with leaders studying in both capitalist and communist countries, and a special relationship with and access to UN sources and support. In this way, the Namibian situation was somewhat unique. We left the country impressed by the initiatives we had experienced or heard about, and by the general atmosphere of enthusiasm and hope.

* * *

Our final discussion in southern Africa was with an Ugandan intellectual who has had extensive experience with both armed and nonviolent movements. Yash Tandon, author of numerous articles and booklets on African peace initiatives, militarism and education, was a trainer for the Southern African Non-governmental Development Organization Network (SANDON).[14] Bringing together a broad range of socially responsible grassroots groups, SANDON operated under the principle that there is strength in numbers–protecting the work and rights of sometimes small, isolated projects. In addition to this development work, Tandon has both been part of and studied social change movements in southern and eastern Africa.

The dialogue began with a review of Tandon's personal experiences: growing up in and fighting against the colonial violence of Britain and the military dictatorship of Idi Amin. Noting that Uganda has been one of the most violent countries in Africa, Tandon placed the roots of this violence within the context of the 1890s global violence of colonialism. A founder of the Ugandan National Liberation Front (UNLF), he was forced into exile in the 1970s. Living and teaching in Tanzania, then moving to Zimbabwe, he commented on shifting ideologies, and his own shifts in tactical and philosophical perspective.[15]

"The whole notion of liberation," Tandon suggested, "gets corrupted by the idea that liberation can only come as the result of the barrel of the gun. I think that there are times in history when people may have to resort to guns–I don't want to be dogmatic about that. Certainly, when a cause is just and the people have to take up arms in a just cause, then–for a limited objective, a limited period and provided that the actions are bound by certain norms–military action may be justified. But what has happened is that in every situation in the struggle against domination and colonialism, a lot of the ideology that we got from Marxist states–the Soviet Union, China, Vietnam–came to Africa in bits and pieces and out of context.

"People talked a lot about the phrase 'power comes from the barrel of gun.' Now Mao Tse Tung said this, but the sentence was actually much longer! He contextualized it, then he qualified it. But those qualifications were forgotten, and people made the 'barrel of the gun' into a dogma. That has characterized the essential aspect of the liberation movements in Africa. Somehow, the military has been raised to a higher social status–undeservedly, in my view–in comparison to all other kinds of contributions that people might make to liberation.

"In Zimbabwe, for example, when there is competition for political or economic resources, there are people who can still argue that 'we were in the bush–we were the ones who were bitten by mosquitoes, and therefore we have a prior claim to resources than those who stayed here.' That ethos is a corrupting one.

"I used to subscribe to the theory that without violence on the part of the oppressed themselves, you can't get rid of the violence of the oppressor. This theory includes the whole idea of violence as a cleansing force, a redeeming force for the person fighting for liberation, a cathartic force that energizes people to higher levels of social existence. I thought that there was some merit to this some time ago. But I've moved out of that feeling in the last decade or so.

"I think that it's a myth," Tandon went on, "to think that you can fight violence with violence. If you look at the existing case of South Africa, there is a lot of violence there–that is true. But we are not talking about violence as it erupts in a society because the social situation is explosive. Here we are discussing violence as a method of struggle against oppression–as a deliberate act. If you were to look at the South African situation and ask yourself the question of the extent to which violence was used as a deliberate strategy of liberation, my assessment is that the large part of the success of the people in South Africa has been achieved through nonviolent methods, not violent methods. In fact, even the liberation movements, which had been talking so much about armed struggle, have been talking about it in the abstract. The most they could achieve was armed propaganda, given the military force that they had. The real results were achieved because of the thousands of people refusing to take trains, boycotting buses, boycotting the payment of rent, taking over civil administration from local government authorities. That is the kind of force that mobilizes the spirit of the people from inside, to say 'We've got to do those things for ourselves because nobody else is going to do them for us.' That is the force that has brought about the end of apartheid in South Africa.

"When you talk about violence as a deliberate strategy, I think you must come to terms with these examples. I can look at my own country, Uganda. At least for the past generation that I have been active in, violence has been a negative force. At one point in time, the Ugandan National

Liberation Front was faced with the situation where a section of the party, a militaristic section, actually took over part of Uganda–a liberated zone. They then demanded that we declare that as a free zone, mobilize the people there, and take up arms against Obote. We had to fight this battle with our own colleagues for seven days, saying 'No, this is not the route we want to go.' We had to go and disarm our own colleagues, and then go into political action. We may not have been that successful, but neither were those who had taken up arms. Today, we can go back to Uganda with some self-respect, and even the respect of others who had been against us–that we had been fairly principled in our position."

I asked Tandon to comment upon how the UNLF came to their conclusions, and eventually developed a shift in their position.

"During that time in the UNLF," Tandon explained, "we came to our conclusions when Frantz Fanon was very popular. We are talking here of the 1970s. The victories that FRELIMO had in Mozambique, or MPLA in Angola, were partly credited to the teachings of Fanon, which suggested a psychological necessity for the oppressed to use violence against their oppressors. For us, then, to have taken the position that was a critique of Fanon in the practical sense was something different. Our approach came not because of any fundamental theoretical insights that we had regarding the nature of violence, but rather because of what we saw on the ground ourselves. We reflected upon what was happening in our country; we had already been in exile for a decade during Amin's time. We found that those who were fighting by political means were somehow regarded as illegitimate. We saw that whole drama, and realized out of our own experience that a route, which bypassed the political struggle, was, in fact, self-negating. So, we made a critique of Fanon. But it was not an awakening that came to us quickly.

"We did not take up nonviolence a priori," Tandon added. "Only very recently, as a movement in Uganda itself, have we thought that it may be useful to look at the writings of Gandhi. But throughout the 1960s and '70s and '80s, we allowed ourselves to be fed by the notion that Gandhi's teachings had a negative effect on the struggles in Africa. We viewed Gandhi as one who had created an atmosphere of passivity, and that the struggle had been prolonged precisely because people had not been encouraged to take up arms. That was the thinking that we went through in the '70s and '80s. So, we didn't read Gandhi, but we have now begun to do so.

"The point I'm making now is that–from personal experience and from my observations–violence is not always needed to bring about real change, and too often violent tactics do not bring about the real resolution of situations."

Beyond the strategic and ideological considerations of the liberation movements, we asked Tandon about the current problems facing African peoples, and the often-violent role of the nation–state. Like his views on nonviolence and armed struggle, we found his concerns in this area to be similar to ours.

"I would accept," he conceded, "that modern nation–states have come to a point in history where they mostly depend on force to continue in existence. This is, I think, a correct description. The state is founded on force. But I don't think that it is a prescriptive fact–I don't think that it has to be that way. A nation-state does not have to be founded on force. Talking prescriptively, I would argue that efforts to do so are self-defeating. Building up military force necessarily arouses its opposite force from the people. Even if the people do not dissolve the military force and overthrow the statist oppression, nonetheless the antagonism that is built by a nation-state that tries to stay in existence through violence will see to its undoing.

"I think that it would be wrong to suggest that if colonialism had not come to Africa, the natural evolution that Africa was going through would not necessarily have produced an authoritarian type of state. The examples of Shaka in South Africa, or the kingdoms in Uganda, were authoritarian too. It's not as if the natural evolution would have necessarily produced a democratic system, because no democracy is achieved without a struggle by the people themselves. Democracy is not achieved by design; it is created by struggle. For sure, there would have been oppression by authoritarian regimes even if colonialism had not come.

"The point about colonialism is that it imposed an alien force–doubly so. Every state power is alien against the people, in my view, because it uses force against the people. It is therefore alienated from the people. But the colonial state is doubly alienated. What has happened after independence is that post-independence governments have taken over the paraphernalia left for them by the exiting colonial powers. In some cases, there have been very few changes in the structures of power–only the faces have changed. Now we have a situation in which the indigenous peoples take over power–with Black faces–but carrying on the tasks of the colonial regimes. That alien force is even more repugnant to the people.

"How to get out of that situation is very hard," Tandon noted. "I have no problem with the devolution of power as a concept. I do think that power is best when it is not centralized, which is fragmented, which manifests itself in different institutions, where there are checks and balances. This kind of power is better than a totally centralized one.

"What I have a problem with is the method by which you go about bringing a devolution of power. In my view, it is not something that can come from simple talk: someone sitting in a room saying 'Now we can decentralize!' The 1960s and '70s were decades when people talked about decentralization *ad naseum*. All the so-called decentralization measures had been ones whereby the gun would come nearer to the village people, but there would be no genuine or corresponding break-down of power. People were still left disempowered. People will only be empowered when there is a genuine struggle against state power, and when they create the basis for their own local power as a result of victories that they win. Significantly, I think, many of these victories have got to be won politically, not simply through military means.

"If you look at empowerment as a process that grows on in history, as a movement–without any finality about it–then you are on the right track. It's a continuous struggle of opposite forces. At a particular point of time, a community may get caught up in struggling–for example–to regain control over the environment: the trees, the wildlife, the land. They are struggling for these resources because these resources have been taken away from them. It's a concrete struggle, it's not a theoretical struggle; it's not abstract. It is here and now, and it relates to their lives today–not tomorrow. Tomorrow, if they gain control over the land, they may use it opportunistically–though at this point in time, their struggle is just. It is a never-ending battle. There is no model to that, and no point in romanticizing it either. It is a struggle that has no dreamy end to it.

"I do, however, believe that–notwithstanding the ups and downs in history (and there have been more downs than ups in the last thirty years of African history)–we are moving in a progressive direction. The illusions of yesteryear have gone. The collective consciousness of the people is better," concluded Tandon, "in spite of the fact that materially they are worse off today. I have no illusions that this will produce something immediately, but at least it creates the basis for the struggle to move on one step further along the way. In my view, at this time, that's all we can do."

* * *

Given the broad, revolutionary visions and ideals existing in the struggles for southern African liberation, Tandon's conclusion may seem sadly limited. More than in any other part of the continent, the liberation movements of the south engaged in a wide range of strategies and tactics, experimenting with a similar diversity of ideological models. It is hard to deny the extent to which the peoples of this region fought for fundamental social change. More than in any other region, the principles of people's war and armed struggle were put into practice. Far beyond the mere rhetoric of some, the movements we reviewed struggled and struggle for lasting conditions of liberty and justice.

In summarizing the costs and effects of these struggles, it's hard not to be carried away by the intense commitments of the organizations and leaders involved. On the one hand, the costs of the terrible terrorism inflicted on Mozambique–and similar words could be said of Angola–make the gains seem sometimes pale in comparison. Namibia, in contrast, appears in a relatively strong place to move–however slowly–towards progressive goals. Zimbabwe may be the most symbolic of the future of the entire region, with an uneven pattern of setbacks and advances.

As nonviolent revolutionaries, we must affirm our solidarity with all of these liberation struggles, and continue our support for social transformation. Their sacrifices should provide inspiration and practical information for all those truly committed to equality. We remain humbled by our dialogues in southern Africa. So much of what we heard reflected pieces of our own perspective; so much of what has been learned has been done so at a high human cost. If, as Yash Tandon suggests, the increasing consciousness of the people provides the basis for future struggle, then perhaps we may take comfort in the very fact of moving forward, step by step. Indeed, that has long been the basis of the Mozambican battle cry, which we must now all adopt as our own: *A Luta Continua!* The struggle continues!

NOTES

1. Interview/dialogue with Bill Sutherland, November 4, 1993, Brooklyn, New York.
2. From "On the Necessity of a Prolonged War," FRELIMO's A Voz da Revolucao (May 8, 1968, Dar), as reprinted in *The African Liberation Reader: Documents of the National Liberation Movements*, Aquino de Bragança and Immanuel Wallerstein (eds.), Zed Press, London, 1982.
3. See, for example, Barbara Isaacman and June Stefhan's *A Mulher Moçambicana no Processo de Libertação*, Instituto Nacional do Livro e do Disco, Maputo, 1980
4. Stephanie Urdang, *And Still They Dance: Women, War and the Struggle for Change in Mozambique*, Monthly Review Press, New York, 1989.
5. As discussed in William Minter's *Apartheid's Contras: An Inquiry into the Roots of War in Angola and Mozambique*, Zed Books, London, 1994; or in Alex Vines' *RENAMO: Terrorism in Mozambique*, Center for Southern African Studies/University of York, London, 1991.

6. Interview/dialogue between the authors and Madame Graça Machel, Maputo, July 25, 1999, 1992.
7. Interview/dialogue between the authors and Dr. Pascal Mocumbi, Maputo, July 24, 1992.
8. David Martin and Phyllis Johnson, *The Struggle for Zimbabwe*, Faber and Faber, London, 1981.
9. Interview/dialogue between the authors and Nathan Shamuyarira, Harare, July 22, 1992.
10. Interview/dialogue between the authors and President Sam Nujoma, Windhoek, August 3, 1992.
11. Interview/dialogue between the authors and Theo Ben-Gurirab, Windhoek, August 4, 1992.
12. Interview/dialogue between the authors and Prof. Mburumba Kerina, Windhoek, August 4, 1992.
13. Martin Prior, "Operation Namibia Escalates Non Violence," *WIN Magazine*, 339 Lafayette Street, New York (10012), April 22, 1976.
14. Professor Tandon is currently Director of the International South Group Network (ISGN), 7 Dougal Avenue, The Grange, Harare, Zimbabwe. ISGN is "borne in the post-Cold War era of globalization, part of the collective struggle for social justice, peace, democracy and humanity."
15. Interview/dialogue between the authors and Mary and Yash Tandon, Harare, July 20, 1992.

CHAPTER 6

TURNING POINTS: SOUTH AFRICA AND THE PROCESS OF LIBERATION

As a college student in the early 1980s, South Africa was a "forbidden planet." The idea of traveling to the racist region was as reprehensible as thoughts of participation in a Ku Klux Klan rally. For a progressive white activist, trying as I was to link my own draft resistance with other grassroots movements, the only South African spokes people that one listened to were representatives of the official UN-recognized liberation movements–the African National Congress (ANC) and the Pan-Africanist Congress (PAC). Several years later, then a graduate student at Columbia University at the time of the student blockade for divestment, I vividly remember the themes of the ANC and PAC messages: "Our Time is Now!"

The Columbia blockade was a dramatic action in the U.S. movement against apartheid, which shattered the myth that students since the 1960s had all become apathetic and self-centered. It exposed the lie that people weren't really concerned about South Africa, and heightened mass sentiment and mass appeal for speaking out against the double-edged sword of racism at home and racist U.S. foreign policy. It brought together young people of all races under the leadership of the Black campus-based organizations.

For me personally, and I believe for others, it helped give human substance to the links between theory and practice, between academic and activist, between far-away foreign and around-the-corner domestic. I'd race from the blockade to a small seminar class I was taking with Professor Hollis R. Lynch, on the links between African-Americans and Africa.[1] The class and the actions had a deeper significance for me because I had recently met Bill Sutherland, a person who himself had been involved in an earlier turning point in the U.S. anti-apartheid struggles.

The year was 1951, when Bill first met Jacob Nhlapo, editor of *The Bantu World*, while in England. Bill was discussing the Peacemaker project with British pacifists and disarmament activists, but was also expressly interested in the African freedom movements. In Nhlapo, Bill recalls, "here was a person who gave me an opportunity to see that–indeed–in one area of the world resistance and the struggle for liberation was going to take the form of a Gandhian's approach." The ANC was about to launch the Defiance against Unjust Laws Campaign.

Modeled after Gandhi's own defiance campaigns amongst the Indian population of South Africa, the ANC had planned for massive non–compliance of the pass book laws, Group Areas Act, and other legal strongholds of apartheid.[2] "Nhlapo had a reputation," Bill remembered, "of being a conservative if not a little bit of an Uncle Tom. Yet here he was, covertly and quietly talking to me in an excited fashion about this Defiance Campaign. He explained who the leadership was and asked what the possibilities were of getting some international support."[3]

"After all, the ANC started in 1912 and some of the people who were in the original ANC had had their education in the U.S. They had come in contact with African Americans in the U.S., and had experienced discrimination and segregation in this country as well as their own. They were the intellectuals and the professional people, and the ANC was very much like the NAACP in its most conservative days. They weren't calling for any great overthrow–they were just calling for an end to the injustice and perhaps a little better political representation.

"I think that it is quite important to point out", Bill continued, "that there has been a contemporary myth regarding South Africa that says 'we tried nonviolence since 1912 and it didn't work.' But that is a very narrow view of South African history, because if you look at what happened with the Zulu Wars and the Xhosa Wars, it is more correct to say that they had tried violence for generations! The 1912 founding of the ANC was after the last big violent push in 1906, and it wasn't until the Defiance Campaign of the early 1950's that active Gandhian nonviolent strategy was used.

"The Defiance Campaign was being pushed by the more militant youth activists of the ANC–the Mandelas, the Sisulus, and others. Manilal Gandhi, the Mahatma's son, was peripherally involved. These younger people were using revolutionary nonviolence to push a very moderate, middle-of-the-road ANC leadership. The older leadership agreed to the Campaign without really seeing the implications of what it meant, and the threat of repression that could follow such a campaign.

"In the U.S. at that time, the Congress of Racial Equality (CORE) was operating out of the offices of the Fellowship of Reconciliation. This was several years *before* the major nonviolence actions in the South–the Montgomery bus boycott, etc. George Houser and Bayard Rustin were the main CORE folks, and I shared with them some of what I had learned in England. I ended up sending the ANC and other South African activists some of the CORE materials, and they in turn began writing directly to George and Bayard. Eventually, we founded the Americans for South African Resistance in the Spring of 1952. Bayard was especially effective organizing with the Harlem-based church people–Rev. Trigg of the Presbyterians and Rev. Adam Clayton Powell of Abyssinian Baptist Church–and our first action was a motorcade from Powell's church to the South African consulate.

"Before Americans for South African Resistance (AFSAR), which included primarily pacifists and church leaders, the Council for African Affairs–an earlier group led by Paul Robeson–had faced severe harassment by the McCarthy anti-Communist crusades. AFSAR, on the other hand, received much greater response and a broader appeal than any of us had ever imagined. People would come up to us, saying 'I'm pawning my diamonds from South Africa to give money to this worthy cause.' We were getting responses from people all across the U.S.

"As the Defiance Campaign heated up in 1953, the South African government instituted the Suppression of Communism Act, and some of the older ANC leaders got scared. Some regulations were put into effect limiting outside support, and they wrote to us requesting that we curtail our solidarity work. I was getting ready to leave the U.S. while all this was going on, but I remember that there were meetings over at Rev. Donald Harrington's Community Church, to broaden AFSAR to focus on all of Africa. And that is how the American Committee on Africa (ACOA) was born."

Once Bill moved to the Gold Cost, he maintained some contact with the ACOA, who–as noted–provided some support for his work in the northern region. When Houser and others came to newly independent Ghana, Bill served as host and contact person. Similarly, as hospitality officer to Nkrumah's All-African Peoples Conference, he helped host some of the South Africans who were able to leave their country at this time of severe repression. The mass arrests and internationally publicized Treason Trials of 1956 made it difficult for many to leave until later years.

Then, in 1960, the massacre at Sharpeville occurred. Often looked upon as the most fundamental turning point of the South African movement, the massacre involved the South Africa Police firing upon a demonstration of unarmed people, an event that sparked militant uprisings across the country. For many, this was the end of nonviolent efforts towards change. It was widely believed that nonviolence, as a tactic, had been tried and failed. Plans for the armed struggle began.

Bill reflected on the shift in strategy. "After Sharpeville, people's confidence in nonviolence was shaken. One PAC member–Philip Kgosane–told me about a demonstration that he had helped to lead. There were thousands of people, including PAC marshals, who would have the man on the right looking into the pockets of the man on the left to make sure that there were no rocks or bricks. They were trying to avoid some "agent provocateur" provocations. When they marched to Cape Town, there were police on the roofs of buildings with machine guns pointing at the demonstrators. The demonstrators called for the freeing of imprisoned activists, and the police said–through bullhorns–that they would negotiate with a select committee, if the demonstrators all went back to their homelands. Once the marchers went back to the various 'native locations', the police immediately surrounded the areas, arresting the leaders and beating up everyone else. One man said, 'I'm not going back to S.A. again without a rifle in my hand. Definitely, for me, nonviolence is finished.'

"And I would say: 'Look, nonviolence is not stupidity! If you've got people–en mass–in Cape Town, willing to confront the police, that's where you've got your strength. Once you're out of the locations, you can refuse to go back–and force the confrontation at the point of your greatest mass solidarity.' In addition, as I've said, people have to have a long-range strategy. Time and time again people would say that nonviolence has failed because a particular action didn't come out the way the organizers wanted it. People just didn't realize their strength.

"My position," Bill still asserts, "is that the Sharpeville Massacre and the militant uprising which followed created a situation where the South African government was almost brought down. The tragic nature of what happened shocked and shook the world. International bankers were frightened, the money was flying out of there, and the economy was significantly destabilized. If it hadn't been for Chase Manhattan Bank's assistance, the government might really have fallen. People confuse defeat with death, and assume that nonviolence is only valid as long as nobody gets hurt or killed. But a militant nonviolent movement must be ready to face casualties, just as those engaging in armed struggle face the possibility of casualties."

In any case, the events surrounding Sharpeville led to the official banning of ANC and PAC, and their subsequent launching of the armed struggle. "After Sharpeville," Bill added, "the exodus out of South Africa became much more than just a trickle." As ANC and PAC bases were being set up in the frontline states bordering South Africa, and international campaigns in support of the ANC and PAC organizations-in-exile were being developed, small but sporadic armed actions did begin to take place inside the country. "We must frankly describe the armed struggle in South Africa as more of an expression of dramatic propaganda, rather than full guerrilla or people's warfare. It's one thing to say that an armed struggle was waged–with a full military and political campaign–in Mozambique by FRELIMO or Zimbabwe by ZANU-PF, and quite another to claim that South Africa went through any period of successful or sustained armed struggle. There were some effective bombings, such as the sabotage of the SASOL plant that was converting coal into oil. But, on the whole, the armed actions were more symbolic than many of the nonviolent actions which took place over this long period."

When, in the late 1960s and 1970s, labor strikes, student uprisings, and the birth of the Black Consciousness Movement (BCM) started up on a mass level, nonviolent tactics were primarily used. Though eventually and occasionally some rocks and bottles may have been thrown, this type of activity–stones thrown against tanks that are leveling communities–is much closer to the Palestinian Intifada, also predominately nonviolent, than to a real armed confrontation.

I remembered a quote from Steve Biko, the leading figure of the 1970s Black Consciousness Movement. "I think in the end there is going to be a totality of effect of a number of change agencies operating in South Africa," Biko noted. "Whether this is going to be through the form of conflict or not," he wrote, "will be dictated by the future. I don't think for a moment that we are going to willingly drop our belief in the nonviolent stance as of now, but I can't predict the future as I can't predict what the enemy is going to do in the future."[4] In 1976, a countryside uprising of students which began in Soweto was put down by brutal force, with over one thousand children killed. In 1977, Biko himself was jailed for violation of the Group Areas Act, and was subsequently tortured to death while held in prison.

Bill, during this period, had started working as Southern Africa representative at the American Friends Service Committee (AFSC), a Quaker-based human rights group. Based in Lusaka, Zambia, and Dar, he was in a position to do more direct and practical solidarity work.

"This was a very interesting and delicate period," Bill recalled, "when you had masses of young people who legitimately felt that, through the Black Consciousness Movement, they had a movement of their own. After the Soweto uprising, they had to flee in great numbers, coming into Botswana. Once they got into the frontline territory, they were being forced to choose between the ANC and PAC, which were the officially recognized movements. One of our major efforts was to try to provide direct material support to these young activists. We were coordinating smaller projects at that time with the established groups–providing medicines or equipment for the ANC and PAC camps. When you came right down to it, though, my major job at that particular period was to get the people of the U.S. to understand and support the struggle against apartheid.

"One issue that came up during my time with AFSC was the concern by some on the AFSC Board that I was making use of the organization to support armed struggle. It seemed that if I said it looks like violence is inevitable in a particular situation in South Africa, I would be accused of advocating violence. I told them I could not say: 'Be not deceived. God is not mocked. That what you sow, so shall you reap–*except* in South Africa!' There was an influential and affluent group within the AFSC with the conscious or unconscious feeling that they could maintain the status quo in South Africa and give it a human face, or make it less violent. It was my conviction that the people must overthrow a system based on greed and racism. Revolutionary nonviolence, as I understand it, takes into account the fact that true liberation must beware of methods that could end up replacing one tyranny with another. But I identify with any people's struggle to get a boot off their necks and it's up to them to decide their methods. I couldn't tell the ANC or PAC to wait until my nonviolent experiment works.

"There were a number of people within AFSC, for example, who felt that sanctions constituted a form of violence. They would've been in favor of Rev. Leon Sullivan's principles of trying to get U.S. corporations in South Africa to hire more Blacks, help ease discrimination, and cooperate with the government on 'loosening up' apartheid. Whereas others of us were listening to people on the ground in South Africa, as well as to the ANC and PAC, whom were all calling for sanctions. Bishop Desmond Tutu told us at the time, 'Let *us* determine how much we want to suffer in order to achieve dignity and freedom.' For us, the corporate participation in the South African economy constituted a greater violence than sanctions, which may have cut down on some jobs, but remained true to a principle of noncooperation with apartheid. Ultimately, we were always able to arrive at a consensus or pull a majority at AFSC in favor of sanctions.

"One of the really positive things that AFSC did," Bill noted, "was regularly nominate Desmond Tutu for the Nobel Peace Prize–for years before he actually got it.[5] I met him in 1978, at a convocation of South African and U.S. church leaders held in New York State. I was so impressed with the way that he told his story–of how he had not really been conscious of the evils of apartheid until the Soweto period. When he saw the police and these huge, monstrous tank-like machines tearing down the townships, looking for kids to kill, that really woke him up. He was always very receptive to working with the AFSC and coming over to the U.S. to help educate people.

"Of course, my Pan-African connections with the South African movements continued after I left the AFSC. In 1983, when I was a fellow at Harvard University's Institute of Politics, they just happened to put me into the same house as Zwelakhe Sisulu, Walter and Albertina's son, who was a Niemann fellow at the School of Journalism during the same year. I was very impressed with the way in which he didn't play the ANC/PAC organization game, as many did. As a member of the revolutionary aristocracy–the Mandelas, Sisulus, Mbekis, etc.–he was much more interested in the unity of the people. We became quite close during that year we lived together, and it all started when I told him about being in correspondence with his father in 1954. 'That was the year I was born!' he informed me."

Now, close to forty years later, Bill Sutherland and I were preparing to enter South Africa, hosted in part by Zwelakhe and the "aristocracy" as Bill called them. With Nelson Mandela, Walter Sisulu and the others out of prison, it seemed to Bill that it was finally appropriate to travel to the one Southern African country he had never stepped foot in. With the travel bans lifted, we nervously prepared to enter this segregated country as an integrated team of reporter-activists. Careful to leave any radical propaganda and the tapes of our other interviews behind, we took our tourist visas in hand, our skeptical questions in mind, and boarded the airline to the country we had for so long boycotted.

* * *

In our travels throughout South Africa, the urgency of the moment was always striking. The South Africa of the 1990's has been marked by fast transitions. As activists from a wide variety of groups and perspectives shared their stories, we tried to understand the common themes or concerns. Certainly our own concerns–on the history of nonviolent campaigns and the role of armed struggle, on the post-apartheid role of the military or the primacy of the nation-state–came through in our questions and dialogues. But the several generations that make up South Africa's core of experienced organizers challenged our own perceptions of how people and movements could work together.

In organizing our notes for this book, it seemed appropriate to begin with a presentation of the three elder statesmen with whom we dialogued: Vice President Walter Sisulu, Archbishop Denis Hurley, and Baba Archie Gumede. These elders all emphasized the long view of the South African struggle, putting the challenges of the moment into historical perspective.

On the eve of the ANC's ascendancy to government, a sense of uncertainty–of nervous expectation that made the air itself appear to tighten–was palpable and constraining. Once inside the power center of the ANC's headquarters in Johannesburg, our discussions with Walter Sisulu, then Deputy President of the ANC, focused on the changing emphasis of struggle over the years. Sisulu, a mentor of Nelson Mandela in his youth and ANC Secretary-General from 1949 to 1959, had spent the years from 1963 to 1990 in prison with Mandela. A co-founder and first Political

Commissioner of the ANC military wing, Sisulu could rightly be called one of free South Africa's founding fathers.

Changing times call for new modes of operation, and that basic fact seemed to create the focus for our discussions.

"The approach is different," silver-haired Sisulu noted, beaming from behind an immaculate desk in the middle of his office. "It is no longer the question of merely howling at each other and wanting to destroy each other as much as we can–you can do that, but you've got to consider that you are on the verge of taking a government. The fundamental question today is the transfer of power from the minority to the majority. It's a complex situation. The distrust between Blacks and whites has grown, at a time when it should be lessened."[6]

Sisulu discussed the ANC's history of organizing–and giving expression to–mass sentiment. "We've had the experience of dealing with the masses of people when they are angry, when the people want to fight, throw stones, and do all the things they did yesterday. We have had a system of mastering peaceful demonstrations even when people are angry. In the last years before majority rule, we've had very strong and powerful actions, mass actions that were able to direct the people properly towards a peaceful solution. We were aware of those who were against us–especially the regime, which had persistently said that mass action leads to violence. But we used the method of mass action because we believed it was a democratic method.

"The violence in the years just prior to majority rule was decidedly different than the violence of the past. It wasn't a violence that came about by accident. It wasn't the same violence of the colonial times of apartheid. It was orchestrated by the old apartheid power structure so that it would undermine the power of the people, and the ANC. It was intended to make the process of negotiating difficult. Our answer was this: we must strengthen our international support. We must be proud of finally getting the real thing.

"We've got to be guided by the concrete situation as it develops now–the transformation that is taking place the world over. We can't use the past; changes are taking place and we have to look at the mistakes of the past and advantages of the present. The important thing is to have an idea–to aim at a more democratic system. When you are emerging as a government, you can't avoid the bureaucratic tendencies taking shape. But to me, the key is in actually looking forward, to a new and more democratic system, having learned from all the mistakes."

Catholic Archbishop Denis Hurley also presented a long view of the anti–apartheid movement, having himself been a part of it for over three decades.[7] As a young white student in Rome in the late 1930s, Hurley's introduction to justice issues was through courses on the social dimensions of the Christian gospel–lessons of a different nature than those faced through practical experience by Sisulu, Mandela, and the young members-to-be of the ANC's Youth League. Hurley recalled returning to South Africa from his studies:

"When I came back as a young priest in 1940, I realized that the South African counterpart to the European problem of capital labor was simply the Black/White problem. That was before what was called apartheid, but not before segregation. South Africa has had segregation right from the start, and what I found when I got back in 1940 was a very, very deeply entrenched attitude of segregation, in some aspects worse than it was during the last days of apartheid, through the early 1990s. I said a few words about the problem of segregation, and gave a few talks, but I realized that these ideas were not at all popular among white people. We of the Catholic Church were very worried about revolution, so when the ANC Youth League began to get confrontational in 1944–45, we stood back rather nervously and did not get involved.

"Already, however, there were some white people whose conscience was beginning to touch them. The South African Council of Churches (SACC)–called the Christian Council in those days–was beginning to notice what was going on. Individual churches also began to make statements. This was a time when churches believed too naively in the power of statements or the pastoral letter, communication of conceptual words to people. They believed far too easily that that would change people. We were much too intimidated by the power of the state.

"As far as the Catholic Church was concerned, I don't think we became activists until after the Second Vatican Council–which was a council of bishops held in Rome from 1962 to 1965. And it was not until the beginning of the 1970s that we, as a Church, asked ourselves: Can we continue with the apartheid structures within the church? Because there did exist separate salaries for white and for Blacks and we accepted that. At the beginning of the 1970s, we began an investigation of the possibility of integrating our seminaries. By the time of the enormous upheaval of 1976–the Soweto Uprising–we had given up our belief in statements and sermons and letters and realized that more had to be done on a practical level."

Throughout the late 1970s and 1980s, the organized church played a growing role in active resistance movements. When a new wave of repression hit, and mass organizations like the United Democratic Front (UDF) were banned–with thousands placed in detention without trial or charge–many leaders of mainstream religious groups took up the call. A multi-racial grouping of South African Christian, Muslim, and Jewish clergy led demonstrations, spoke up in favor of international sanctions against South Africa, traveled around the world to provide information about what was going on, and–in some cases–even faced arrest in nonviolent civil disobedience actions. Archbishop Hurley attested to some of the philosophical questions that were raised by these actions.

"There were always little groups within the church–going back about twenty-five years–that got involved in what you might call nonviolent resistance. Yet the church as a whole didn't have any plans or patterns. The institution had become far too accustomed to living with what you'd call the structures of violence–structural injustice. The circumstances that surrounded us in the late 1970s, however–the way the state reacted against the young people after 1976–just disgusted church people. They couldn't accept it, so they took a principled stand: enunciating where the church stood, cheering for the young people, befriending them, protecting them whenever they could.

"The massive direct actions in 1992," Hurley continued, "leading up to the transfer of power, seemed at the time like the best way within South Africa. With so many people involved, the problem was to keep from becoming violent–on the side of the people and also on the side of the police–who are so used to using strong-armed methods over the decades. Those methods have been very much part of our culture and life-blood: the male, acting-out of the South African Police. The root causes of violence–even the clashes between the Zulu-based Inkatha and the ANC–have been exploited, to a great extent, by the police force.

"When we were marching everywhere and church people were called out to march in the front ranks, there was a great spirit among us. I enjoyed being in those marches–it was vital and alive. Now, all over the world, issues of liberation theology and nonviolence are big topics of debate. I don't know if the debate is very great in South Africa, but those theologies have come to stay, *because* of the existence of oppression. Pacifism, I think, is quite an important debate, but the situation of the church as such is that it's slow to reach definite conclusions."

The third elder that Bill and I spent time with was Archie Gumede, former co-chair (along with Walter Sisulu's wife, Albertina) of the United Democratic Front.[8] Gumede's perspective reinforced a sense of strategic pragmatism underlying the conversations with Sisulu and Hurley, but from a grassroots point of view. Meeting at his modest home in a township outside of Durban, Gumede stressed the building of community-based organizations as a key to liberation.

"I've been in the struggle for fifty years! My first involvement was with the ANC in Pietermaritzburg in 1942 or '43. Towards the end of World War II, I was asked to be the secretary of the local branch. It was before the attempt of Germany on Russia, and the Communist Party locally had been pursuing the line that the war was an imperialist one, and the people should not take any part in it. But then Hitler attacked Russia! At the time, we were not so much anti-national or anti- international politics, but we did have our own local projects. For example, there was a proposal at that time that African women should be subjected to health inspection by doctors before they entered employment in the urban areas. That was an indignity that we objected to, because it was based on the perception that

Black people were the ones who imparted venereal diseases so the lives of the white people would be put in jeopardy.

"The Defiance Against Unjust Laws Campaign in 1952 came about mainly when the ANC Youth League was formed by folks not satisfied with the way the ANC was proceeding through passing resolutions, pleading for this or that. The unjust laws targeted were the pass laws, segregation in the post office, and the Group Areas Act. There wasn't a Group Areas Act–restricting Black people to live on the poorest land in townships–until 1946, when the National Party came to power.

"When we were dealing with the pre-war Smuts government there was a possibility of pressure being effective. In my view, the fact that Smuts was in touch with world opinion and had been a participant in the drafting of the UN Charter of Human Rights, made him sensitive to external opinion. But the National Party and Malan were not worried about external opinion. When they discussed the repression of Blacks by whites, they said it was natural! They'd use the Bible and the story of Ham and Shem and Noah, saying that Ham was condemned to be the heaver of wood and the drawer of water. If a person believed in the equality of human beings, that made him automatically a communist. They were very critical of the American Constitution and the Declaration that all men are born equal and free.

"The Indian people were the first to resist the Group Areas Act. We should always have in mind that the Defiance Against Unjust Laws Campaign had as a precedent the campaigns of Gandhi in South Africa in the early 1900s. That made us believe that it was always possible to bring about change through making those kinds of sacrifices–being in prison, being beaten with a sjambok. The Youth League was made up of people who accepted the Gandhi method as a strategy, and they influenced the ANC to accept these tactics. So in 1948 and 1949, as the Nationalists were taking over, there was a treasury of Gandhian experience.

"One organizing problem that we faced was that in applying apartheid, the Nationalist Party had set up these strata: at the bottom were the Blacks, next were the Indians, next were the Coloreds, and the whites were on top. So they developed antagonisms among the various groups, granting some rights to one group and not to another. In many respects, the Indians were better off than the Black people, because they were not forced into townships and they were able to open businesses in the urban areas." Also, as organizing and the Defiance Campaign mushroomed, repressive laws increased. "Formerly, if there was an act of trespass of the segregation law in the post office, there would be a sentence of three months–the same if you broke the curfew laws. But if you were convicted because you deliberately broke the law in an attempt to change it, you would be sentenced to three years. This meant that if you participated in the Campaign, you must be prepared to make a much greater sacrifice. And people were not ready for that! By 1953, the campaign died down.

"Then, Professor Z.K. Matthews proposed a Congress of the People–bringing groups together. That was a wonderful campaign. We went around to the people saying: 'Now you come to this Congress and you tell us what your proposals are and what we should do.' We had to go out and educate the people that way. People came from all over the country. I was very busy working as an organizer at this time.

"It was out of this Congress," Gumede recalled, "that the Freedom Charter was produced and adopted. And that was the reason that people were arrested and the Treason Trial took place. The argument of the government was that the Freedom Charter–which outlined people's rights and equalities–could not be achieved except through violence. So advocating the Charter was advocating violence. No one in the ANC had been talking about the use of violence at that time. Although it was reported at the trial that one of the accused had said 'When we say nonviolence, it means violence.' And one of the 'experts' for the government at the trial did say that in communism, nonviolence is violence. The Treason Trial started in 1956 and went on for several years. It raised the consciousness of the people to a much higher degree than it had been before. The trial gave so much publicity to the people's demands, that many more people became aware.

"Then came the State of Emergency in 1960. So many people were in prison! Not that they had done anything–but the government claimed that they were in the ANC army.

This was after Sharpeville, and a big gold mining disaster in which a large number of people had been killed. People like Chief Albert Luthuli, who won the Nobel Prize for peace and was an ANC leader at the time, were arrested in Durban. Large numbers of people marched peacefully into the center of Durban and Cape Town, facing the machine guns of the police.

"Leading up to Sharpeville, the ANC had passed a resolution declaring actions throughout the country. There was to be a showdown regarding the pass laws, and on a particular day actions were to be stepped up. People were supposed to go to the local commissioner's offices and demand the abolition of pass laws, then they were to go to the provincial officers to make the same demand, and then eventually to bring the demands to the capital–Pretoria. The demands would come first, and eventually the passes would be destroyed and people would be arrested. The Pan-Africanist Congress (PAC) decided upon another strategy–they were going directly to the police station and face arrest.

"Now in Sharpeville, there had been a lot of disruptions for some time. There had been a bus boycott going on and the bus owners were using provocative methods to end it. The people of Sharpeville had been more politically aware than people in other areas. They went to the police station in great numbers and I don't know whether the police were taken by surprise, but they panicked and then shot at people indiscriminately, shooting many people in the back when they were running away.

"They did this because the only thing the Boers knew in the treatment of Black people was violence. The Afrikaner always did what is known as a 'Kaffir Pak': when an African man or boy did something wrong on a farm, the white farmer would invite his neighbors to come to the farm and they would tie him to an ox wheel and lash him. And all the time he is being struck, he is supposed to say 'Danke, Baas'–which means 'Thank you boss.' This mentality, that the Black man must always jump at the white man's call, is something deeply ingrained in white people–even to this day.

"Anyway, there was supposed to be a day of mourning for people killed and wounded at Sharpeville, and hundreds more were imprisoned. Thousands of unemployed people were rounded up and put into prison. And money was flowing out of the country after Sharpeville. The government could have been overthrown. Even the Prime Minister–Verwoerd–was shot! At that time, I was picked up early in the morning and taken to prison. It was the second time that I had been taken to prison early in the morning, the first time being at the time of the Treason Trial. After Sharpeville, I was in prison for six months.

"Just after 1960, there was a conference at which the question of continuing nonviolence was reassessed. It was felt that something really had to be done to effect the state. What was in mind was some action, which would not involve killing people–the feeling against killing people was very strong. So it was decided that there should be this campaign of sabotage–the railways, the telephone lines, the electricity lines, etc. Creating these kinds of problems might cause the government to change its policy. Shortly after that, in 1961, the ANC armed division *Umkhonto we Sizwe* (MK)–Spear of the Nation–was started."

We asked Gumede to reflect in hindsight on the thirty-year history of armed struggle. "As far as effective attacks on the South African economy," Gumede replied, "MK achieved what could only be called flea bites. Attacks on shopping centers, malls, and other places like that have had very little effect on the South African economy. Until you breach the walls of the economy, you are not really achieving anything. The young people went into the bushes, and a lot of them became bored with life in that situation. They realized that they could be doing better things with their time than they were doing. One thing that happened was that a large number of really intelligent young left the country for good. But in my opinion, the armed struggle did have some effect in showing that people could resist oppression. It boosted moral. People have felt that the ANC has fought for them."

Unlike many of his generation, Gumede was neither thrown in jail with long-term sentences, nor did he flee the country and join the movement in exile. So when the mobilizations of 1980s grew into the UDF, he was in a position to take an honorary leadership role even though it meant facing another trial for treason. The UDF was originally coalesced to protest against the Tricameral Parliament proposal–that Blacks, Coloreds, and Indians would have their own separate and unequal governments alongside of the all-powerful white one. By the late 1980s, the UDF had brought together a broad grouping of anti-apartheid forces–from various ideological tendencies, mainstream institutions, and diverse communities–growing into the Mass Democratic Movement which was an important factor in the unbannings of the ANC and PAC, and the release of Mandela, Sisulu and other political prisoners. We questioned Gumede on the significance of the UDF period, and on some lessons for the future.

"The UDF," Gumede underscored, "was able to communicate democracy to the people. It really communicated the idea of equality–participation–so that there was a level of participation across all barriers that the ANC has not, to my mind, been able to achieve. Even in the communities–the church organizations, the social organizations–all these organizations really felt a part of the UDF. There was no question of *this* person being *the* leader. It was a question of what needed to be done. Things were done through workshops that were really in the hands of the people themselves, so that people did not feel that there was an organization there to tell them what to do and what not to do. There has to be unity in the community, there cannot be conflict. We can only get rid of conflict if there is agreement by the majority of the people that there must not be this conflict, that they don't want it."

* * *

Another generation of activists we interviewed spanned a wide range of opinion and perspective, each working for the advancement of their own communities. From Zwelakhe Sisulu to Black-Consciousness-oriented Rose Ngweyne of AZAPO, from former Inkatha leader Oscar Dhlomo to IFOR pacifists Richard Steele and Anita Kromberg and Anglican church leader Emma Mashinini, the common element amongst these organizers was their life-long investment in the struggle, and their commitment to social transformation. We began by traveling to the Indian community of

Durban, discussing methods with a woman who, in addition to her illustrious family history, has made her own important mark.

Ela Ramgobin Gandhi, member of the Natal Indian Congress and granddaughter of Mahatma Gandhi, focused on her own work with the ANC through the armed struggle and mass action periods. "As you know," she began, "the history of the Gandhi family's political and social involvement begins in South Africa.[9] Even before I went to the University, I was very interested in communities and community relations. I eventually became a social worker, though I do not like the traditional social work–which is just charity. I am interested in community development, and concerned with self-sustained communities meeting their own basic needs–like education, health care, employment, etc. Unless people have those things, there is always going to be a violent society or potential for a violent society. My political involvement has been with civic organizations, enabling communities to become empowered, engaged in mass action and even resistance."

Bill reflected on the conflicts between federal governments and local needs, recalling a story from India's independence movement. As India was about to become free, Gandhi apparently told a group of leading congress party officials: "Don't take power–go back to the village republics." His concern was that the National governmental structures would be corrupting and distracting from the basic problems of the people. But the Congress Party members said to him: "You don't want us to take power *now*, after all we've been through?!!!" It seemed like an unreasonable and unrealistic request to them. I asked Ela Gandhi to ponder this dichotomy.

"A number of the young people in the movement," she asserted, "have said that the way the new constitutional policies have been set up are most democratic. If you look at the sacrifices that some of the South African leaders have made, you can see that they are concerned and committed people. For instance, Mandela and Tambo could've been among the richest people in South Africa today, building upon an already thriving law practice, but instead they chose to remain in prison and in exile. There was one Afrikaner–

Bram Fischer–who was put in prison when he could have been one of the highest people in government, but he chose to die in prison. With that kind of leadership and that kind of background, I feel that the ANC will serve the people well.

"Of course, unless there is redistribution of wealth, the major problems will continue. The rich will get richer and the poor will get poorer. It will be the monopolies against the people, because at the moment there are about eight companies that own eighty percent of the wealth of the country. They will have to give up some of that wealth.

"I believe in nonviolence," she stated, "but I knew an ANC person who died recently after killing a lot of people. I knew that he was only eighteen, and that Inkatha killed his parents. His house was burned down, and he decided on that day that he was going to kill all who were responsible. When the apartheid police came, they just shot and killed him. They came to the caravan where he was staying and completely shot it up. People said that it was just full of holes–that is how the police behaved in this country. And when that happens, what do you expect people to do? Even in India, when things like this happened, people just took to arms because of the provocation.

"The ANC leadership has praised the people for showing discipline and restraint. An organizer for the Women's League said that our children were faced with the bullets of the police, and as they grew they were affected by this violent society. She said that we want nonviolence. We don't want a violent society, we want a peaceful community, and the people have shown that we can live in peace. But as long as police kill our people, and our children see this, it is difficult for us to bring them up with nonviolence. The leadership itself, however, has already passed along the message that this kind of discipline is what is necessary.

"As far as *Umkhonto We Sizwe*, it is a difficult question. I can't say that the armed struggle was responsible for bringing the apartheid government to the point of negotiations, or whether it was the economic boycott and other nonviolent actions plus the pressure from the fact that the entire rest of Africa was free. I think that the armed struggle was one of the factors. What I have seen of people who have come back is that many of them have been traumatized by their experiences–like a lot of what you probably saw among the soldiers that came back from Vietnam. We have counseled many returning exiles and MK members in our social service agency. There are some who have really developed through study–they actually read Gandhi while in exile! So there have been both good and bad effects of these experiences."

Since she was active in UDF groups before the unbanning of the ANC, and clearly had worked closely with the ANC since its return, I asked her to comment upon the breaking up of the UDF civic organizations. Her conclusions were pretty direct. "I think that it was very bad, because those structures were most important for the future of South Africa, even with the change of power... I can't see that a change of power at the top is going to bring overnight changes. Until we can get the affluent people to lower their standard of living, we won't see many changes. This is the big issue, and it is a world issue.

"We have been saying all along that there is a need for a strong civil society. In other words, the struggle does not end with the change in power. People have to organize themselves until there is a strong civil society, which will always insure that the government, whatever government is in power, actually meets the needs of the people. I think that we need strong civic organizations, strong trade unions, and strong women's organizations. Without those, we won't really be able to effect changes. You can't expect two or three people in government to do the job. It has to be the people themselves. Even in the Gandhi system, he said that the villages should be organized. He went right to the grassroots and talked about organization of the villages. I feel that it's exactly the same here–we must begin to organize people at all levels, right from the grassroots. People then need to take the necessary actions, in order to get results."

Helping to train people to be ready to take the necessary actions has been the life work of Anita Kromberg and Richard Steele, two white staff people for the International Fellowship of Reconciliation (IFOR).[10] Along with the War Resisters International, the IFOR South Africa chapter has struggled to be inclusive, sensitive, and committed to solidarity and self-determination as well as nonviolence. From

Bill's history with A.J. Muste to my own struggles within WRL and WRI, discussions with Anita and Richard felt comfortable and familiar.

"I think that nonviolence" Richard began, "is extremely important–on two levels. One is that nonviolence in South Africa has always, from a practical and a strategic point of view, been a dominant mode of the struggle for liberation. Violence has been a more symbolic element in the struggle. Strategically there is no question that here, nonviolence has been the dominant tactic–in terms of strikes, boycotts, civil disobedience actions, and such. Most importantly, however, I think that nonviolence is something that holds out the possibility for reconstruction. It has within it the Gandhian sense of a constructive program combined with respect for individuals in service. The fact that nonviolence holds the seeds for reconstruction makes it, from my point of view, very relevant as a way forward. I don't have enormous hope that it will become a predominant mode, because I don't see any country in the world where it's actually the predominant mode. But it is going to play an important role in the future."[11]

"On a practical level too," Anita added, "nonviolence does offer some hope for people–out of the horrendous experience of violence. People hadn't realized what the consequences could be in making an ideological choice for violence–such as the massive level of crime. I understand why people can't say 'we chose violence for ideological reasons.' It's difficult to admit publicly and possibly some people never actually discussed it.... I must note, however, that we very rarely have this kind of discussion. We don't preach nonviolence; we hardly do any kind of training or talking about it. What we do is our political task–which in our case is anti-militarization, anti-war, support for conscientious objection, and conscientizing the white community. And we have good relationships with comrades, you might say, in the anti-apartheid movement. They respect the work we do and we respect the work they do. That doesn't mean we don't have a critique about violence, but that's a point we don't often make to them."

"That was behind my comments," explained Richard, "of violence being a valid choice as part of a spectrum–and not a choice I make, but one I respect another person making if it's out of their life experience. We have not yet run a single workshop on principled nonviolence in such a context, because we've not been asked for that, and we've not sought to impose it. We've run workshops on planning nonviolent direct action and there are a hundred strategic reasons why nonviolence can be effective and productive without ever needing to introduce the moral or spiritual dimension. We have worked on the strategy of nonviolence, and we have tied ourselves up in knots and bent over backwards to explain at the beginning of every workshop that we accept that our commitment to nonviolence comes out of our life experience and we are not about to judge people who make a different choice. We can concentrate on this area of resistance, namely, nonviolent struggle."

Emma Mashinini–co-worker of Archbishop Desmond Tutu and historic trade union activist–is certainly one example of a committed organizer who came to nonviolent action from a pragmatic perspective. Mashinini's autobiography, *Strikes Have Followed Me All of My Life,*[12] which documents the South African labor movement, was a banned book in South Africa. She discussed her decades of experiences in various anti-apartheid structures and the new prospects for meaningful reconciliation.

"I started out as a garment worker, and because of apartheid I found that many people were not organized. Because of what was called job reservation, there were jobs, which were not done by Black people, but by whites. When we started seeing a few Black people in the center of town–in the big supermarkets, in the department stores–we took an interest in them and a concern to see who organized them. So I founded a union of shop workers. This particular union flourished and became South Africa's largest and most powerful union until the 1988 formation of the mineworkers union by Cyril Ramaphosa, now ANC Secretary-General. Even now that union is still functioning, and has had many contacts with international unions all over the world, commercial and allied worker's unions.[13]

"And I was put into prison for my union work. I was a trade unionist for thirty–three years, and after that I thought: 'Now I am going to stay home!' But there was a vacancy for someone to fill within the Church of the Province of Southern Africa, which is the Anglican Church. Coming from the trade union movement to work for the church, I could not imagine having a role to play. In our time, when people see something holy, they've got to go on their knees and all that. It did not fit into my militancy at all. But people insisted, and I did take on this job as coordinator of Justice and Reconciliation and Peace division of the church, for the whole of Southern Africa.

"The most important thing which really is stealing and taking everyone's time just now in South Africa is the violence. The violence has overtaken any other project or work that was done. I've just come from a meeting now where people were speaking about monitoring groups, and that's not for me. I'm not interested in monitoring violence. My main and great interest is in a peacekeeping force, so that we don't have to monitor.

"We have a problem with education," Mashinini reported. "Our children who have been in the countryside have not been going to school for fifteen years. We have a whole generation of future leaders who have been deprived of education. We have problems with homelessness–both before and after the return of exiles. And if that is not enough, now we've had an added problem of drought and we can't say that apartheid is responsible for that! There are many other areas, which we ought to be focusing on, but because of apartheid you forget about everything else. We are miles behind in dealing with AIDS, for example, because all our energy is spent on dismantling apartheid.

"There will have to be many programs and trainings, many organizations. One of our slogans is 'For Reconciliation with Justice.' And we are faced with the same very new issues. Before, we were working as Africans, as oppressed people against apartheid. There was nothing like: 'You are Inkatha and you are part of the Azanian Peoples Organization (AZAPO) and you are ANC and you are PAC.' You just lived on the street where you lived and that was what was important. Now, there is too much division amongst ourselves according to which organization we belong to. We've never, however, had a fear of the tribalism that has appeared elsewhere in Africa. The division we faced in the early 1990s had been more political or criminal than tribal. For example, they say that everyone who is Inkatha is Zulu and everyone who is ANC is Xhosa. I wake up one day to find myself being Inkatha! And there are many of us who feel this way. I worship together with the Zulu Inkatha leader Buthelezi because he's an Anglican and I'm an Anglican. He is Zulu and I am Zulu, and we can meet easily and frequently in church, but not in any other sphere."

Knowing that the police force under apartheid helped foster some of the criminal elements and ethnic antagonisms, which led to violence, Bill asked Mashinini about her experiences with the police.

"You need a police person that you can go to and say 'I have a problem.'" Under apartheid, she noted, no African person could do that. "Our police were no different from those police in Los Angeles. You know that happened with Rodney King in Los Angeles! I was in the United States, and I said 'Now, I'm at home! It looks like I'm back home!' Everything has got to change ....

"There was one policewoman–which is, in itself, a rare thing–who noticed me when I was in prison, deteriorating and dying in my cell. She came on Thursday, which in South Africa is a mother's union day. This day is when all the women in a church get together to pray, wearing a special uniform. She came into my cell wearing her police uniform, and she locked the door and took off her police uniform, and out came the church uniform which she was wearing underneath! And she said, 'Here, doll, let's pray'–and I could see that she wanted to help. This person was police, except that she was a policewoman. Even though I had to go to a clinic for tortured people when I was released, had it not been for this woman, I'm sure that I would have died.

Mashinini continued to emphasize the significant role of women. "I boast that, throughout the whole world, the women in South Africa have been very powerful. While most of the men were in prison or exile, who brought the struggle to the point of democracy? The women! We did these things not under the flag of women's rights, but under the flag of human rights and people's rights. I have attended very many world conventions, leading the South African delegation. In almost no part of the world has there been a woman leading a delegation in the world forum. The women in South Africa have really played a very important role. Can you imagine that when Nelson Mandela and Sisulu came out of prison, they did not wander in the streets, they went back to their homes–homes that had been maintained by women. They went back to their homes and found their children educated.

"We know that our men are selfish. Our men–Black and white: even our Black men would stand together with the white men and sort of look back on the women. Even the ANC is a bit of a men's club. But we don't want to fragment our struggle by saying that we are especially focusing on women's rights. The younger women stand up. And the women in my age group" Mashinini concluded, "have been very powerful. We have been deprived, we have been provoked, and we have had to fight back. We have helped to lead the struggle."

A similar perspective is held by Rose Ngweyne, coordinator of the AZAPO Women's Organization, with whom we had a brief conversation. "Women are not appreciated at all," she suggested. "Traditionally, we as women are not supposed to be actively involved in any decision-making, even if it could mean the family. A woman's word will never be listened to. This is how we brought up even our children; they were not into respecting us because of the discrimination that there would be between a girl and a boy's bringing up by their mother.[14]

"The community as a whole is suffering so from this. The whole education structure is set up in a way that women are being discriminated against by their family. At the moment, we are dealing with the type of women who are helpless because of what has happened with education. They were taught from childhood that the only thing they can mastermind or do is domestic work. Domestic work is the highest paid of all possible jobs for these women. And a lot of families are headed by these women, who are the supporters of the poor in this country."

The AZAPO women's organization was founded in 1989, and follows the Black Consciousness/Black Power perspectives of Steve Biko. Active in setting up numerous grassroots community projects, they have attempted a lot for a small, national grouping. In addition to a health care public education campaign, which focuses on detection and treatment of breast cancer, they have set up an Adopt–to–Educate program, which tries to get young people back to school. Finding it important to focus primarily on women, they have set up several day-care centers, and have tried to relocate and help orphans and homeless children. Though many community programs have also been headed by activists with an ANC perspective, one fundamental difference has been about strategic process: does one concentrate all energies on governmental changes and the ending of apartheid, or diversify efforts to revolutionize various constituencies within society?

"As AZAPO, we have never been against negotiations as it is," Ngweyne commented. "We've simply felt that negotiations should be done in a way that both parties would come from positions of relative power. As an organization, we feel that if the ending of apartheid is just to be adding Black faces to parliament, then people are going to be as oppressed as we are now. We thought that negotiations would be one of the ways we could overcome the problems in this country, and we don't believe that armed struggle is the only way to gain our victories. But there are issues of structural violence and day-to-day violence that must be dealt with."

From the other end of the political spectrum, working primarily with national parties on electoral issues, comes Dr. Oscar Dhlomo–founder of the Institute for Multi-Party Democracy, and former leader of Inkatha. Bill and I were suspicious of anyone with links to Inkatha, with their history as the main promoter of tribal divisiveness and ethnic violence. In Natal, where Zulus make up the majority of the population, Inkatha's leader–Gatsha Buthelezi–has always played up his "chieftaincy" and royal position in the South African political scene. Though claiming to differ from the ANC regarding, among other things, advocacy of armed struggle, Inkatha rallies feature self-described warriors wielding "traditional cultural symbols"–spears and other weapons! The fact that the apartheid government allowed these demonstrations to take place when other peaceful protests were being severely repressed, and that the Inkatha warriors often used their weapons in clashes with pro-UDF and ANC supporters, was only one indication that collusion between Inkatha and the apartheid regime was taking place. Now it has been clearly documented that Inkatha had been the principal agent of the apartheid regime in opposing and repressing the ANC and other liberation movements. Oscar Dhlomo's main claim to legitimacy was his break with Inkatha. We approached him carefully, attempting to get an insider's view of the history of the group most responsible for what outsiders liked to call "Black-on-Black tribal violence," but what we believe to be more comparable to the internal political differences that existed within the tribes of Europe at the time of World War Two.

Bill challenged Dhlomo about Inkatha-apartheid relations: "Haven't there been revelations about financial support from the apartheid government going directly to Inkatha–not just locally and not just recently? The accusation has been that Inkatha all along was working hand in glove with the racist government!"

"Yes, you can't escape those kinds of accusations once you are discovered," Dhlomo admitted, "even if you are discovered ten years later.[15] One pathetic piece that Inkatha's scandal exposes," he continued, suggesting a personal ignorance of the Inkatha–apartheid collusion, "is something that I was going to pass on: the lack of democratic ethic inside the leadership structures of Inkatha. Decisions that should have been made by the major body were made by one person, Buthelezi. These decisions were totally at variance with the known policies of the organization. For instance, the financial policy was that you don't receive funds from the South African government. If it had been done democratically, I would have been the second person to know. I remember clearly a rally in King Park, my last rally in Inkatha. It was quite a shock to learn after I left that that rally was funded by the government. One incident, out of the blue and to the amazement of many people, in the midst of tension and violence, was when President De Klerk spent June 16, 1992–the day set aside to commemorate the Massacre at Soweto–giving an address to the KwaZulu Parliamentary Assembly. It looks to me more and more like it is adopting a right-wing stance on a number of issues.

"I doubt that the Inkatha of today would be interested in training in nonviolence! But I remember that I was personally involved in a program that would have done exactly that. Professor Henrick Van de Merve of the Center for Intergroup Studies, an Afrikaner Quaker, was going to conduct it. But we couldn't raise funds overseas for the training. For Inkatha to say that they are nonviolent today is just an empty slogan. And Inkatha doesn't represent the majority of the people. That's an image that was created. The fear is that, with polarization, the Inkatha leadership might exploit the ethnic question. Certainly, if you took a poll, the majority of Zulu people would not be in Inkatha. They are in all of the various organizations–including ANC. Zulus are the largest ethnic group in South Africa, numbering about seven million. But Inkatha does not even have three million members."

The Institute for Multi-Party Democracy (IMD) has attracted some attention and participation from a wide variety of groups. In that sense, Dhlomo's concerns for tolerance and dialogue have been addressed. He explained IMD's philosophy and mission: "When I left party politics in 1990, I went around the country, calling workshops together, telling people in all walks of life what I thought would help us in the establishment of an organization. The idea was that it works for the promotion of tolerance, work in educating people in the basic democratic tenets and work ultimately for national reconciliation from our divided and polarized past. There was support for this view, and great emphasis on total nonalignment. So now, we stand totally independent. We launched IMD in Cape Town, February 1991, and it was quite an event, which was reported on for many many weeks. For the first time, we were able to bring together parties that had never been seen under one roof before: the National Party, the ANC, the PAC, the Communist Party, Democratic Party, Inkatha, and AZAPO. Everybody attended–the unions, businesses–and at that time it was really quite a miracle, quite unique.

"Since then, we have tended to get involved in the democratization process, training in leadership, holding focus meetings on a specific democratic issue. Our conferences always have an underlying principle that there must be multi–party. There must be all the parties involved there," Dhlomo concluded, "and fortunately we have had very good cooperation."

The IMD has continued to monitor events in South Africa, serving as a forum for critiques of the ANC-led government. Though maintaining an apparently nonpartisan approach, it is hard not to question the long-term motivations of someone associated with anti-liberation forces for so long. On the other side of the African political spectrum, Bill's friend Zwelakhe Sisulu has spent a growing amount of time monitoring the events of free South Africa from his perspective as the head of the South African Broadcasting Corporation. As editor of the *New Nation*, he was one of the country's top journalists in the last years of apartheid. As son of Walter and Albertina, he had literally grown up in the struggle, and had a unique insider's view of the leadership of the liberation movement. As a former Harvard fellow with Bill, the two of them could speak freely about the issues involved in the transition from liberation movement to government authority.

"One of the weaknesses, I believe, in the ANC's approach to negotiations," Zwelakhe began, "was our 'over-opportunity.' The commitment to negotiations became so complete that we believed it would only take a few months for the process of transformation. In retrospect, it was an incorrect view, and what happened for a time was that we ignored mass struggle. We had a situation where leaders were negotiating with leaders and the mass of the people were not part of the equation. That certainly was a serious error.[16]

"At the point of the Boipatong Massacre in 1992, it became clear to us that negotiations were now being waged not as a peace process but as a war process, and that sitting in negotiations at that point would not make sense. I did believe that, even when negotiations broke off, we had the capacity to change things–that is, to actually force the apartheid regime away from using negotiations as a war process. But the only way we could force them was through mass action, peaceful mass action.

"Ultimately, all of us were convinced that the answers lay in negotiation. We all recognized that there was no alternative for this country. It was a very difficult situation, because if the ANC continued to negotiate and there was violence, the ANC looked bad. When the ANC pulled out of negotiations and the process became protracted and more people died, the ANC still looked bad. So it was a very tricky situation we had to deal with. The regime itself was conscious of this, because it was doing things to empower its own position at the negotiating table. And one powerful element it had in its armory–that we didn't have–was the violence.

"The early 1990s were a difficult time, and there was no doubt in my mind that the violence we were going through was going to have a profound impact on any culture that emerged, even in the post-apartheid society. One of the dangers of this society is that all the killings have now become statistics and we no longer have the ability to see these figures as real people do. We had people who came to the *New Nation* office to tell us the most horrifying stories.

"One woman told a story.... She was in her house at 7 o'clock in the evening and a group of people came. They shot her 18-month-old son through the window. They shot her husband. Then they demanded that she retrieve the bullet from her husband's skull. She tries to do this–in vain–and when these people leave, she runs outside hysterically and finds people from a police vehicle. She pleads with them to help her. And mockingly they say: 'Why don't you put your husband in the wheelbarrow and take him to the hospital?' And in her confused state, she does exactly that. She loads the husband and the kid on this wheelbarrow and carts them off to the nearest clinic. But, of course, by that time they are long dead. Now I tell this tale just to show how awful the violence had become. I said to myself, 'What has this experience done to this woman? What has it done to the other child, who was trapped in the house when this happened?'

"When the violence started, it was very coherent, and it was clear to us that the state was involved. But what happened next was that the violence gained a momentum of its own, to the extent that really no one was in control. When the violence starts, it may be a difference between two individuals or two groups, but ultimately it assumes a political character. A good example of this is in the ANC–Inkatha conflict. Inkatha is actually numerically very small; it can't match the ANC. But the strange thing is that we found Inkatha mushrooming in areas far from KwaZulu, with people calling themselves Inkatha not because they had any formal links to Inkatha, not because they identified with its political objectives, but because it's an identity in contrast to the ANC. 'If you are ANC, then I have to be Inkatha.' That was why we had a situation where it seemed that the main conflict was between Inkatha and ANC.

"In addition to the state-initiated violence under apartheid, there were a number of other dynamics that came in. Millions of people were unemployed. The collapse of the homeland economies led people to flock to urban areas. And the economic paralysis in the entire region led people to flock here–from as far away as Zaire. One of the major problems that confronts us is that we can't guarantee that mass action is going to be peaceful because, given the dynamics in society, the level of violence is so high.

"Of course, mass action is also something which will help to rebuild grassroots structures. Nothing is as good as a campaign to help you build structures, particularly a campaign that is likely to draw broad support from the community. And an international presence also helps to reduce violence. The presence of the international community during mass actions would not stop the violence, but it would have an inhibiting effect on the racist regime."

I asked for more information about the grassroots structures–how they worked during the 1980s and why they did not continue through the '90s.

"I think the apartheid government strategy was very clear," commented Zwelakhe. "First, smash all the grassroots structures. Then, introduce reforms so that there is a completely new political culture. That is what happened. We had a situation where we had no structures on the ground. The ANC was unbanned and we had to start from scratch to build ANC structures. At the same time, you have all these problems of unemployment and violence. The violence, among other things, is designed to show people that the ANC can't protect you. Even holding a meeting becomes difficult. If you are in a vigil and somebody just walks in and wipes people out with an AK-47, then even the holding of meetings is difficult. I'm talking about in-house meetings. One has seen families withdraw into themselves, whereas previously the entire street–in a sense–would be one family.

"Let me tell you about a strange experience. I attended a funeral and I noticed that while we were praying there was a car that was being burned next to the grave. So I asked people, 'What's happening?' They explained to me that this is something that has been happening in Soweto. The person we were burying was apparently a car thief, and the new subculture demands that his comrades must steal a car that very morning and damage it. Now I'm saying, this is a manifestation of the disintegration that has taken place in our community. In the earlier days, that would never have happened, because we would not have tolerated it. We, the community, would not have tolerated the situation–where our traditions of burying people are vulgarized and defamed.

"Some of these things happened with the connivance and collaboration of the apartheid police. The phenomenon of car thieves or so-called jag rollers–these are youngsters who drive flashy cars and they go into schools and abduct women and girls and rape them–we have found that most of them get their arms from the police. In turn, they organize stolen cars for the police. We had a situation where Soweto police stations were basically controlled by white people who came in the morning at 8 a.m., and at 4 p.m. they went home to their safe areas. We were left in the hellhole without any policing. The police force is something that is here to stay. One would say that the important thing now is that the police must be people who come from the community. Then those people would have a stake if there were peace in the community.

"I live in Soweto," Zwelakhe stated, returning to my original question. "We had a situation where we actually controlled the community–and we were able to do that through the block committees, so that each member of the community was answerable to some structure. We did not even need a police force, because the community was in charge of itself. All those structures, of course, were smashed during the 1986–1987 State of Emergency, where most activists were taken into detention. I was in jail then. Soon after the State of Emergency was lifted, before we could even build new structures, the ANC was unbanned. It was no longer a question of reviving those structures, but starting from scratch setting up structures for the ANC and other organizations. It was at that point when we clearly saw the hand of the Apartheid State–moving in to set violence in motion. Then they withdrew, as the violence picked up a momentum of its own."

"People were shooting at random, but as I said earlier, ultimately, it assumed a political character. We grappled with this problem–you know, 'What is to be done?' We tried a number of things, when people spoke about setting up defense units. But often that type of tactic becomes even more dangerous, because you are confronting a state that is powerful. If you set up the armed structure, you actually give them a pretext to act against you. I am saying, quite frankly, that it was a war that we could not win using violence. We had to find other means."

Zwelakhe's stories were yet another expression of the pragmatic need for nonviolence. His conclusions demonstrated that the search for alternative methods must continue.

* * *

During the summer of 1985, just after the Columbia divestment movement had made all the headlines, I found another link to my twin interest of draft resistance and African liberation. By this time, my U.S.-based interests had expanded considerably beyond the anti–registration movement, and I had been elected the National Chairperson of the War Resisters League–focusing on disarmament, war tax resistance, international solidarity, as well as anti-military resistance. A growing movement of whites in South Africa, it seemed, were getting together in a mass-based campaign to say 'No!' to the military and to the apartheid system. This group, in my evaluation, could be a model to anti–militarists worldwide; they put into practice a politics that was profoundly anti-racist and critiqued the cycle of violence as well. The End Conscription Campaign (ECC), as this new organization was called, was an important group to work with.

I actually had gotten a glimpse of ECC–in–formation one year earlier, on a study trip to Zimbabwe. While discussing local politics with U.S. author Julie Fredrikse,[17] she noticed my tee shirt with a broken rifle on it, and suggested that I meet her husband, a South African military refuser who was in contact with some other refusers on holiday or in exile in Zimbabwe. Their new organization just in the planning stages, they discussed how military service was one of the few material prices that white South Africans had to pay to maintain their vast privileges. With regional wars and a home-based Black movement heating up, they could use this hardship on young white males to encourage resistance and split the South African Defense Force. The war in Namibia, after all, was being referred to as South Africa's Vietnam. Through this political opening, public education on the evils of apartheid could be brought to a more mainstream white populace. When a notice of the official ECC launching reached my WRL mailbox in New York that summer, I wasted no time sending telegrams, letters, and packages of support materials.

Seven years seemed like a lifetime later. By the time Bill and I reached Johannesburg during the summer of 1992, the ECC had gone through a cycle of transition paralleling the changes in South African society: they had grown into one of the major vehicles for white resistance, had been especially targeted among whites for detentions, had been banned, then unbanned.[18] With significant international attention, including two WRL-sponsored U.S. tours, the ECC–along with the UDF–had helped to break the media "white-out" during the State of Emergency of the 1980s, and got information on what was happening inside South Africa out to world attention. Then the unimaginable happened–Mandela and the others were released, the ANC and PAC were unbanned, and it was clear that apartheid was about to fall, soon. By the summer of 1992, the ECC was finally diminished to a small group of pacifists and conscientious objectors. The African leadership was leading as never before, and was clearly about to take power.

Meanwhile, campaigning among whites in the U.S. about the links between racism and militarism had brought about substantially less dramatic results. Faced with a predominantly white peace movement which seemed unwilling to learn some fundamental lessons of history, many supported the ECC as an anti-draft group only, hoping that the South Africans would eventually declare themselves to be pacifists, but never really committing themselves to work on anti-apartheid causes. The arms race, after all, had to be our main focus–it wasn't *our* job to be doing solidarity work. Others in the U.S. couldn't understand what a fellow white person could tell them about racism. After all, the argument went, racism is the issue that we deal with every time we "do outreach" to a Black person, inviting them to attend our conferences and tell us a little bit about their situations.

Still others heard the message, but had difficulty giving full support without first pigeonholing the ECC: Are they ANC? Are they nonviolent activists? Some of these questions, especially those concerned with how respectful and informed ECC was of the situation of South Africa Blacks, were certainly relevant. People with those concerns found out that most of the ECC leadership was in fact under the leadership of UDF structures, and that for agreed-upon strategic purposes the ECC as a whole was not to be linked to any other coalition or group. U.S. activists with this depth of understanding turned out, unsurprisingly, to be the most supportive of ECC and UDF efforts.

With the end of apartheid now near, I looked forward to reuniting with old friends–a younger generation of activists schooled, like myself, in the struggles of the 1980s–and finding out how they were fitting in to the transitions taking place. One, Laurie Nathan, ECC's first National Coordinator, and the main international spokesperson for the group, had become the Director of the University of Capetown's Center for Intergroup Studies. Adele Kirsten, ECC's second National Coordinator, had spent the latter part of the 1980s as a staff person for the Five Freedoms Forum (FFF). FFF's political principles included the freedom from want, the freedom from fear, the freedom of speech and association, the freedom of conscience, and the freedom from discrimination. By 1992, however, Adele had become active in a local branch of the ANC. We picked up our discussions where several of our other dialogues had left off–reviewing the break-up of the UDF and of local community structures.

"When we look at the unbanning of the ANC," Adele began, "I think we can't just take the timing as coincidental. The government knew that they were unbanning the ANC into a climate, which was at its worst, in some sense. Even though things had begun to reorganize, we had just passed through a terrible period, with hundreds and thousands of people in detention and great repression. People were beginning not to trust anyone. There was a work style of not sharing information, working on your own, which doesn't help facilitate an open and democratic style. A lot of people–in the community–were scared. Before, people were fired up, ready to join the struggle; with the repression, people were much more anxious and much less easily drawn in. Obviously, during the repression there wasn't very open recruitment, because one had to have very tight structures. By 1989 and 1990, things were beginning to reform, people were beginning to organize again, but there hadn't been sufficient time to really consolidate those old structures.[19]

"Then everyone was being pulled into the reorganization of the ANC. There were lots of debates in the early days of 1990, when groups like the UDF were saying: 'Do we discontinue, do we actually close?' A lot of people were saying that we mustn't, because we might need the networks and contacts we've established. But others said that this was the moment we've been waiting for. The ANC is here now and we must put all our energy into the ANC.

"There was a lot of tension then, with questions of how to integrate the exiles coming back and how to integrate the varying styles of work. I think that it's lessened now, but there was a lot of jockeying for position. Many people who had really given themselves to the struggle saw a position with the ANC as a reward for all their work. People coming back from exile had a sense that there had been a hell of a lot of exciting stuff that had been happening here, but that a lot of the skills and the styles of operating were foreign to them. Some came back to the country feeling insecure that they didn't have the networks and connections that activists inside the country had. Yet they wanted to hold onto their positions of power as well.

"Even in 1986, some people were asking: 'What happens when the ANC gets unbanned?' But we couldn't visualize it, it was not a priority for us. We thought that maybe it was going to happen at some time in the future, but we weren't sure. In retrospect, it was one of those things we couldn't talk about. Perhaps if we had had more awareness, more sense or guidelines of how we'd do this, these tensions would not have happened. The ANC in exile, of course, wasn't just from the 1960s movement–it included activists from the 1970s and '80s as well. People from exile spoke so much of Oliver Tambo–how he was a man of the '60s, but when the first wave of activists started leaving the country after the Soweto Riots in 1976, he was someone who managed to hold the ANC together and incorporate different styles of political thinking and strategy."

Though Adele does not like to use the word pacifist to describe herself, she does consider herself to be committed to nonviolence. Given her long history of anti-militarism work, we were especially interested in her thoughts on MK, and the armed struggle in general.

"I think it's generally accepted," she commented, "that the MK was basically a propaganda arm of the ANC. But it worked. It was effective in the sense that people did fear attacks by the ANC. Internally, people had the sense that the ANC's armed wing was much bigger and more effective than it was–even though they didn't see anything more than the SASOL bombing or blowing up of a few police stations. It was an effective strategy, it definitely did contribute.

"Of course, a lot of people will talk about the lack of structure on the part of MK, or a lack of motivation of MK people, who had to sit in camps for years, not actually doing anything. This has had a really negative effect on those people–who left the country particularly to take up arms, and ended up not taking up arms. A lot of them feel like the people inside the country did a hell of a lot more to bring about the end of apartheid, while they were back in the camps. We've had to deal with a kind of disillusionment and some anger towards the ANC.

"The ANC had to both prepare for taking power and to build the structures up again. Some people at the top level may not be committed to doing that, because they have been in exile for too long and are tired. They want power, and in some respects I can understand that. I don't think that going back and rebuilding structures can take the place of taking control–the rebuilding of structures will take longer. Clearly, in power, the ANC is not going to be able to deliver all the goods–in housing, education, etc. The period between the first and second elections is going to be very important because energies are going to have to go into building and structures. The ANC is conscious of the needs, having observed what's happened to so many other countries after independence.

"I think that we will evolve into a social democracy," Adele predicted. "People have looked quite seriously at Nicaragua, trying to understand why the Sandinistas lost their election. My sense is that one of the reasons people voted for the UNO party was as a way of registering their dissatisfaction with the Sandinistas. Then it became a groundswell, and somehow people didn't intend that it should move so far so fast. Nevertheless, people need a channel to say 'we're not completely happy with how our government is running things

"I guess a question a lot of us are asking is: Is it possible in the current situation–not just here, but anywhere in the world–to have the kind of national political structures that actually facilitate communication between government and the masses of people?" When Bill and I met up with Adele in 1997, as we discussed the process of reconciliation and demilitarization, that same question still loomed.

One of the most dramatic examples of strategic community organizing in the 1980's was the development of a mini-city at Crossroads, a squatter camp of people who refused to move back to the townships despite the government's threats and bulldozers. The chief doctor at the makeshift Crossroads medical clinic was also one of the white community's most outspoken draft resisters, Ivan Toms. When we caught up with him in 1992, he was a director of the National Progressive Primary Health Care Network. We began reviewing the grassroots dynamics of the 1980s, this time focusing upon training and discipline, and went on to discuss some thoughts for the future.

"We saw some of the most intense direct action in August and September of 1989 in Cape Town, when the oppression and repression in other parts of the country was much harsher. We all went together to the white beaches and got ticketed and baton-charged, with helicopters to blow sand in people's faces–to blow us off the beaches. But there was real follow-up in the churches, with Desmond Tutu very involved, and trainings in nonviolent direct action. We went back to the beaches a month later and just kept up the pressure, until there was a kind of insurrection between the political activists in the church.[20]

"That whole period was incredibly effective. We held the first legal march in Cape Town, with 30,000 people and even the Mayor attending. It was what we had been aiming for, and we were planning to go on and March on Parliament. We called it the People's March, because we knew that there was going to be a confrontation, and that the police would bring out the water cannons with purple dye. When the cannons came out, we all sat down–I remember holding these two quite old nuns, who were almost washed away by the water cannon! A friend of mine actually got on top of the water cannon and took control of it for awhile. He turned the Cannon on the Nationalist Party itself, which made it all so incredible because the police planned that if you were found with purple later, you'd be arrested!

"We were back there the next week–it was a real, sustained nonviolent action. Part of the reason that we could do it in Cape Town was because there was less oppression going on. There was other violence elsewhere, like what was going on in Natal. So part of the question, in a way, is whether there is enough space to take on nonviolence. I think, in South Africa, that has always been the difficult question. When the state response or police response has been to kill people, it has been quite tough to keep any sustained nonviolent action going. In the Western Cape, the police pressure has been less than elsewhere–with people not dying in detention, with involvement between Blacks and Colored, or Blacks and whites. So that was one period when I felt that sustained, disciplined nonviolent action occurred amongst a cross-section of the population. Masses of people could be toi-toiing (dancing) along the beach, and there was enough discipline and control to do that, rather than things just blowing up.

"Part of the changes that occurred in the early 1990s," Toms continued, "centered around the lack of idealism. People had become demoralized, especially white progressives. They thought, at best, that what we're going to get is a Black government, but that we're not going to get full liberation. After all these years of struggle, that's a harsh reality. Basically, people are tired.

"Back in Crossroads, when bulldozers were threatening us with demolition, that's when the community stuck together and could really work well. There was discipline, and the committee would report back to the community. When the pressure was off, greed took over. People not used to a lot of money would take the money for a school and give half to the school and keep half for themselves. That started to develop, and I think that kind of thing began again in the early 1990s. Some people are beginning to live in expensive houses and really make it financially. Yet for a whole generation of Blacks, there has been no schooling and no future. That's the problem that an ANC government or any government is going to have to deal with–there are going to be angry young Blacks who have no future because they have no skills. It's going to be hell, because they have given a lot for the struggle and they are probably going to get very little out of it.

"It's true that power corrupts–corrupts ideals, and even can corrupt some really good people. They take the easy way out. I've been through this whole thing, thinking: 'You know, I want a decent salary. I deserve certain things.' Finally, I don't know what to do, because at a certain level, I still want to keep that commitment that I had. I've had to look at the conflict going on within my own self, and I'm in a much better position than people who have big families and a lot of financial commitments. So I am trying to regain some of my idealism, even in a situation which is not so idealistic. I say to myself: 'That's what kept you going before, don't lose it now.'

"I think that many people now, because of their disillusionment, can't cope with nonviolence. I don't know how people survived in some of the townships at the time of transition, with brutal, brutal violence. You'd see young men, women, and children standing around, and it didn't touch them–it left them cold. How can you stand around and watch somebody burning? Where have we gone to as human beings? The commonplace of violence – that's a really scary point where we are at now. If someone mugs you, no one comes to your aid because people are scared. They probably say to themselves: 'That's your bad luck, having money on you,' So there is an acceptance of an endemic violence–by children, especially–which is quite scary.

"We've seen the carry-over of the violence of apartheid, now in crime: bank robberies and the hijacking of cars where young people are using AK-47's. Angry youth, who were comrades but now are no longer disciplined comrades, are involved in some of that crime. There seemed to be a massive increase in crime, because of the availability of weapons and the economic situation. It seemed really hard to survive, as violence had become the norm. It's going to be a post–apartheid problem, because the new government is not going to be able to deliver everything. So the situation will continue, and there will be more justification for saying: 'To hell with it, back to the rule of the gun.'

"In a sense the Black Consciousness Movement created a pride in being Black and a sense of self worth. But when people's self-worth is low, we see internal repression being bigger than external repression. People have internalized this sense that they are not good enough or that they are not good at all. I saw a lot of that during my work in Crossroads. Members of the staff who had the skill to do things would often back off and ask me to do them. It was a sense of insecurity, quite deep, which would spark off at the most unusual times.

"Part of the problem, on the other hand, are some white progressives. They have brought to the struggle–because of their skills–quite a lot of influence, power, and leadership. I think that's quite rightly being challenged now. It's hard. I find it hard, when you have to redefine your role into a background position, dealing with people who are not as skilled as you–at least initially. That causes a lot of frustration because white people have assumed privileges as if they were rights. Whites in the professional class usually don't have the same level of fear, but lower class and working class whites are terribly afraid.

"But I am still incredibly hopeful," Toms concluded, "about the possibility of really dealing with racism in this country. Partly I am hopeful just because of the statistics–you have such a massive Black population, who obviously ultimately is going to have power. There is a big enough white population–with an incredible amount of skills and economic power–that you can't just say 'to hell with it.' Likewise, whites can't make–as in America–just token appointments of Blacks to high positions, effectively making sure that the power remains where it is. You cannot simply co-opt Blacks into the system. So I think that the possibility for examples of real non-racism in this country are very positive, and that the ratios are right for it. I've always felt very strongly that the Afrikaner Calvinist has a better potential ultimately to be more integrated than the English-speaking activist, once they accept that its God's will."

* * *

One institution with a long history of accepting and advocating that an end to racism is God's will is the South African Council of Churches (SACC), formerly under the leadership of Afrikaner radical Dr. Beyers-Naude. I first met SACC's Assistant Director, Rev. John Lamola, at the end of 1985 in Vedchi, India–the place of Gandhi's birth. The venue was an ashram hosting the War Resisters International triennial, and the occasion was the first African participation in WRI in many years–since the early explorations by Bill Sutherland. I had urged the ECC activists I was in touch with to attend the WRI gathering in person, and–once we got through Indian protocol, which had disallowed South Africans from traveling in and out of the country because of sanctions and a travel ban–two ECC organizers, one Black Sash representative, and Lamola were the four South Africans selected to attend. Schooled in Black Consciousness philosophies, John had critiques and questions about Gandhian philosophy, but was interested in learning as well as teaching. When we met again in 1992, his experiences had enabled him to get a unique series of perspectives on violence, nonviolence, and the future of South Africa.

"Remember in 1984 and '85," he began, "we had ideas and ideals about violence and nonviolence. Remember, that was also a very difficult time in South Africa, and I was fortunate to have gotten a job with SACC, as a field worker for the Department of Justice and Reconciliation. The Department was basically dealing with intervening on issues of injustice, violence, and human rights, and I found myself working with people who were very angry. It was quite a challenge to be able to rationalize, to think, and to say that no matter what happens; we have an ethic of nonviolence as the way we deal with our problems. Coming back home from India, it never would have been easy to implement, because 1986 was a very brutal time in the struggle. It was clear that the South African apartheid regime, especially when the State of Emergency was declared, was not going to be moved. Many of us doubted if nonviolent action, which we had thought we could implement, would work.[21]

"To an extent, for instance, we had the UDF, which was a mass organization that clearly had a tactic which was different from the ANC, which was engaged in armed struggle. When the UDF was banned, in a way that was a closure of a hope of nonviolent action. Serious questions were asked of what options the people had. Of course, we had identified economic sanctions as an alternative to the promotion of armed struggle, as a means of moving the apartheid regime. But many of us were led to question whether there was a simple choice between violence and nonviolence.

"We were beginning to work on the theory of a just revolution. We were saying that the just war theory indeed has many flaws, ethically and historically. You cannot fight a just war in a nuclear age. We reviewed the European conflicts, the international conflicts, and finally the South African national conflict–where a state is taking up arms and brutalizing the very people whom the state is supposed to protect. Therefore, in this context, it could be argued that people have the right to stand up and defend themselves by whatever means are available to them. Those were some of the ideas that we were discussing through 1987.

"In February 1988, the ultimate happened: I was forced into exile. I learned about the reality of the ANC that I had been theorizing about–the armed struggle–and it became part and parcel of my life. I lived in exile, shared comradeship with the guerrillas, and with the people who were involved in planning the military activities of the ANC. By some coincidence, and because of my history, I got to be appointed to head the Department of Religious Affairs that the ANC/MK had just started, and I acted as a chaplain.

"There was so much to understand, about the experience of going to live in Zambia among the young South Africans who had left the country mainly in 1986–'87. One thing was to underline the damage apartheid has done to a people, which can never fully be told. Some of us who were chaplains had to bury young people in exile, away from their families, where it was impossible to contact parents. We saw so many gifted young people who had grown up in cities like Johannesburg, being forced to live in remote, rural parts of Zambia. Also, there were so many complications of living under the government of a political organization. The ANC provides your food, your clothes, your everything, even the passport in your pocket. To live in that kind of situation is quite illuminating, but it makes one angry about what our people had been reduced to by the apartheid system.

"Another incident which was still being furthered by the apartheid regime while we were in exile was the constant fear of raids from the South African Defense Force. There were all kinds of activities by agents of the regime–like the poisoning of waters, bombs being found next to ANC nurseries. For me, it underlined that we must use whatever means available to resist these people.

"But as a chaplain, I had the privilege of listening to people talk about experiences. I shared my life with young people, and some older than me, who had been to Angola, who had been soldiers, who had fought in real battles that my country didn't really know about. Some of these young people had seen their friends with their heads cut off by the Angolan rebel army UNITA, some had spent years in a military academy in Yugoslavia or the Soviet Union, trained as soldiers. Many of them, due to the nature of *Umkhonto We Sizwe*, were amenable to a very strong combination of the political and the military. Political education in the camps supported the old consciousness of responsibility towards others–simple things, like supplying food or transport to needy people. Still, the experiences gave a window into living under a government of people who had been militaristically trained. And when you are in a militaristic atmosphere, where people have learned that orders are given and orders are obeyed, you learn to work within that bureaucracy.

"Through my contacts with the international peace movement, I read a lot about militarism, but I never knew what it really was until I was there. Hearing stories about what people have gone through made me realize that war is not what we write about. Violence is not what you can write about. Living in exile was a shocking experience–where you had to live with guns around you, whether you liked it or not, whether you were trained or not.

"I tried to create theological sense out of the ANC's armed struggle," Lamola continued. "I wrote a number of articles where basically my line was that we cannot use the word violence indiscriminately when one is talking about a conflict between what the ANC is facing and what the South African government is doing. You cannot imply that the SADF and MK have equal power, given the nature of the struggle that people are waging. Also, some of us were able to investigate the ANC mode of waging struggle. There was a code of conduct, for example, which all MK cadres had to adhere to. The ANC, at the political leadership level, had determined that the armed struggle was part of, and a complement of, the political struggle. Every MK unit was made up of three persons–a logistics person, a reconnaissance officer, and a political commissary. The ANC leadership also made a calculation that they were going to wage the armed struggle in a way that produces political results for the future. For instance, there was a directive that said there must be no indiscriminate attacks directed at white people, and that no civilians in general should be targeted. Particularly white civilians must not be singled out simply because they were white. The argument was that we cannot have this if we hope to be an organization which one day is going to come to power and present itself as an alternative to the apartheid regime.

"On the basis of those considerations, I was able to express the mood I had of revolution. What is in me is the awareness that one cannot talk about violence and war unless you know what war is. We had a hospital where I was making trips to comrades who had been wounded, offering hope in the utmost fear. Moreover, I found people suffering from all sorts of difficult hurts which were visible, but also psychological and psychotic problems which people had across the board. When I came back to South Africa, I was not excited at all when we talked about war, when we talked about action, because some of us know that there's a price to pay. You can't stand up against an evil system without paying a price."

Bill and I asked John to recount some of the conditions just before he left the country, and how things had changed by the time he got back.

"1986, I think, was the height of mass rejection of the apartheid regime," he replied. "From 1984 on, there were eruptions all over the country, and people were moving–taking chunks of power from the regime. We had street committees everywhere, and the idea that it was time to make the South African government ungovernable. The violence that was there was the violence from the regime, of massive repression. There was a nationwide state of emergency, and we only know now what was happening at that time. It was a terror what happened, the most brutal and fearful thing. When we look back, we used to say 'How did we survive?' Two hundred thousand people or so were kept in prisons, in remote places, under horrible conditions. There was a whole atmosphere that there was nothing you could do. After that time, violence was not an option–you couldn't defend yourself. You couldn't come and talk about nonviolence. We didn't have the means to fight.

"There is some criticism, at that time, of the ANC: 'Where were you then, and why didn't you give us arms, because you could have had resistance?' One answer that the ANC gave us was that, after the signing of the Nkomati Accords in Mozambique, the ANC was forced to move its military bases. The massive internal uprisings in the country were undercut by what was happening in Mozambique. The ANC and MK bases lost their only direct border with South Africa. There is another excuse also, which is most truthful: the ANC had lots of problems in its military wing. Now, I'm not saying that there should have been an armed uprising.

Maybe it's good that it didn't happen, and that the ANC was not well-organized militarily at that stage. The analysis, however, is that that was a time when mass action should have been coupled with armed struggle, because the theory that the ANC had developed was that MK must be there to defend the people's struggle.

"I came back to South Africa in July of 1991. At that stage, we were all putting on a mode of reconstruction. We had a country that had been ravaged by conflict, and the perspective was to be positive. There were slogans that we had to move from a cult of resistance to a culture of reconstruction. We have been involved in trying to nurture a negotiation process. In a way, negotiations make up a world alternative to violent conflict and recriminations.

"What we quickly realized, however, was the fact that politicians are politicians and, even when they negotiate, they have a hidden agenda and limitations of how far they are going to take it. The violence that had robbed us of so much was obviously of a different nature. We were no longer dealing with violence being something between the regime and the forces of liberation, but with something within the Black community. Fortunately, it didn't take us long to understand–and we have tons of corroborating proof–that the South African government was fomenting this violence. In the course of negotiations, it became very clear that the regime was not sincere, and wanted to keep white power in a different guise, in a new constitutional dispensation that could be worked out. There was a sense that we should have continued the fighting and taken over the country. We had support, like the PAC, who were systematically bringing up that spirit. The collapse of the official negotiations–the Conference on a Democratic South Africa (CODESA)–proved all that.

"For us, one problem at the intellectual level is that of ethical dogmatism. I think that one can hold ideals but not subscribe to a dogma. I hold to the ideal of nonviolence, because I want to see people using nonviolent means. But I refuse to declare myself a pacifist because I have learned from religion that a commitment sometimes becomes more important than one's goals. Once, some people were trying to train and teach people nonviolence in the townships, and they went nowhere because all that was important to them was to remain a pacifist. All that was important to us was to get rid of the system of apartheid.

"Yes, violence can be a way of life," Lamola summarized. "And I know that pacifism is a way of life. But the strategy of a revolutionary must be to make revolution a way of life."

Nozizwe Madlala Routledge, the second of the younger generation of Black activists we dialogued with, is one comrade who clearly considers herself a life-long revolutionary. Attending the WRI triennial in Belgium in 1991, she spoke eloquently of the quick changes going on at that time. With news of the proposed ANC constitutional reforms–including gay rights and women's rights clauses–she participated in discussions with a South African delegation considerably larger than the one at the triennial five and one-half years earlier. By 1992, she was an official representative at the CODESA meetings. When we met with her in Durban, she told us of her life in the struggle.

"My original involvement was only at the university, in student politics. I got involved with the whole issue of 'Bantu' education in 1971. I had met Steven Biko when I was at school, and I got involved in the South African Student Organization (SASO). It was really a learning period for me, because I had grown up in a quite isolated situation somewhere in the rural areas on the south coast. Life at that level was simply about survival.[22]

"We were expelled from university in 1973, after a boycott of classes. By that time, I was heavily involved with SASO–up until it's banning in 1977. A lot of our work was just getting together and talking about our problems. But we also had winter projects–for instance, we were involved quite a bit with the community in the area of the original Gandhian Settlement. We were involved in a clinic, we went to neighboring communities to find out their problems, and helped with housing and basic needs.

"I got most directly and heavily involved in the leadership of organizations in 1980, when a women's organization had just formed in Durban. It was formed around the commemoration of National Women's Day, and the original 1956 Women's March to Pretoria. At that time, 20,000 women from all over the country marched to the capital to protest against the extension of pass laws to women. In 1980, we were very small, but we linked up into the Natal Organization of Women, and then with other women's groups around the country.

"In 1983, we joined the United Democratic Front. We were involved in our own programs as a women's organization in the Region, but also in the national programs of the UDF. We felt that our issues affected us as women, and that we were also a part of the overall oppression of the whole of South Africa. I think that is why we felt strongly that we should be part of UDF, although we were independent and we did our own thing.

"As far as the experiences of CODESA I, I personally got the feeling that the South African government representatives were very arrogant, that they hadn't reached the point where they were really prepared for sharing their power. For most of us, the experience of negotiations was a new one. At a certain point, you realize that the negotiating council itself is the site of the struggle–because you feel, sitting there, that what you are negotiating is a life and death kind of thing. You start out with principles you want, you've been involved with the struggle for particular reasons, you want change–you want transformation. When you are talking, you don't want to see a situation where the very basis of the struggle is just lost. So, I think that negotiations become the site of struggle in a different form.

"The dream that one has is of a society where each individual is respected, and feels that they are a part of this country and can contribute something towards the building and the development of the country. Black Power and Black Consciousness was an important part of our struggle because we needed to evolve and develop a positive image of ourselves. My underlying position is to relate to all human beings as equals. But one needs to go through stages of anger–especially if you have been dehumanized in the way Black people have been dehumanized. Just like, as a woman, I think that it's important for women to accept themselves and to develop a positive image, in order for us as women to relate to others on an equal basis. So I don't see it as a contradiction, having believed in Black Consciousness and now being involved in a nonracial organization."

The nonracial–or multiracial–group that Nozizwe is involved with is the South African Communist Party (SACP), of which she is a Central Committee member. But the swing from Black power to communism is only one transitional bridge that she sees no contradiction in: Nozizwe is also now married to a white man, and together they attend, along with their two children, the small Durban Quaker Meeting. She described her eclectic philosophy to us:

"The main thing for me is that I see our struggle as a struggle for peace. Because of this, the nature of our contradictions arises out of our very experiences. The driving force for my involvement is that everything one is doing should eventually achieve justice and freedom. For that reason, I feel I can go to Quaker Meetings as well as belong to the SACP.

"The liberation movement in this country, including the SACP, dealt with the state by adopting violence as a means of achieving our aims. But I strongly believe that that path was chosen as the last option, and not because the people believe that the struggle has to be violent. As I would see it, nonviolence would be the preferred strategy of dealing with the problems. But then the situation sometimes requires that we resort to violence. I don't think that the aim of the liberation movement was to have a situation where people would lose their lives. Once people get involved, however, with commitment and feeling, then they may feel that if it comes to that, it's just part of the struggle.

"In terms of the SACP's visions, we have–through the experiences that other Communist Parties have had in other countries–reviewed our situation very seriously. In our branches and regional structures we have been debating several issues, and we think that socialism still is a system that can lead us to the kind of society where people benefit from the work that they produce and they are treated as equals. Of course, it is a process, and we are involved in the whole process of democratizing our society. It involves making sure that the people have rights, including the right to express themselves and to participate in a meaningful way."

Along with Nozizwe, another participant in the 1991 WRI triennial in Belgium was Sandile Thusi. A student activist from Durban, Sandile's intensity and energy are quickly apparent. An early claim to fame for him, however, did not involve something he did, but rather something he refused to do: Sandile was one of the longest hunger strikers in South Africa's prison movement of the late 1980s. I had first come in contact with him when he was still in detention, and a small WRI delegation to Durban was able to visit him. Vietnam veteran Greg Payton, who represented WRL to the WRI and also works with U.S.-based Black Veteran's for Social Justice and the AFSC, traveled along with WRI staff person Howard Clark to help bring news of Sandile's condition to world attention. They met him shortly after he had concluded his last fast.

The Belgium triennial, therefore, was something of a reunion for the three of them, with Greg and Howard admitting that they couldn't have predicted that in so short a time Sandile would be able to travel internationally! For Bill and me, getting to see Sandile one year later, on his home turf at the University of Natal, was another concrete indication of how quickly changes were taking place. Given the important role that political prisoners have played in the South Africa and global revolutionary context, it felt appropriate that this, our last discussion in South Africa, was taking place with one such prisoner.

"I got involved through being engaged with the youth organization of my church, the Evangelical Lutheran Church," he began. "Then one day came the Co-President of the UDF, Baba Archie Gumede. It was after a raid in Mozambique, when a few of the ANC people there were almost killed, and they were arranging a commemoration within our church. When I looked into the program of the UDF–it's principles–I found it very compatible with my own ideas.[23]

"After that, things started to go haywire in South Africa as a whole. In 1984, I found myself in detention for two days. The Security Branch people were convinced that I was coming from Angola, undergoing military training. They even visited people within my neighborhood and went around asking about me. I was released after they were convinced that I had never been anywhere outside of South Africa, and that the only time I was not around my home was because I was out with the church youth organization.

"In 1985, Mrs. Mganya, the women whose house we were using to meet in, was murdered. Her husband had already been murdered by the Security Branch people. Shortly after her murder, an attack was made on my home, and I lost my brother in that process. I left home then and stayed in a residence where Black medical students were accommodated. I took refuge there until I managed to go back home, about 1986.

"I enrolled in the University of Durban and I was there only two months, as a first year student, when the declaration of the State of Emergency was made. And, bingo! I was taken into prison on July 10th and stayed there until June 12th of the following year. We set up an orientation committee as an organized structure inside detention, because we realized that there were older people, fathers, who were perhaps 65, and married people, and younger people who had to be converted to understand why they were in.

"We wanted to train the minds of all the detainees to understand their mission, the reasons why they had been detained, and their conduct in the future. We wanted to explain to them why we were engaged in the struggle. Some of them, funny enough, were detained because the Security Branch could not find the people they were looking for in their family, so they just took who they could find till the other person surrendered themselves in exchange! Hostages!

"I was involved in a committee as liaison with the prison authorities, and at the same time I was organizing prayer services for people inside prison. We tried to follow the example of people like Archbishop Tutu, Allan Boesak, and other church people who were committed to the question of getting rid of apartheid.

"When I was released, very late in 1987, I could not go back to the University because it was mid-year and they were not conducting summer classes. I was approached by the folks at the National Education Crisis Committee (NECC), who asked that I assist them in setting up a project which looked at alternative options of education, trying to blend the academic style with the popular education that was familiar within our own ranks. So I joined them in August, and worked for a few months, consulting people at the grassroots level. But in June 1988, they picked me up again–back into detention.

"This time the chaps were serious about interrogating me, in an intensive way. They told me that they were going to throw the key away, that there was nothing they could do with me now. When they detained me in 1986, I stayed there for a whole year, and started all the trouble that was taking place in prison. Therefore, there was nothing they could now do to me because I was undependable, and they were going to throw away the key.

"As the interrogation went on, I realized that they didn't understand me, and really didn't have any idea at all what to do with me. I was trying to do my best to convince them that we were not just engaged in the struggle because there was some sort of conspiracy from the former Soviet Union to overthrow the regime. It was a practical fact that with the conditions we were living under, there's going to be struggle. Some of us, I tried to explain, were even in detention because of our Christian convictions; that's why we're involved in struggle. But at the end of the day, I really gave up and realized that there's nothing one can do to convince these people. It was interesting to notice how racist they were, even in their treatment of some of the Black Security Branch officers.

"They said that they could not take me to a local prison. After three months of interrogation, they told me that the commander of the prison didn't want me because I was a troublemaker, so they sent me to Pietermaritzburg. There they placed me among hardened criminals, and eventually in an isolation cell. I was not allowed to go the library or get books, or read newspapers. I was allowed to go to a doctor once a month, but I was having problems with visitors because my family was in Durban. When I raised the question of attending church, they said that this was out for me, and since I was a communist, I didn't have to pretend any longer! They were really trying to drive me mad.

"Most disturbing to me," Sandile recounted, "were the conditions that the other prisoners in there were placed in. Some were chained to the doors for twenty-four hours a day, and were given only one meal a day. Many were attempting to commit suicide. It was not surprising, in the midst of the night, to hear people attempting to kill themselves. In the morning, I'd see blood flowing on the floor from their cells. Somehow or other they managed to find instruments to try to kill themselves. One guy managed to find a broken glass, and cut himself but did not succeed in killing himself. They allowed him to stay there for hours, in front of me. Every time I watched, life was going out of him, but he managed to survive the ordeal. It was driving me mad, and I realized that it was part and parcel of torture, psychological and otherwise.

"After six more months, they mixed me with the other detainees. By that time, after only a week, we decided to embark on a hunger strike. Some people had been in for two years, others three. One chap was saying that he was arrested in 1985, appeared in court in six months, then released. That very night, while having supper, the security police came to his home and arrested him again. We realized that we had to do something about our condition. We couldn't depend on the question of court applications, because the state was closing every loophole in the courts. We had a number of debates, like: Did the Security Branch have anything to lose if we died? We decided that we had no other option but the hunger strike. We informed our lawyers and relatives that this was the position we were taking, and made arrangements to contact other support people on the outside. Letters went out to the local organizations that we belonged to.

"After 14 days, most of the striking detainees were taken out of prison. I was taking only water, three times a day. Finally, after having undergone a hunger strike for thirty-eight days, I was released under very severe conditions."

The hunger strikes of 1988 and 1989 are often cited as one of the last straws that led to the lifting of the State of Emergency and unbanning of the banned organizations. A dramatic and desperate campaign, prisoners from jails throughout the country participated in the coordinated strikes. Sandile, one of the earliest and longest strikers, told us that he was motivated, in part, by anger. "I was depending on the idea that at this stage in history, they would be in serious trouble if they let me die! Many people began to pay a lot of attention to my case. The entire university community was involved in a march against detentions, and others were coming in just to offer prayer. Even some of the policemen who were guarding me at that particular time began to change.

"After my release I was in a dilemma. I'd not been staying at home for more than three years. Going back home now, and being under house arrest, could be committing suicide on my part. If I broke the regulations, I could go back to prison for five years. I couldn't stay with more than four people, I was not supposed to leave my local area–so I couldn't go to church and couldn't consult with my lawyer. Regarding my education, I was told that I was not supposed to read or write anything at all. I was supposed to report to the local police two times a day, and I had to take a taxi, because the bus has more than four people in it! Sometimes the cops would come around at midnight, to check if I was home, waking my entire family. Eventually, I'd make coffee for them, invite them in–once we talked for more than an hour amongst ourselves!

"I stayed with these regulations for almost a month, but then said–come what may–I was tired of the regulations and had to move out of my family house. When I came back to some of my comrades, I said: 'Look, I need to study nonviolence.' A number of studies have been done about violence, concentrating on the statistics and the number of people who have died or have been banned. But there has been little study on the social level of how people and institutions like education have been affected."

In the course of study, Sandile became a leader of the local Dispute Resolution Committees that tried to resolve community-based problems in a positive way. In the violence–torn region of Natal, this work was especially difficult and important. "It was a really hard struggle amongst our friends–especially the youth," Thusi commented, "to convince them that we need to go and talk. When the peace initiatives started, there were many meetings held, including consultations with Inkatha. It was a dilemma for me–why should we engage in this thing? I was fighting hard not to be influenced by what happened to my family, or me but to think broader than that. I managed to come to a decision that, truly, in this nation, no one wants war.

"On the issue of peace, the fact is that there is an advantage I have from being personally affected by the violence itself. I've lost a brother. I've lost a home. If I speak about peace, no one is going to say to me: 'It is because you have not suffered what we have suffered.' Every time, when I talk, everyone knows that I've lost a lot in this violence. Eventually, it turned out that I was the only young person in the district-wide resolution committee. I found myself sitting among very elder people from my own ANC organization, Inkatha, the Security Branch, the SADF, and the KwaZulu police. I was the one trying to reconcile things!

"It is a fact that armed struggle itself was engaged in, and arms were taken up against the regime, because all other avenues had been closed. Then there were those within their own areas, like whites within the ECC, who decided to go to prison for refusing to take up arms, as a sign of commitment to getting rid of apartheid. The racist regime always said that violence is not a correct method, but–oh my God! Who are they to tell us how we are supposed to conduct ourselves in struggle? We must come to a point of understanding: What does it take to come out with methods of inflicting pain on another human being? What is the force behind the power that a person can be able to defile another person's thoughts? A lesson that we have learned is that we should never forget what happened. That is also where the forgiving part will come from.

"We can't afford to stoop to the level of the enemy," Sandile stated, beginning to slow down after more than two straight hours of talking to us under the hot sun outside of the University. "The mere fact that we've gone so far is because we are morally justified in engaging in this struggle. It is because we have held the moral high ground. It was not just a matter of being correct, but of morals themselves and of how we conducted ourselves. We, ourselves, need to be exemplary, and not only to our own people. We want to correct a wrong, to show that South Africa is the Freedom Charter State; that South Africa belongs to all who live in it–democratic, united, nonsexist. These must be our principles, and not just something theoretical."

* * *

Since our visit to South Africa in July of 1992, an avalanche of events has taken place, which are a challenge to evaluate. After the revival of mass democratic action, state-instigated violence and terrorism was reduced to the extent that the African National Congress leadership felt justified in resuming negotiations. Chris Hani, however, an outstanding ANC leader of the younger generation whom many considered the logical successor to Mandela, was murdered under mysterious circumstances just after we left. Eventually, the world looked on as an election was held, judged free and fair by foreign observers. All attempts, both organizational and individual, to derail the negotiations leading to the elections and a coalition government failed. The inauguration of Nelson Mandela, leader of the majority party, was magnificent, with outstanding dignitaries of the world in attendance–including Cuba's Fidel Castro.

A follow-up visit in 1998 demonstrated in very human terms the extent of the transitions–at least as far as personnel. Sadly, Archbishop Hurley had passed away, as did Archie Gumede–one day before our visit. At Baba Archie's funeral in the township of Clermont, mourners wore shirts with the words "Gentle Giant," commemorating a man who lived a life consistently fighting for peace as part of the struggle for justice. Most reflected upon the fact that, for once, a township funeral took place where the deceased had at least lived to see the dream of a free society.

Both Ela Gandhi and Nozizwe Madlala have become ANC Members of Parliament, working hard to balance their work with their communities and the pressing responsibilities of building a central government. Zwelakhe Sisulu has left public service to go into the private sector. Laurie Nathan's Center for Intergroup Studies changed it's name to the Center for Conflict Resolution, and his work has included helping the Minister of Defense write the nation's white paper on military policy–an unusual role for an anti-militarist![24] Adele Kirsten still works with non-governmental peace campaigns, now heading up Gun Free South Africa, while Richard Steele has taken a step back from direct peace work to become a homeopathic doctor, promoting different, though related, forms of healing. We heard that John Lamola has gone into the world of business, working, in fact, with the arms industry. Dr. Ivan Toms, however, has stuck to his basic politics, but has become Head of Health Services for a major section of the city of Capetown. And Sandile Thusi is now Deputy Head Clerk of the City of Durban, a position which puts him at the very top of the civil service in that city, where his considerable organization and people skills can be used for the benefit of all citizens. Most recently, in July of 1999, Nozizwe Madlala made the international headlines when she was appointed Deputy Miister of Defense; few commanders of armed forces have ever been rooted in Quaker Convictions.

Whatever the enormity of the changes in South African society, however, many problems still exist. Immediately following the official end of apartheid came a heightened threat of violence from the white right-wing, as well as the demand for real change from the Black majority. The trade union movement remains independent and vital, and has maintained close ties to the ANC-led government. As opposing elements of the population fight for a maintenance of the status quo or for faster policies promoting justice, the need for difficult government decisions and for an independent progressive movement remain burning social issues.

The nature of violence has changed–from the major crime of apartheid inflicted upon the majority to more mundane and common criminal acts perpetrated upon all, unsuccessfully controlled by a police force still corrupt after decades of racism. Struggles to change the economy, for 350 years geared towards serving a privileged minority, show how difficult it is to bring justice for all over a short period of time. The establishment of the Truth and Reconciliation Commission (TRC), under the Chairmanship of Archbishop Desmond Tutu, has been a unique attempt by the actual victims of terror and oppression to take the initiative in healing through revelation, redemption, and reparation. In contrast to Western notions of retributive justice, the TRC has returned to an African tradition of restorative justice.

As Bill and I shared our own notes of our dialogues, we reviewed how activists had met and were meeting the challenges of the past. We had spoken to socialists, anarchists, revolutionary Pan-Africanists, and nationalists. Those interviewed described themselves as supporters of the armed struggle as well as pacifists, church activists and trade unionists, politicians, and those skeptical of liberation through negotiation and electoral means. Yet despite the differences in approach, people across the political spectrum remained flexible and pragmatic regarding the processes for future change. In addition, a set of common themes and concerns had emerged: How could both mass action and negotiation be made meaningful as tactics? Why were the community structures of the 1980s let go, and how could they be rebuilt? What were the roots of violence, which would transcend the ending of governmental apartheid, and what could be done to address this institutional violence in a post–apartheid South Africa?

NOTES

1. See, for example, Hollis R. Lynch, "Black American Radicals and the Liberation of Africa: The Council on African Affairs 1937-1955," *Cornell University Africana Studies and Research Center Monograph Series No. 5,* New York, 1978.
2. A number of volumes document the inter-connected strategies experimented in this period by the Indian and African movements in South Africa, most recently covered in Enuga Reddy and Fatima Meer's (eds.) *Passive Resistance 1946: A Selection of Documents,* Madiba Publishers/Institute for Black Research, Durban, 1996. *A critical analysis can be found in Maureen Swan's Gandhi: The South African Experience, Raven Press, Johannesburg, 1985; a worthwhile primary source on the earlier period is M.K. Gandhi's Satyagraha in South Africa, Navajivan Publishing House, Ahmedabad, 1928.*
3. Interview/dialogue with Bill Sutherland, November 15, 1993, Brooklyn, New York.
4. Steve Biko, from "Our Strategy for Liberation," an interview conducted and published by *Christianity and Crisis* magazine and by the Episcopal Churchmen for South Africa, and reproduced in Biko's posthumous

anthology *I Write What I Like*, Harper and Row Publishers, San Francisco, 1986, p. 149.

5. As a recipient of the Nobel Peace Prize in 1947, the American Friends Service Committee is eligible to nominate candidates for the prize each year. *Involved in anti-apartheid work and general African solidarity, the AFSC still monitors conflict and change in Africa, helps to organize occasional Africa Peace tours of the U.S., and produces materials; their U.S. office is located at 1501 Cherry Street, Philadelphia, PA 19102-1479, [http://www.afsc.org].*
6. Interview/dialogue between the authors and Walter Sisulu, Johannesburg, July 30, 1992.
7. Interview/dialogue between the authors and Archbishop Dennis Hurley, Durban, July 31, 1992.
8. Interview/dialogue between the authors and Archie Gumede, Durban, August 1, 1992.
9. Interview/dialogue between the authors and Ela Ramgobin Gandhi, Durban, August 1, 1992.
10. Though the International Fellowship of Reconciliation office in South Africa is no longer operating, IFOR (Spoorstraat 38, 1815 BK Alkmaar, The Netherlands) still conducts African-based nonviolence trainings throughout the continent.
11. Interview/dialogue between the authors and Anita Kromberg and Richard Steele, Durban, August 2, 1992.
12. Emma Mashinini, *Strikes Have Followed Me All My Life*, Routledge, New York, 1991.
13. Interview/dialogue between the authors and Emma Mashinini, Johannesburg, July 29, 1992.
14. Interview/dialogue between the authors and Rose Ngweyne, Johannesburg, July 29, 1992.
15. Interview/dialogue between the authors and Dr. Oscar Dhlomo, Durban, July 31, 1992.
16. Interview/dialogue between the authors and Zwelakhe Sisulu, Johannesburg, July 28, 1992.
17. Included amongst the extraordinary political journalism written by Julie Frederikse is *South Africa: A Different Kind of War*, Beacon Press, Boston, 1986.

18. ---, *Out of Step: War Resistance in South Africa,* Catholic Institute for International Relations, London, 1989.
19. Interview/dialogue between the authors and Adele Kirsten, Johannesburg, July 28, 1992. Adele is currently national coordinator of Gun Free South Africa, which shares office space with the peace group Cease-fire at: P.O. Box 31532, Braamfontein 2017, South Africa, [gunfree@wn.apc.org].
20. Interview/dialogue between the authors and Dr. Ivan Toms, Johannesburg, July 27, 1992.
21. Interview/dialogue between the authors and Rev. John Lamola, Johannesburg, July 29, 1992.
22. Interview/dialogue between the authors and Nozizwe Madlala Routledge, Durban, August 2, 1992.
23. Interview/dialogue between the authors and Sandile Thusi, Durban, August 1, 1992.
24. The Centre for Conflict Resolution publishes *Track Two,* (c/o University of Cape Town, Private Bag, 7701 Rondebosch, South Africa) a quarterly journal on innovative and constructive approaches to community and political conflict.

CHAPTER 7

THE PAN-AFRICAN EXPERIENCE: GLIMPSES THROUGH THE DECADES

The world is just beginning to realize, with the advent of Afrocentric history, the length, and breadth of Pan-Africanism throughout the centuries and throughout the world. There were, of course, historians in Africa, Europe and the U.S. who had written extensively on the subject, but their works have been deliberately ignored or disparaged during the last two centuries in the attempt to justify the practices of slavery, colonialism and the continued exploitation of people of African ancestry. Even today, there is an attempt to bring back the real revisionist history and pseudoscience of the 1800s, as charlatans like Charles Murray gain mainstream attention for their "bell curve" genetic theories.

An honest accounting of recent history suggests not only the importance of Africa's contributions, but also the consistency with which Africans on the continent and throughout the Diaspora have attempted to link up. The African American-African connection has been generally based on a set of mutual needs and interests, growing out of common experiences of oppression and cultural denial. Though problems have existed at times, the most significant examples of contemporary Pan-African relations are more positive than negative. One such example occurred after Bill Sutherland had moved to newly independent Tanzania.

In September of 1964, Bill had an experience that was to exemplify the opportunities he has had to serve as a liaison and host between African and African American peoples. At a party given by the Algerian Embassy in Tanzania, Bill met a visiting activist who was just completing his first tour of the Middle East and Africa: El Hajj Malik el Shabazz, the man known as Malcolm X.

"He had full participation in this party" recalled Bill, "without drinking, without dancing, but just fully enjoying others doing their thing. Malcolm remained out in the kitchen, but would talk to people as they came to refresh their drinks. He was perfectly at ease.[1]

"My meeting with him there resulted in my being his chauffeur for the next week, because he was staying at the Deluxe Inn in Dar and didn't have any transport. Although he had sessions with people in government, including President Nyerere, he apparently wasn't put in the category of V.I.P. official visitor. I did attend meetings that he had with TANU people, at the home of the most prominent woman in TANU, Bibi Titi Mohammad. He also met with members of the African American community, and spent quite a bit of time with some Harvard volunteers who were teaching at a school for refugees near Dar. A lot of his most lively discussions were with these white folks from Harvard, which was noteworthy because so many of the followers of Malcolm–particularly during that period–didn't want anything at all to do with white people. Malcolm, on the other hand, was willing to carry on conversations with everyone. Another session that I attended was at the Zahir Restaurant in Dar, with Chucha Hunonu. Chucha was a member of the Unity Movement of South Africa, which was one of the smaller revolutionary groups, closely associated with the Trotskyists. It was 3 o'clock in the morning and the animated discussions were carried on over plates of shrimps and rice.

"Malcolm discussed with me some issues the significance of which I didn't realize at the time. He was already talking about the Organization of Afro-American Unity (OAAU) and immediately started to work on the OAAU upon his return to the U.S. When in Tanzania, he was quite full of his recent trip to Mecca, where he began to realize that there were white people who were Muslims–from various parts of the world–that he could relate to. When we had a discussion about whites, he told me something which indicated where he was at that time. He wouldn't have put it quite this way, but I'll paraphrase: 'I don't trust those who are willing to die for me, I trust those who are willing to kill their own. If I were to think of a white man I could relate to and trust in and believe in, for example, it would be radical U.S. abolitionist John Brown.'

"Malcolm also talked about the attempts on his life. One attempt had apparently just taken place in Cairo, Egypt. He spoke of other attempts, which had taken place while he was in Europe. At that time, he didn't talk as though he suspected the Nation of Islam of any involvement. He really suspected that the U.S. government was trying to assassinate him.

"In terms of general impression, Malcolm was a person who was constantly exploring, constantly alive, not afraid to talk with anyone. He talked to everybody in his own quest for answers. An example of his insight and humor at the time had to do with his telling me about his relationship with my brother-in-law. He and Otto–my sister Muriel's husband–had gone to school together in Boston, and when they met down at the 1963 March on Washington, Malcolm was just hanging out at the hotel where Otto and Muriel were staying. Malcolm saw a CORE button on Otto's lapel; it was a picture of white and Black hands, shaking. Malcolm said: 'You know, you are wearing that as though it has some positive meaning, but just look at which hand is on top!' Of course, the white hand on the button was on top.

"One of Malcolm's favorite lines in beginning conversations with people in Tanzania was 'I know that you don't like to hear this, but....' Then he would go on. Unlike many of his followers, he was always ready to enter into discussions with anybody. He had the kind of confidence, a kind of vitality that was different from many other famous people. Most leaders are great when they are on stage and into their act or their speech, but when they come off the stage they are really not ready to have lively discussions with people. In fact, they are often quite exhausted. Malcolm, in the short time that I was with him, never seemed exhausted. He was always full of life, always extremely interested in his surroundings and in the people he was with.

"I was really very shocked, and felt a significant sense of loss, when less than a year later he was assassinated in the U.S. I had been working in the Tanzanian Ministry of Culture, and something interesting happened in the months just before Malcolm's death. The Vice-Chancellor of the University had received a letter from the American Society for African Culture (AMSAC), saying that they were sending my friend James Farmer over for a trip through Africa. Farmer was the head of CORE at the time, and I had known him from my own days in CORE. When the Vice-Chancellor asked me to coordinate the trip, I agreed, though I had no official clearance to do so. I arranged for him to meet Nyerere, who suggested that it would be good for Jim to see Zanzibar. At government expense, they flew him over on a charter plane. I found out later that Malcolm X felt that Farmer had been sent over following his trip to 'clean things up' and present more of an American establishment point of view. I think that the two of them straightened it out a little bit later on, when Farmer came back to the States. But all of this must have happened at the very beginning of 1965.

"The AMSAC, like the African American Institute today, really started off with the initiative of Black intellectuals and artists. But because they didn't have funds, in a very short time they were co-opted into getting funds from official and semi-official U.S. government sources. I don't believe that James Farmer himself really played the role that Malcolm suspected him of playing, although he did agree to come to Africa under those auspices. I do think that Farmer expressed himself rather frankly about the racial situation in the U.S. Nevertheless, as a nonviolent person and the head of CORE, he was seen as a more 'appropriate' person to speak from the U.S. government's point of view. He clearly didn't have the outright confrontational attitude of Malcolm.

"Malcolm was, undoubtedly, the leading representative of the struggle in the U.S. for the African liberation movements of that time. He did, after all, speak before the Parliament of Ghana, and was invited to do that. Although he had a less public role in Tanzania, he was speaking to the leaders of the labor movement, the women's movement and to many government leaders. I'm sure that, just on the strength of his position and his personality alone, he was by far the most impressive of all the African American leaders. We do have to remember that when he was killed, there were expressions of sympathy and sorrow and anger from African leaders across the continent.

"Earlier, Martin Luther King, Jr. was the African American who had been the leading representative of the struggle in the U.S., but with the growing acceptance of the need for armed struggle among the African liberation movements King's approach was seen as less relevant. One must still recall that Nkrumah invited King to Ghana's independence celebrations in 1957, where a dinner was arranged between him and Julius Nyerere of Tanzania. King was unable to accept our invitation to the Positive Action Conference in Accra in 1960, but sent Rev. Ralph Abernathy in his place. Three years after Malcolm's murder, I met up with King in London when he was receiving an honorary degree. We talked a bit, and Martin shared his feelings that he had not followed-up as he should have on his earlier African interests. He suggested that he would like to make an extended trip to Africa later in 1968, and asked one of his assistants, Rev. Rutherford, to begin working with me on how this could be done. Tragically, later that year–before these plans could be finalized–King was also killed. Flags flew at half mast in most African countries."

* * *

The most significant turning point in the history of the Pan-African movement of the post-independence era was the convening of the Sixth Pan-African Congress (6-PAC), not surprisingly held in Tanzania. The Pan-African Congresses had a significant and long history, because they practically chartered the growth and development of Pan-Africanism worldwide. Bill and I had already discussed the contributions of Nkrumah and George Padmore to the

Pan-African movement as a whole, so his reflections on the people and events leading up to 6-PAC focused upon other figures.

"In reviewing the history of the Pan-African movement, we could go back as far as Edward Wilmont Blyden and the biography written by your former teacher and my friend Professor Hollis Lynch,"[2] Bill reminded me. "But perhaps it is enough to begin with W.E.B. DuBois and Marcus Garvey, whose picture was on the wall of Nkrumah's home before independence. Some have described the movements in which they played a major role as elitist (DuBois) and populist (Garvey). I don't think that this view is quite accurate. Although it is true that the movement DuBois joined (initiated by Henry Sylvester Williams in 1900) had congresses of prominent people from the Diaspora and Africa, it's major concerns had first to do with justice and then with independence for the people of the continent. Garvey's main concern, on the other hand, was people of African descent in the Diaspora–their rehabilitation and return to the continent. This is not to say that Garvey did not communicate with African leaders as well. I heard of his correspondence with the Kenyan leader Harry Thuku in the 1920s, as well as with some South Africans. One interesting aside is the story of Ho Chi Minh's contacting of Garvey in Harlem when Ho was a seaman based in New York. We must also not forget Paul Robeson and his Council on African Affairs–begun in the 1930s–which worked diligently for African peoples until repressed by the McCarthyism of the 1950s.

"There is no question that the key Pan-African Congress of the DuBois group was the Fifth, held in Manchester, England in 1945.[3] There, Africans who were to be major players for independence–such as Nkrumah, Jomo Kenyatta of Kenya, Harry Nkumbula of Northern Rhodesia–strategized with those of African ancestry. Representatives from the Diaspora included DuBois, George Padmore, Ras Makonnen from Guyana, and Dudley Thompson from Jamaica–all of whom, particularly Padmore, were to play important roles in Africa later on.

"The All African Peoples Conference (AAPC) called by Nkrumah in 1958 with Padmore as the chief organizer represented a shift from 'color' Pan-Africanism (people of

African ancestry) to 'continental' Pan-Africanism, concerned with freedom from colonialism. I first heard those terms from my good friend the late Professor St. Clair Drake–an African American of West Indian descent who spent a number of years teaching in Africa. Several African leaders, despite the shift, felt a strong bond with Africans of the Diaspora because of their experiences of discrimination in the United States and their associations with African Americans.

"Kwame Nkrumah, as has been noted, invited W.E.B. DuBois to live in Ghana. At this time, there were other African Americans heading for Accra, many of whom had taken an active part in the demonstrations at the UN when Patrice Lumumba was murdered. Among them were the writers Julian Mayfield and Maya Angelou, and the artists Tom Feelings and Kofi Bailey. Maya had a close relationship with my late wife Efua, and wrote many articles about Africa upon her return to the U.S. Dr. Alpheaus Hunton, who was a colleague of DuBois, also arrived at this time and started work on the Encyclopedia Africana with some Ghanaian academicians. Some of this group formed an informal kitchen cabinet, which met with Nkrumah from time to time.

"My own association with these major figures over the years has been both direct and indirect," Bill continued. "I used to see Paul Robeson's wife, Eslanda, at a mutual friends' house. I met up with Paul Robeson, Jr. in the 1970s in Detroit, where Mayor Coleman Young held a series of events that began to reestablish Robeson, Sr.'s contributions. I met DuBois with his wife, Shirley Graham DuBois, at a party hosted by *Monthly Review* magazine in New York City in the mid-1950s.[4] I saw Shirley again with Amy Jacques Garvey at the AAPC in Ghana. Later, Mrs. DuBois went to join her son David in Cairo, Egypt; she had lived in Ghana with W.E.B. until he died–staying on after his death till the overthrow of Nkrumah in 1966. Shirley and I became good friends because she visited Tanzania often while working on a young people's biography of Nyerere. The Chinese Embassy in Dar-es-Salaam always treated her as a V.I.P. because of their great respect for W.E.B. David, who took the name of DuBois although he was the son of Shirley's first husband, has been a colleague of mine over the years; I've served on the board of his DuBois Foundation.

"Dudley Thompson of Jamaica has the distinction, as far as I know, of being the only person who attended the Fifth, Sixth, and recent Seventh Pan-African Congresses. One of the lawyers who defended Jomo Kenyatta, Dudley has also been a Minister and diplomat for the government of Jamaica. My more personal associations have been with Caribbean intellectual C.L.R. James, George Padmore, and Ras Makonnen. James and I were neighbors in New York's East Village in the 1940s, meeting up later in Ghana and Tanzania. I once arranged a meeting between him and Nyerere, which I also attended, that was stimulating and often hilarious! James spent his last days in London, where I saw him occasionally; he visited me when I was ill and in the hospital in Washington D.C. and presented roses to my daughters. James–though known as a formidable figure–was always very kind; I miss him very much.

"Ras Makonnen was another kind of character altogether. Owner of a restaurant in Manchester, he was the logistics person at the 5-PAC. Later, Nkrumah put him in charge of the Africa Affairs Center in Accra. When Nkrumah was overthrown, Jomo Kenyatta secured his release from Ghana and brought him to Kenya, where he remained till his passing. 'Mak' was a wonderful raconteur, with whom I spent many fascinating hours."

Basing the Sixth Pan-African Congress of 1974 in Tanzania was indicative of the high esteem in which Nyerere and Tanzania were held by the African Americans who, in fact, initiated the Congress.

"Some people who were formerly involved with SNCC were able to interest C.L.R. James in the prospects of a 6-PAC," recalled Bill. "Courtland Cox, and several Afrocentric student activists who had worked closely with Stokely Carmichael, traveled with James to Tanzania for a preliminary visit with Nyerere. In 1972, Nyerere agreed that the party–TANU–and not the government, would serve as host of the conference."

Since TANU was the ruling party, and Tanzania was a one-party state, the lines between the two were always somewhat unclear. The 1972 agreement, based in part upon the organizers' preferred emphasis on the people rather than the state, was to foreshadow future splits. As a longtime advocate of Pan-Africanism, and a figure knowledgeable in both African American and Tanzanian affairs, Bill was asked to represent the Tanzanian government's interests in building for 6-PAC and was transferred to the Ministry of Foreign Affairs. In actuality, this post placed Bill on the hot seat–between the younger SNCC folks whom he did not know all that well, but who knew that he was under Tanzanian government employment, and some Tanzanian officials who were somewhat suspicious of Bill's allegiances to his colleagues from the U.S. "They were kind of circling each other and I was in the middle," as he put it. Despite his good relationships and past history with both Nyerere and James, there was little that Bill could do to cut through the complicated dynamics and miscommunications that followed.

"At first," Bill reflected, "I was very enthusiastic about the Call to the Congress. After a long period of waiting, while others were to have drafted the announcement, James himself finally authored the Call. He called for a people's Congress, to be held in Tanzania because of its example of self-reliance. There was a theme presented on the importance both of self-reliance and of the Pan-African technical transfer of skills. From James' point of view, the real emphasis should have been upon peoples' movements rather than on government initiatives. So many governments in Africa, he suggested, had been the agents or the co-exploiters of their own people. There should be a line of steel, he suggested, drawn against them. That was the basis upon which James wanted to make the Call: to revive the spirit that had been there at the time of the Fifth Pan-African Congress.

"What actually took place was that the Congress organization, which began with TANU as host, immediately began to raise some complicated questions. If it was going to be a people's Congress, for example, what role would various African heads of state get to play? Do you even invite them? What happens when, as in several cases, heads of state are also the leaders of various mass political parties? The organizers tried to work out some method whereby government officials would serve as patrons–in a role more like figureheads–and that sponsors would be the key people in the grassroots Pan-African movement itself.

"As time went on, however, it became more and more evident that there was a real problem between these two basic ideas. Many of the people who were most interested in Pan-Africanism were the dissidents within their own countries–directly fighting against their governments. From the Tanzanian perspective, the identification of the TANU party with the government led some overseas officials–particularly in Guyana, Jamaica, Trinidad, and other parts of the West Indies–to put pressure on the Tanzanian government. They said, 'What are you trying to do here? Are you simply putting together a conference of parties of the opposition? You're basically aligning yourselves with the people who are trying to overthrow us!' In the end, the Tanzanian government felt that it had to step in and subvert the original idea. The final 6-PAC became somewhat of a mini-Organization of African Unity, where all the heads of state were invited and felt welcome to come.

"Just to be clear, I'm not saying that the original purpose was totally foiled. Since African Americans and Africans had been seeing each other through the eyes of whites for so many years, a large group meeting face-to-face would invariably mean that many misconceptions would be dispelled. And beyond the 'governments vs. peoples' split, there were all kinds of other conflicts going on. Among the U.S. participants, there was the whole conflict between the cultural nationalists and the people who were Marxists. The two main leaders in this group of about two hundred African Americans–which, by the way, was a real force because all of the other delegations had only between ten or twenty people–were Amiri Baraka, at that time a strong cultural nationalist, and Owusu Sandaki (Howard Fuller), who was seen as more of a Marxist. There was no Black Panther Party presence *per se*–in fact, the majority of the delegation was in the cultural nationalist mode. The cultural nationalists happened to be the people with the money and the time to take international trips! It's always easier to be a cultural nationalist and live your own comfortable life, than to be a revolutionary. But the Congress was an educational experience for everybody, and it was the beginning of Baraka's change-about to a revolutionary socialist position.

"I felt at one point, prior to the conference, that I really should have resigned as the liaison to the Tanzanian government. As far as my friendship with C.L.R. James was concerned, I was upset that he was going around the whole Pan-African world spreading the news of one type of Congress, while an entirely different kind of meeting was in the making. When James discovered how the conference had been changed, he actually refused to come. I discovered that I was in the wrong place at the wrong time, and there wasn't much of a role that I could play.

"Interestingly, Nyerere's opening speech was quite frank in saying that the Congress should not be a government affair. The governments, though they were there, should not have the control of the Congress, Nyerere suggested. The African Americans and other grassroots activists should have the right to speak. In his talk, Nyerere was invoking the tradition of the Pan-African Congress movement itself. He was also saying that Africans and people of African descent were not the only ones oppressed in the world, that there were other people who had a history of oppression. Color prejudice, he noted, was a peculiar kind of oppression. As long as it existed, he stated, people must get together on the basis of race to fight against it. But both Nyerere and Sekou Toure, President of Guinea, called for a Congress that would include an understanding of the broader revolutionary and class issues. Both of them were very clear that Pan-Africanism must not be defined as narrow cultural nationalism. This came as quite a shock to a number of the African Americans who had come over.

"C.L.R. James, choosing not to attend, certainly felt that there had been a betrayal, but not by Nyerere. In fact, it was the people who had originally called upon him to serve as 'venerable elder' who failed to keep him properly informed, so that he had been going around speaking for one kind of Congress while another kind was in process. I don't think that James felt in any sense antagonistic towards Nyerere; he felt much more antagonistically towards his own people.

"Generally speaking, the 6-PAC was riddled with complications and conflicts! There was some propaganda, for example, that some of the socialist countries considered Pan-Africanism itself to be suspect. Somalia was in the Soviet orbit at this time, but when the Somali delegation met the African Americans, they got along well and invited a number of them to come to Somalia. It was clear that they felt they had been propagandized. The African Americans who came to the Congress got a breadth of vision of African people who were in the majority in their own countries, and didn't have the same kind of psychological feeling of being a minority. The Africans didn't have to struggle in the same way to maintain their identity. There were delegations of North Africans who were very, very strong on the point that race should not be the major issue. Therefore, they were a little upset that representatives at the Congress included aboriginal peoples from Australia–who had nothing to do with Africa, but who happened to be dark-skinned. Others felt strongly that Pan-Africanism should be a matter of Blackness, and this grouping was not happy to see North African peoples of Arab descent present at the Congress. Then, Mozambique's FRELIMO representatives, as well as some other socialists and communists, were trying to gain control of the Congress in order to play down the race angle. For them, examining the questions of race and class meant making sure the class issues were dominant."

In Bill's report immediately following the Congress, he wrote the clear statement: "This was *not* a Congress of peoples' organizations." Nonetheless, looking at whether the Congress reflected the historical reality of the time, he also noted that "with its delegations from thirty-six politically independent African and Caribbean nations and ten liberation movements, 6-PAC represented achievement beyond the wildest dreams of the 5-PAC organizers. 6-PAC reflected fairly accurately the major forces at play in the Black and Third Worlds in its composition and the power of Marxism in its resolutions." Believing at the time that "effective work (could) be done if the naturally allied progressive forces come together without fanfare," he suggested that meetings be organized "by a group relatively free from diplomatic and protocol pressures, but who would have access to peoples' organizations of similar ideological persuasion." Unfortunately, no meetings of this type were to take place.

Repression and war on both sides of the ocean left groups focusing upon the problems and survival issues particular to their areas. Of course, throughout the period following 6-PAC, the Africanist momentum did continue to develop.

"Since the Sixth Pan-African Congress, there has been a movement–right up through the 1990s–to define Pan-Africanism in a more holistic way. We have tried to look more strategically at how we can work together. There's a lot of feeling within and amongst African leadership that there can be a cooperative role played by people within countries like the U.S., putting pressure on their own governments in support of African interests. Salim Ahmed Salim–the Secretary General of the Organization of African Unity (OAU), for example, is very strong in his recognition that there are important roles that Africans in the Diaspora can play. I think that there are a number of people, and I count myself among them, who would say that there is great validity in having a Pan-African movement which will work with other movements in the world that face similar problems due to what I call Pan Europeanism: the capitalist, colonialist, Eurocentric model. These forces in the world that are opposed to what has happened and is happening to our planet have got to combine. It's not a question of setting one group against or above another.

"There were elements of discussion on this within the building for the Seventh Pan-African Congress. Twenty years after the Sixth, the Seventh Congress–which took place in Kampala, Uganda in April of 1994–looked at a kind of Pan-Africanism which would not be exclusionary, but would try to combine with other oppressed peoples, with people's grassroots movements wherever they are. Like the Sixth, the Seventh Pan-African Congress was initiated by a small group, among whom was Tanzanian Marxist the late Abdulrahman Babu, who had excellent relations with Yoweri Museveni, President of Uganda.[5] Museveni agreed that the Government of Uganda would host the Congress, although there was considerable unease among some members of the preparatory committee at accepting a government as host. One notable member of the committee who put forward this critique, Horace Campbell, correctly predicted that the Ugandan government's Congress chairman and representatives would have disproportionate influence. As is often the case, he who pays the piper calls the tune. The decision to hold the next Congress in three years time in Libya reflects the power of money in decision-making, along with the continued collusion of governments.

"It is true that there was far more freedom of speech and representation of dissident groups at the Seventh than at the Sixth. Flare-ups amongst contesting groups in the Sudan and Somalia were frequent, and there were heated differences among the U.S. delegates–as usual! There was a lot of behind-the-scenes fighting between Malcolm's widow, Dr. Betty Shabazz, and Minister Akbar Muhammad, the Nation of Islam's international representative (the conference was held before the reconciliation between Shabazz and Farrakhan). The battle as to who really represented Pan-African forces in the Diaspora was intense among several competing groups, but fighting was particularly bitter between Kwame Ture (formerly known as Stokely Carmichael) and Abdul Alkalimat (Gerald McWhorter). Beyond ego, Kwame Ture felt that he had been on the Pan-African scene all this time.[6] Alkalimat was coming in with a group of trade unionists, having concentrated on the U.S. scene, with more of a Black/U.S. perspective."

Bill mentioned that another Congress delegate from the U.S. was the dynamic Dhoruba bin Wahad, who had been a spokesperson for the Black Panther Party during the early 1970s. Having spent most of the years between 6-PAC and 7-PAC in prison–framed as part of the U.S. government's Counter Intelligence Program (COINTELPRO)–he was one of the political prisoners and prisoners of war for whose release I had done some organizing. One of the most extraordinary moments of my recent life had been sitting in the courtroom when his case was finally overturned, and–after nineteen years in prison–Dhoruba was released on his own recognizance. I'd had the honor of meeting and working directly with him after this time, and introduced him to Bill shortly before 7-PAC. At 7-PAC, Dhoruba energetically worked to put forward the struggles of the over one hundred political prisoners still held in U.S. jails.[7]

"President Museveni's speeches to 7-PAC emphasized that the new Afrocentric movement was a positive development, but what was really needed was for Africa to catch up industrially with the rest of the world, not to concentrate on the cultural aspects of struggle. We must not blame our present conditions, he suggested, on the history of the past: If there's a drunk in the gutter and he's robbed, the robber is wrong but he didn't cause the drunkenness. As with 6-PAC, there was a diversity of ideological perspectives, with no definitive or unified perspective clearly worked out. A number of us had been co-opted to serve as the Committee running the Congress, and it was finally left to a groups of "elders"–including Babu and myself–to attempt to reconcile the different drafts of the Conference statement which had been distributed. The final statement was basically a call to fight against the recolonization of Africa by global capitalism. It repeated the theme of the call to the conference, put out by Babu: Don't Agonize, Organize!"

* * *

From almost the start of Bill's setting up residence in Tanzania, a growing number of organizers and organizations set up shop in Dar, working to build bridges between people. "There is a general impression," Bill noted, "of Africa as being disunited, with people always fighting. Western observers love to talk about tribalistic in-fighting and inter-African conflict. The mainstream media does not recognize the great cooperation and sacrifice that's been made by different African leaders and people, in order to help their fellow Africans. We already talked about Ghana, and how much Nkrumah did, founding the African Affairs Center. We discussed how much of the resources of Ghana he put at the disposal of movements struggling for independence. We also discussed how, between 1965 and 1968, Dar had become the center of Pan-African activities. The Organization of African Unity (OAU) had been set up in 1963, and soon after that the OAU established its Liberation Committee, headquartered in Dar. South Africans were coming out in great numbers, living in camps in Tanzania. As we know, there was some military training of South Africans, preparing for the armed struggle. The Tanzanian government was making great sacrifices. The Portuguese colonialists, for example, were furious that Tanzania–on the very border of Mozambique–was helping the Mozambican freedom fighters. The Portuguese actually bombed the southern part of Tanzania several times during the period before Mozambique's independence.[8]

"I remember drives for aid to the liberation movements of Africa, where the Tanzanian peasants throughout the country were making their small but significant contributions, so that the liberation of Mozambique and Zimbabwe could be helped. The diplomatic services of Tanzania throughout the world used their facilities to support the African movements and countries who were not yet free. You have to remember that Tanzania is a very poor country, so these acts of solidarity represented real sacrifice. Zambia was also following this same example; each time a country would become independent, it would offer it's help to movements of other countries not yet free.

"Outstanding assistance and sacrifice was also *given* by Mozambique and Angola, once they became independent in the mid-1970s. Mozambique suffered destabilization and what is euphemistically called low intensity conflict–carried out by Rhodesia and South Africa–as it provided refuge and rear bases for the Zimbabwean and South African liberation movements. It is fair to say that Mozambique never fully recovered from the atrocities of destabilization perpetuated by the minority white regime while the young government strove to fulfill its Pan-African commitments. The same has been true for Angola, which suffered greatly from Western-supported attacks from South Africa and Zaire, as it maintained support for the Southwest Peoples Organization (SWAPO) in it's struggle for the independence of Namibia. In very real and material ways, Pan-African cooperation grew to quite extraordinary measures, but this has never been played up or well-documented."

In the context of this Pan-Africanist material aid, another key African American internationalist figure emerged on the Tanzanian scene. Robert Franklin Williams had headed up a chapter of the reformist National Association for the Advancement of Colored People (NAACP) in Monroe County, North Carolina in the early 1950s. After repeated attacks from the Ku Klux Klan and other white supremacist groups, Williams organized a militia, becoming one of the first Blacks of his era to advocate armed self-defense. Though criticized by the national officers of the NAACP, Williams became a hero in many circles, eventually publishing his views in *Negroes With Guns.*[9] Forced into exile, he and his family lived first in Cuba and then China, publishing a journal–*The Crusader*–for distribution to Blacks in the U.S. New radical movements were emerging after the murders of Martin and Malcolm, and a revolutionary nationalist grouping named the Provisional Government of the Republic of New Afrika (PG-RNA) was formed. The PG-RNA, which advocated (and still believes) that the southern "black belt" states of the U.S. should separate to form an independent nation, named Williams as their first President, in exile.

"By the early 1970s, Robert Williams was considering going back to the U.S.," recalled Bill. "First, however, he came to Tanzania, with the idea that possibly he would live in Africa, after his time in Latin America and Asia. The first time I met him, he came alone, and he met with Nyerere and various other leaders. Somehow, the chemistry was not quite right between them, and I think that he himself was quite ambivalent about whether or not he wanted to go back to the U.S. and face those hassles, or to start a new life in Africa.

"I think that he expected a little warmer reception than he got when he arrived in Tanzania. He wasn't well known in the same sense that Malcolm X was well known. He had, of course, been in China over a long period of years and had been a celebrity there, along with his family. The one thing he appreciated in China was that they gave him special attention and yet, at the same time, didn't try to control him. He was putting out his little magazine. He was meeting with visitors all the time, and it was clear that he was not a Marxist-Leninist by any stretch of the imagination. Yet he was impressed that the Chinese did not try to manipulate him or dictate to him.

"Of course, with the Cubans he had become disillusioned. He had felt that there was a lot more racism in the Cuban society than they were prepared to admit. I don't think that it had so much to do with his feeling that they were trying to manipulate him, but rather that they did expect him to–on his own–toe their line. There were definitely some hard feelings when Williams and his family left Cuba, but that wasn't true in China at all. Even though he was not quite in line with Mao's positions, there was a sense of mutual respect, and that included when he decided that he had to leave.

"While alone in Africa, he did some quite adventurous things. He bought a motorcycle and traveled straight through Tanzania, down to Zambia and back again! He told me about his experiences, and one of them involved going through a game park at dusk and twilight. It was almost night, and as he was traveling, he saw a great cheetah running alongside of him. It was a bit disconcerting, he confessed, going forty-five miles an hour, with this cheetah easily racing along with him, not having any problem at all!

"He decided to stay in Tanzania for awhile, and proceeded to send for his wife and two sons. He asked if I could accommodate them, and for a short time the whole Williams family stayed with me in Dar. One thing that he claimed–and I think it was probably true–was that this Chinese ship which was engaged in delivering cargo made a special diversion to the harbor in Dar-es-Salaam in order to drop his family and his personal things in Tanzania. I was impressed with his two sons, who would be in the house speaking Chinese to each other at one moment, and would then be in yard, discussing things in rapid-fire Spanish the next. They really didn't stay long enough in Tanzania to learn much Swahili, but they were clearly having a unique international experience.

"Williams' wife, Mabel, and his sons went back home to the U.S. ahead of him. When he was about to return, he took a flight from Dar-es-Salaam to London. As he was about to get on a TWA flight from London to New York, he was taken off that flight and–after some questioning–was told by the British authorities that they would keep him for the night at Pentonville, which he thought was a hotel, but turned out to be a jail! I was in the U.S. at the time, and I had been in touch with Mabel. She was understandably upset, and told me what had happened. I immediately got in touch with my friend Jimmy Plinton, the key African American in TWA at the time, who had a special public relations position. It was a position common among corporations who were trying to respond to the civil rights movements, in response to affirmative action issues, where African Americans were hired to trouble-shoot anything having to do with race. I told Jimmy what had happened to Robert.

"I happened to be on my way back to Africa anyway, so I took off a little ahead of time and made a stop-over in London. I got in touch with Tony Smythe, who used to be with the War Resisters International, and who was working for the British Civil Liberties Union. We gathered our forces to challenge the government, went to Pentonville, and visited Robert. The British authorities were about to return him to Dar-es-Salaam.

"They said, 'All right, Mr. Williams, we're taking you now to put you on a plane back to Dar.' Robert just sat there and quietly said: 'Well, O.K., go get the undertaker, because somebody is going to die here tonight. I don't know who it's going to be, but....' He made it clear that he was not going back to Tanzania!

"They left him for awhile, and in the meantime my friend Plinton had been sent over by TWA. The upshot of the whole affair was that TWA put on a special plane, which had nobody on it except Robert Williams, Plinton, the pilot, and a couple of security men. They flew him back on this special TWA plane–direct to Detroit.

"I remember that we were trying to argue with the British. We said, 'Look, you say that you are afraid that this plane is going to be hijacked, that Robert is a terrorist. But why is this man going to hijack a plane that's going to where he wants to go? He wants to go to Detroit to join his family, and that's where the plane is taking him!' Of course, there were some ridiculous things that were happening in the world at that time. Another Williams, for example–who was no relation to Robert–happened to be on a TWA flight that landed before Robert's plane. This poor Mr. Williams got off the plane and was immediately surrounded by all these FBI men, and he didn't know what was going on! Once Robert did return, he was welcomed by the movement and harassed by the government. Ironically, a little later on he was called upon to testify or speak *in camera* to some Congressional committees. The fact that he agreed to testify made him look very suspicious to a lot of people who thought that there was some kind of deal that he'd made, because he was officially still a 'fugitive' from American justice.

"A more accurate interpretation, I believe, is that Robert Williams actually served as an emissary of the Chinese government to the U.S. government. This was a period, remember, of strategic significance for U.S.–Chinese relations, just before President Nixon's trip, ultimately resulting in normalization of relationships between the two countries. I believe that Robert brought some key messages to the U.S. government from the Chinese leadership. It is true that his case was eventually not prosecuted, and he ended up teaching somewhere in Michigan.

"I always had feelings of high respect for Robert Williams, as a person of integrity who believed in fighting the battle his own way. Just as I have associated all my life with people in the liberation movements who believed in armed struggle, I believe that differences must not stop us from looking at the essential violence of the society in which we live. Robert and I and so many others in the Pan-African movement shared these basic beliefs, and I felt quite brotherly towards Robert–in part because of my own experiences as an African American growing up in the U.S.A."[10]

In addition to providing logistical support for the passage of African Americans, Bill also participated in a growing number of Africa-based Pan-African projects. The Black Faith and Black Solidarity Conference of 1971 brought together clergy and lay people, Black power advocates and those exploring an African version of Latin America's liberation theology. U.S. scholars James Cone and Gaylord Willmore came to Dar to collaborate with those exploring similar connections on the continent, such as a Zambian Bishop who combined Catholicism with traditional African religious practices.

"I was paired with a Tanzanian Catholic priest as the opening speakers," Bill remembered. "In essence, we just compared notes. He told about the way in which Black Tanzanian Catholic pupils were taught that the U.S. south was filled with happy slaves, who were gradually converted to Christianity–and how beneficial it was for Africans to have come to America. I, for my part, talked about the Tarzan image: the Africa that we learned about in the U.S. We discussed how long it took us to realize the truth, the fact that we were seeing each other through white eyes.

"It was a very important conference because it didn't simply bring together theologians, but brought in young activist types as well. Ron Daniels, for example (now of the Center for Constitutional Rights), was there, as was Owusu Saudakai and other prominent people on the move. These people were really interacting, pushing the church to take more radical stands, including reparations and other strong activities which were characteristic of the 1970s."

The early 1970s also saw the advent of the Pan-African Skills Project, set up in the us to channel material and technical support to Africa. Founded by Irving Davis, the Project was able to get money from church and other sources to assist in the effort. The Harlem-based Patrice Lumumba Coalition of the 1980s and 1990s grew, in part, out of these efforts.[11]

"There were so many African Americans who wanted to make some contribution to Africa, and who were highly skilled," Bill explained. "We had a roster of people of various professions: engineers, doctors, etc. Somebody visiting Tanzania latched onto the idea that I should do a tour of the U.S. to recruit more African American support. At this time, Nyerere was still really gung-ho for the idea of Africans from the Diaspora coming to Africa. He always had time to see Harry Belafonte or Coretta Scott King. He would meet with the Black church activists and others whenever he visited the U.S., which was often. There was enthusiasm in the air, along with the encouragement from Nyerere.

"Nyerere's people in the lower echelons of government and TANU were, however, very very upset. They felt that the African Americans who were coming over represented a threat to the domestic power structure. They feared that the highly skilled and capable African Americans would work themselves into powerful positions within Tanzanian society, and that their African ancestry would make them difficult to dislodge. So, the bureaucrats sabotaged the effort–either by dragging their feet, losing files, trying to prevent the highly qualified people of great integrity from getting in. Often the hustlers and pimps and those who could bribe an official did get in–which, of course, gave a most negative picture of African Americans. Despite the bureaucrats, however, a 'heavy trickle' of people who wanted to work in Tanzania did eventually come over.

"The climax came in 1974. It was around the time of the Sixth Pan-African Congress, and there were some neo-Garveyites who wanted to come and live in a village near Butiama, home of President Nyerere. They had, in their luggage, a number of guns. Well, the bureaucrats immediately concocted the idea that African Americans were coming over as agents of the CIA, to sabotage and overthrow the Tanzanian government! They really put this idea out. There was a move on African Americans throughout Tanzania, and a number of them were put in jail without trial. If any African American had a gun around, or even a walkie-talkie, they were imprisoned. The majority of these people had come over through the Pan-African Skills Project, including some very good folks. Jim Campbell, an excellent teacher and personal friend of mine, was put inside. It was quite a tragic moment. Tanzania had represented, for the African American community, what Cuba represented to the left in general: a sign of hope and possibility. After these incidents, there was tremendous disillusionment.

"I went to Nyerere and to Vice-President Kawawa to see if I could diffuse the situation of having so many African Americans arrested–to get these people out. But I had a definite impression that Nyerere felt he couldn't spend any more of his political capital on this. He needed his people–bureaucrats and all–to run the government, and they were clearly opposed to the Skills Project. They were the ones sabotaging it, but it was too much for him to directly confront them, considering the other responsibilities he had to face. Eventually, the Project went down the drain, which was quite tragic for all of us involved.

"It was, for me and in general, a very sad time. I will say this, however: the government did respond to our appeal on the prisoners, and everybody was released within a short period of time. There is even one somewhat humorous story connected to their release. We had a committee going to Vice President Kawawa, who was apparently the government official in charge of these matters. One of the women in our delegation–Edna Mayhand–had just had a baby, and she came with the little child to the meeting. We made the appeal, and Kawawa was shaking his head negatively, saying 'I don't think I can do anything. . . .' All of a sudden, that baby burst out into the loudest wail that you can imagine! You could actually see Kawawa changing his mind: well, maybe he *could* do something. I've always said that Edna pinched that poor kid! So, the situation turned out OK for most of the individuals involved, but our Pan-African efforts had suffered a definite setback."

* * *

Throughout the ups and downs of Pan-African relations, the Organization of African Unity (OAU) has nevertheless served for thirty years as a forum for cooperation and collaboration between nations. Incorporating a political spectrum from left to right, which is as diverse as the politics of Africa's governing elites, the OAU has been able to accomplish some notable achievements. Not least of these, from a Pan-Africanist point of view, was the great assistance afforded to southern African freedom fighters by the front-line states. Economic projects, which have drawn together inter-state cooperation, including the Southern Africa Development Coordinating Committee (SADCC), have largely grown out of discussions initiated at the OAU level.

We talked with OAU Secretary General Salim Ahmed Salim about his own history and perspectives, as they related to his work for the OAU. "I got involved with what I call the struggle for Africa's independence," he began, "at a very young age–as a high school activist in the Zanzibari student movement.[12]

"I was the vice-president of the Students' Union. In my early days, I was also interested in journalism because of my involvement in the independence struggle. 1960 to 1963 was a most interesting period, though I had been involved in the youth movements since 1958. I was, of course, inspired by what was going on in the continent. Those were the days when our heroes were people like Jomo Kenyatta in Kenya and Kwame Nkrumah in Ghana. I was struck by this whole idea of Pan-Africanism.

"I remember taking part in a demonstration condemning the disappearance and subsequent assassination of Patrice Lumumba. Our heroes were not heads of state but heads of movements–individuals who identified themselves with the struggle and who were tortured in the process. There were stories of Algerian women who resisted all kinds of torture, yet kept on struggling. Those were the things that really inspired us. We of the younger generation were very idealistic.

"After '64, I left what I call classical politics and entered the field of diplomacy. I was involved in diplomacy from 1964 to 1980, as an ambassador from Zanzibar to Cairo, Egypt. After the union of Zanzibar and Tanganyika, I became the first ambassador of the United Republic of Tanganyika and Zanzibar. It was a very good experience for me, because I was in Cairo when a number of major events took place. The Second Conference of African Heads of State and Government was held in Cairo in 1964. I was telling Egyptian President Mubarak the other day that it was fine that we went to Cairo for the 25th OAU summit conference. I was there in 1964 when the organization was formed, and was happy to go back in 1993 as Secretary General for the 25th Session of the Organization of African Unity.[13]

"From Cairo a number of significant things happened: after the 1964 OAU summit, there was the Nonaligned Conference. All these were major events for young Africans like myself–young people who had no experience in diplomacy, and who went to Cairo as militants. When I first went to Cairo as ambassador, I was still a student! From Cairo I went to Chad, then I went back home, and finally I went to the UN in New York. I spent almost eleven years as Tanzanian ambassador, and was also accredited to the Caribbean, Jamaica and Cuba."

Bill also recalled that Salim had been Tanzania's Ambassador to China, and was one of the leading advocates for "red" China's admission into the United Nations. When China was finally admitted, Salim was seen dancing in the aisles of the General Assembly! This enthusiasm earned him the enmity of the United States, and was a key factor in his defeat as a candidate for UN Secretary General at a later period. Salim's time in New York, however, afforded him other opportunities.

"My stay in the States helped me in many ways," he noted. "Meeting and working with African Americans brought the whole question of Pan-Africanism into sharper focus for me. It was the late 1960s, during what I'd call the resurgence of the civil rights movement. One felt a great sense of identity. I also became involved in Pan-African concerns at this time, because I became the chairman of the United Nations Committee on Decolonization. My eight years with the Decolonization Committee gave me a chance to become involved in the liberation struggles throughout southern Africa.

"Those were the days when the struggle intensified in countries like Seychelles, like Comoro, like Zimbabwe, Namibia, Mozambique, Angola, Guinea Bissau–all these countries were not independent. Those were the days when Rhodesia's Ian Smith used to boast that there would be no majority rule in a thousand years. That period served as a good education for me, a good practical training, and exposure to the struggle of our people–because you cannot be Pan-Africanist without being in the struggle for African dignity, in the struggle for freedom.

"Nowadays, I think of decolonization in two distinct phases. The first phase is what I would call classical decolonization. This phase includes the political liberation of our people from colonial domination, and the provision of possibilities on the part of our people to develop, to take care of our own affairs. That was a major step. When you consider that inherent in the colonization process also was the denigration of the identity and the dignity of our people, I think one must not underestimate this important part of our people's struggle. Despite many mistakes that have been made by post-independence nation-states, it is important to understand the significance of our struggles for freedom in extremely difficult conditions.

"The mistakes lie in not getting to the second phase, and completing our decolonization. Having conquered our past, we should have capitalized on our gains and proceeded to embark on the logical sequence of classical decolonization–the socioeconomic development of our people. The problem is that, by and large, there has been a failure in many of our societies to allow our people to be in a position to express themselves, to be the masters of their own destiny. Sometimes, in the name of nation building, people have committed some of the worst atrocities on the African continent. There have been cases of simply not enabling people to participate fully in the social, political, economical development in society. That is the problem.

"Some regimes have been simply determined to ignore normal basic rights of our people, often using the most incredible of justifications. Some people generally believe that too much freedom; too much latitude, could lead to anarchy, or could lead to too much liberalism. Therefore, it's been feared, instead of concentrating on nation building, people will be concentrating on the luxuries of freedom. But there is no luxury in freedom! Your are either free or not free!

"Another significant problem of our current period is that we have paid too much lip service to the question of unity. In concrete terms, we haven't moved sufficiently. When the OAU was formed, there was talk of economic cooperation, there was talk of improving telecommunications, and there was talk of improving transportation on the continent. There was talk of inter-African trade. In my view, I think there is no way this continent can feel free and can really make itself relevant in the world unless we do so in unity, unless we correct the mistakes of the past and really begin to cooperate.

"But hitherto, for a long time, the question of cooperation has been given mere lip service. Despite all the talk about inter-African cooperation, or inter-African trade, the reality of the situation is that there is much more interaction between Africa and the rest of the world than there is amongst the African countries. Despite the old talk about how we need to be self-sufficient, we still are dependent on imports for fifty-five percent of our food requirements! This is very unhealthy, because Africa can't afford to do that. Africa *can* afford to feed its own people. We have failed to live up to the ideals and expectations of the original Pan-Africanists, to think of ourselves as Africans rather than simply as Tanzanians, Ghanaians, Egyptians, and so forth.

"I think that we talk Pan-Africanism, but we practice nationalism–and, at times, a narrow nationalism. Europe has been more and more coming together, the Americas have been talking in terms of larger entities, but Africa has still been talking in terms of individualized African countries. This has just begun to change, especially at a 1992 meeting in Abudja, when we agreed to establish an African economic community. That was a very major development. Now we must put into practice economic regionalism, because the world of smaller entities is gone. We need not only to *think* as Africans, but also–by our actions–to practice what we preach. It is in the larger interests of our people to think in terms of Pan-Africa and East Africa or Southern Africa, than it is to think in terms of individual nation-states."

We asked Salim about the root causes for some of the nationalistic and repressive mistakes he referred to. "The reason for repressive governments in Africa," he continued, "has its roots in Africa's historical development. The governments that Africa has been bequeathed all have a history of authoritarianism. My concept of government when I grew up was something that had instruments of power–the police, mobile forces, or colonial armies. In most African countries, there was not a judiciary that had equitable standards of democracy and justice.

"We inherited governments that were associated with authoritarianism. Some people accuse Africans of being repressive by their nature–but that is absolute crap! We inherited this. Of course, that does not mean that what we inherited we should have followed. This is not a justification of why our countries deny human rights today. But it is a factor that people must not underestimate.

"We in Africa have got to evolve systems which are in conformity with the basic principles of a democratic society. These principles are accepted internationally and are universal in character. They include: the right of people to decide their own times of conflict, to be able to change their leaders freely, democratically; the responsibility of governments to be accountable to their people. Mind you, all African governments, without exception, are signatories to the UN Declaration of Human Rights. The Declaration of

Human Right is universal. It has provisions for the rights of assembly, the rights of association, and for freedom of choice. But Africans have gone further that that. In addition to being signatories to the Declaration of Human Rights, we also have the OAU Charter on Human and People's Rights. Going beyond the question of human rights, we have included the right to work and the right to enjoy a decent standard of living. These are things which African governments are, in principle, committed to.

"You ask some African intellectuals how many of them have really read the Universal Declaration of Human Rights, to which Africa is committed. How many of them have gone through the OAU Charter on Human and People's Rights? My argument is that we have to abide by the accepted norms of democracy. Beyond that, every society must evolve in conformity with its own history, its own values, and its own culture. You cannot say that what is applicable in London, or what's applicable in the United States, must, *ipso facto*, apply in the same way in Tanzania, Kenya, or Uganda. If you do that, you are going to get into trouble.

"What we have begun to do in the OAU, especially during the reorganization of the Secretariat in the early 1990s, is to set up a special section in conflict prevention, management, and resolution. Now that's a very heavy agenda because when you say you want to prevent conflicts–and prevention is always better than the cure–you have to be on constant follow-up. You have to have an early monitoring system, an early warning system to tell you what is happening where. The best guarantee to avoiding conflict is to create institutions in each society where people become paramount. Therefore, if you do not assist in the efforts by the people to change society without violence, then there is always the possibility that we will have civil strife with far reaching repercussions.

"The history of this continent has clearly demonstrated that African leaders have always preferred nonviolent action. That is why you find that many countries, in their struggle for freedom, have struggled with what Nkrumah called positive action-demonstrations, marches, etc. The African leaders only had to resort to arms when all others avenues were blocked. It's extremely important to create a climate where it is possible for people to resolve their problems through negotiation, discussions, mediation, arbitration, and reconciliation, rather than through the force of arms. That is a universally accepted proposition.

"What we have to do is to create the mechanisms to make that possible. African leaders have generally accepted the responsibility that my neighbor is my brother–that we cannot afford to behave like ostriches and say that whatever happens in other countries is simply their own business. Since Africans will talk in terms of a larger family, wherever the lives of Africans are affected anywhere it must be the collective business of all Africans. What we are trying to do as far as conflict management and conflict resolution is concerned is to consider those principles in a very broad sense. We want to create conditions that would make it possible for Africa to concentrate its resources for the development of Africa. To do that, the elements of justice and equity must be taken care of. The best guarantee of justice is to ensure that our societies are truly democratic.

"Finally, if we are to achieve the objective of creating more humane societies, we must involve the ordinary African, and we must do this through non-governmental organizations–through civic institutions, though universities, centers of learning, and professional organizations. This mood of a new Africa–a more cooperative Africa, a more conscious Africa, a more sensitive Africa that respects human rights–must be an all-encompassing movement within the continent itself. I've always said that, as my major achievement, I would like to see the OAU become more relevant to the ordinary African.

"My biggest goal is for the ordinary African to see that he or she has a stake in the OAU. First we must start from within Africa–through the creation, for example, of national commissions on human rights. We must create national chapters and grassroots initiatives, working for African integration. Tanzanians must feel that it is in their interests to work together with Kenyans, Ugandans, Mozambicans, or Zambians. We must be able to identify ourselves by proclaiming 'This is our continent, we are African.'

"All the peoples of our continent must know the responsibilities of government, and know his rights or her rights.

These rights cannot be violated with impunity. People must be able to take entire governments to court, if they violate the basic norms and the basic principles of human rights. I think that the leadership in Africa has no option but to follow these principles. The momentum on the continent is so powerful. The time for despots is over."

It is difficult not to want to agree wholeheartedly with Salim's optimistic assessment. Though we fear that forces beyond the will of the people–including the massive pressures towards capitalist structural adjustment by the major economic powers and international lending agencies–make the future possibilities more difficult and more limited than Salim suggests, we are generally inclined to share his positive approach. Both a pragmatic "good business" orientation and a principled socialistic orientation could lead towards inter-African cooperation along the lines of the Pan-African ideal. Of course, those contrasting approaches do not share equal commitments regarding the need for decolonization and democracy, which are prerequisites for a Pan-Africanism that applies to more than just the elites.

If Pan-Africanism is to remain true to the history and progressive movements of Africa, it must be rooted in anti-imperialist as well as anti-authoritarian principles. The greatest possibility for this, we believe, is produced by the coming together and working together of a broad range of people: through grassroots organizations, international congresses, and non-governmental projects. Our work must focus upon a broad range of human needs-as diverse as the freedoms we fight for.

NOTES

1. Interview/dialogue with Bill Sutherland, December 3, 1993, Brooklyn, New York.
2. Hollis R. Lynch, *Edward Wilmont Blyden: Pan-Negro Patriot*, Oxford University Press, London, 1967
3. See Hakim Adi and Marika Sherwood, *The 1945 Manchester Pan-African Congress Revisited*, New Beacon Books, London, 1995
4. *Monthly Review* (122 West 27 Street, New York 10001) continues to publish important articles on Africa,

including the recent appraisal of "Amilcar Cabral: An Extraction from the Literature" by Sylvester Cohen (December 1998), and a 1999 feature on the Truth and Reconciliation process in South Africa.

5. Babu, often characterized as Tanzania's most leftist politician (see Resnick's *The Long Transition: Building Socialism in Tanzania*, Monthly Review, New York, 1981, or Bienen's *Tanzania: Party Transformation and Economic Development*, Princeton University Press, New Jersey, 1970), was involved in many Pan-Africanist efforts, putting forth the need for an African interpretation of Marxism, as in his *African Socialism or Socialist Africa?* (Zed Press, London).
6. The outpouring of solidarity as Kwame Ture succumbed to cancer in 1999 underlined his stature as the leading Pan-Africanist, at least within the U.S. and parts of West Africa. A *Black Scholar* Tribute Issue devoted to Kwame (Vol. 27, Nos. 3/4, P.O. Box 7106, San Francisco, CA 94120) was published in 1998, printing a number of his key speeches. *The All-African People's Revolutionary Party (CP 965, Bissau, Guinea Bissau, West Africa; PO Box 300, New York 10027, USA) continues to build chapters throughout three continents. Abdul Alkalimat, based in Chicago, has written and edited several important works, including Perspectives on Black Liberation and Social Revolution, Twenty-First Century Books, Chicago, 1991.*
7. Campaigns for the release of the over one hundred U.S. political prisoners–including many former Black Panther Party members and journalist on Death Row Mumia Abu-Jamal–have been represented by the Jericho Movement, P.O. Box 650, New York 10009, USA. Dhoruba himself, now published–along with Mumia and Assata Shakur–in *Still Black, Still Strong: Survivors of the War Against Black Revolutionaries*, Semiotext (e), New York, 1993, has set up residence in Ghana.
8. Interview/dialogue with Bill Sutherland, March 22, 1994, Brooklyn, New York.
9. Robert F. Williams, *Negroes With Guns*, Third World Press, Chicago, 1962

10. Robert Carl Cohen, *Black Crusader*, Lyle Stuart, Inc., Secaucus, 1972.
11. The Patrice Lumumba Coalition (PLC) continues to organize community-based forums on a wide range of issues relating to the Pan-African community of New York. The recently published Smith and Sinclair book, *The Harlem Cultural/Political Movements*, Gumbs and Thomas, New York, 1995, covers some of the history from which PLC grew, and includes some work by and about Elombe Brath, PLC's coordinator.
12. Interview/dialogue between the authors and Salim Ahmed Salim, Dar es Salaam, September 10, 1992.
13. Several special publications were produced in tribute to the OAU's twenty-fifth birthday, including Kwesi Krafona (ed.), *Organization of African Unity, 25 Years On: Essays in Tribute of Kwame Nkrumah*, Afroworld Publishing, London, 1988. See also Zinaida Tokareva's *Organization of African Unity: 25 Years of Struggle*, Progress Publishers, Moscow, 1989.

CHAPTER 8

PAN-AFRICANISM CONTINUES! SOME RECENT EXPERIENCES

On a 1998 trip to South Africa, both Ela Gandhi and Nozizwe Madlala–two ANC Members of Parliament with portfolios that included, respectively, review of labor and land issues–looked questioningly back at us as we asked them about the compromises their new government has made with big business. "Well, what do *you* suggest?"

Recognizing that the greatest threat to humanity today is the tidal wave of globalization of the world markets, we have tried to suggest that, while we certainly have no clear or easy answers to the basic question posed, there are some possibilities to be found in experiences of "positive" globalization. It is clear that in South Africa, as elsewhere, people are being crushed between the millstones of monster corporations on the one hand, and locally-based outbursts of reaction–such as the world crime wave, drug use, and prostitution–on the other. Using our own experiences with grassroots movements as a guide, examples of positive globalization can be found where an international array of academics and activists have come together towards common goals in truly transnational campaigns.

Three samples of this positive global spirit, growing out of direct action movements in Africa, were presented by us at the 1998 International Peace Research Association (IPRA) conference held in Durban. Nkrumah's Positive Action conference, the anti-nuclear Sahara Protest teams, and the global anti-apartheid movement all show how, in limited ways, the interests of big business have been at least temporarily thwarted. A more current example can be seen in the postponing of the Multilateral Agreement on Investment, a strong initiative of the IMF, which was delayed (if not halted) by vigorous global networking, mainly through the use of the computer-based "world wide web."[1] Without being unrealistic about the long-term economic capabilities of mass-based movements, further exploration along these lines is certainly an imperative.

The attendees of the IPRA conference, for the most part, accepted the traditional definition equating globalization with global capitalism, noting–as did Ugandan policy development analyst Catherine Odora Hoppers–that it was simply "a continuation of the war that began with colonialism and never ended."[2] There was some exploration, however, of the possibilities for economic alternatives. Togolese Professor Diyanama Ywassa, an IPRA vice-president, focused her comments on the ever-increasing global arms trade, suggesting that most countries act in a schizophrenic manner regarding arms merchants. Talking of peace while dealing in the weapons industries, Ywassa asserted that "peace cannot be achieved if one is producing the means to kill and destroy."[3] As with our other dialogues, practical suggestions for confronting the dominant business or governmental powers were few and far between. Sudanese statesman Frances Deng told stories of positive personal experiences working towards equitable dispute resolution, but had few words on the larger issues of political or economic justice. John Amoda, a Nigerian scholar who has researched the role of UN peacekeeping, admitted that progressive movements have little competencies in the area of promoting lasting peace making, especially as peace relates to a more equal distribution of resources. But Dr. M.V. Naidu, editor of the journal *Peace Research*, suggested on a more hopeful note that a Gandhian model of constructive work could defeat the current process of globalization. "There are," Naidu presented, "two ways out of the current crisis: de-industrialization, and a re-humanization of science and technology."[4]

Naidu's comments echoed–in part–a proposal for a reinvigorated Pan-Africanist approach, written by Bill Sutherland prior to the Seventh Pan-African Congress. Underscoring some of the more practical needs of the current period, Bill suggested that "in the 1990s, Pan-Africanism must determine what its relationship should be to other movements to save the world from the consequences of Pan Europeanism. Prominent among these are the environmental movement with its political expression of Green parties, the women's liberation movement, the Non-Aligned Movement, and various other movements concerned with the realignment of socialist forces in the world. These movements appeal to a much broader constituency than the Pan-African movement."[5]

The revival and extension of the Pan-African movement, Bill noted, must be based both upon the realities of continued racism worldwide, as well as upon the potential motivation amongst African peoples to challenge current realities and struggle for global institutional change. In addition, Africa continues to have, in Bill's words, a "great need for appropriate *higher* technology–leading to real development in environmentally safe ways."

* * *

Our 1998 visit to South Africa coincided with the culmination of the work of the Truth and Reconciliation Commission (TRC), a group strongly charged and committed with finding a way to peace in a society with many unresolved social conflicts. Many "wishful thinking" scenarios have been put forward, and one journal we read upon entering the country even suggested that a magic wand had been passed over the continent of Africa! "How else," the magazine editors asked, "could a country as reviled as South Africa under apartheid suddenly be led by Mandela–the hippest president in the world!"[6] But the hard work of searching for peace, while still inching forward on matters of justice, is in many ways symbolized by the post-apartheid efforts.

Opening the IPRA gathering was a symbolic hug of reconciliation, where two former opposing "warlords" of the neighboring district of Mpumalanga discussed how frank dialogues and a look at long-term goals helped develop the current climate of rapprochement existing between the ANC and the Inkatha Freedom Party. Though observers of apartheid-era politics might find cooperation with the collaborationist Inkatha hard to stomach, Mpumalanga Mayor Meshack Hadebe clearly articulated the need for peace in the communities if efforts for greater justice are to prevail.

The work of the TRC, gathering information and passing preliminary judgment, has been one of controversy and contradiction. TRC Chairman Archbishop Tutu worked to hold together a diverse staff and commission structure, amidst skepticism from abroad and from some sectors within the country. Though the TRC has made it impossible for apartheid apologists to claim that the acts of brutal repression were isolated incidents carried out by rogue officers, it is still not uncommon–especially outside of South Africa–to come across the opinion that justice has been traded in for truth. Hearing often-painful testimony of torture and murder, the Commission has recommended amnesty to only a small percentage of those who have applied, and is in the process of reviewing its recommendations for reparations.

Tutu asserted that the Commission offered restorative justice, in keeping with the traditions of African jurisprudence.[7] Lying somewhere between the militant's hope of revolutionary resistance and a liberal's desire for minor and unthreatening reforms, the challenge of reconciliation in South Africa is being met in unique and creative ways. Perhaps, born out of pragmatic necessities, new methods of struggle may be developed. Tutu has suggested that "instead of violations of human rights" (which have clearly continued since independence in both revolutionary and non-revolutionary African regimes); "here there will be restoration of the moral order and respect for the rule of law."

TRC investigator Zenzile Khoisan, a radio journalist not noted for reporting the news from a rose-colored perspective, recounted for us his own positive outlook on the future, based in part on the work of the TRC. Though his emphasis is on the "getting at the truth" aspect of TRC's work, the process of change which the TRC has helped open up allows for other progressive possibilities. "The new era that will dawn," Zenzile shared, "will be an era of one of the strongest and deepest anti-neocolonial struggles that we have ever seen, a point of optimism in the worldwide socialist movement based on a new internationalism."[8]

Archbishop Tutu also spoke of his positive feelings, and of the place of South Africa in a new international setting. In a private meeting on the day before TRC members from around the country came together for a month-long deliberation on the writing of their final recommendations report, Tutu reflected upon how reconciliation has effected the possibilities for the future of South Africa. Much was learned and improved, Tutu admitted, when the TRC reviewed similar processes in Chile and elsewhere. But much still has to be done. When U.S. President William Clinton met with the Archbishop on his visit throughout Africa, Tutu suggested to him that much of America and Europe could benefit from a process of reconciliation and truth.

* * *

Local efforts for liberation and peace were highlighted for us in 1996, when we took part in a conference bringing together activists from French-speaking Africa. Again, the building of civic structures took precedence over many other issues discussed. In this grouping, however, critiques of the army ran high.

When being picked up at the airport to attend an international anti-militarist conference, one does not necessarily expect one's host to be stopped by military roadblock on the way to the conference center, asked to get out of the car, and quickly frisked for weapons. At night, however, in the Central African country of Chad, these personal interventions seemed commonplace. We were already used to the slight delays when, several miles further down the road, the driver was again stopped so that the car could be looked over for guns, rifles, or ammunition. The eighth biennial gathering of the International Conscientious Objectors

Movement (ICOM),[9] held in Chad's capitol city of N'Djamena, took place in this context of militarism seldom experienced by most peace activists of the north.

The ICOM conference marked an important first. Of all the European and U.S.-based international peace associations, ICOM was the first to hold its general meeting in Africa. Though a growing number of these associations have placed an increased emphasis on the situation in Africa, none have ventured to call upon their members to travel to the south. Despite the actions and conferences held under African sponsorship in the 1950s and early 1960s, the major anti-militarist groups of the north have found reason upon reason to keep their meetings regionally based. Logistical problems and political uncertainties in African countries are always cited as logical obstacles, and the high costs that northerners must pay to travel south is also usually mentioned. But, as in the WRI Triennial I attended in 1982, the international peace meetings have remained largely Eurocentric, devoid of the perspectives, history, and wisdom of the African experience. ICOM '96 held out the possibility of something different: a handful of northern activists would meet in a majority–African setting to discuss and exchange common problems and diverse strategies.

"The army has always been seen as a cause of the violence within society," commented Enoch Djondang, head of the Tchadian League for Human Rights (LTDH). Making the links between the violence of the military and the structural violence existing in society was a hallmark of the reports of all Chadian delegates to ICOM, and of the conference participants in general. These links were made, however, not without considerable risk: an LTDH founder was killed by security forces in 1992. Tchad Nonviolence (TNV), in fact–the host group for ICOM and an affiliate of the WRI–made their first public declaration as a result of the assassination. "We have become well-known in the population," noted TNV President Brigitte Djionadji, "because the people of Chad hate weapons and are tired of weapons and war."

In Chad, though there is a high percentage of desertion from the military, many of those who leave take their weapons with them and turn to criminal activities. Neighboring Benin, in contrast, had an extensive forced military service under a Marxist government of the 1980s. According to Aboubakar Baparape, representative of Benin's League for the Defense of Human Rights, popular resistance was based primarily on a rejection of militarism, and those who refused service were sent to far-off work camps. Today, the camps have been shut down and a process of pluralism created, with over eighty political parties in that small, West African country. Though the International Monetary Fund and World Bank policies in Benin cause economic devastation, a political opening has definitely taken place. "The question of conscientious objection," Baparape concluded, "can play an important role in the process of democratization."[10]

The leader of the Congolese League for Nonviolence, Jean Makoundou, noted that many "make their professions" based upon violence towards others. Reviewing the ethnically rooted civil war, which raged through Congo-Brazzaville in 1993, he explained that groups of youngsters who had been involved in militias at that time–and who had developed a bad reputation for violence–were now integrated into the Congo's national armed forces. "All over the world," Makoundou lamented, "people are talking about peace but preparing for war. But there can only be peace through nonviolence."[11]

For Bill, the conference represented another sign of hope, and a coming full circle from his days as a conscientious objector in the U.S. It was a refreshing opportunity to meet with dozens of grassroots activists–many from African countries where we had had little contact–who were beginning to develop organizations and strategies based upon Pan-Africanism and nonviolence. As he took to the plenary, respected as a veteran activist and elder, he reflected upon his broad range of experiences. He remarked upon the recent declaration of Africa as a nuclear-free zone, reviewed the crisis in Rwanda-Burundi, spoke of the movements against French nuclear testing in the Sahara, and of the long fight throughout the continent and the Diaspora for the freedom of South Africa.

Calling on participants to transcend barriers of geography, race, and identity, Bill complemented the gathering as an historic one. "This meeting," he said, "represents a revival of the spirit of nonviolence in Africa, and a revival of the networking that can and should be done. Our dream is to remove these meaningless boundaries," he concluded. "We must remove the boundaries of language, remove the boundaries of nationalism–in Africa, everywhere–and have the people's movements, as represented at ICOM, determine our own destinies."

* * *

As we have worked to prepare the conclusion of this book, as headlines scream out at us of the horrors of the day, we continue to come across new examples that provide hope in desperate times. These small, oft-unnoticed, largely unreported–upon initiatives, statements, or stories provide the seeds for future movements that must ultimately reach deeper in making the changes only dreamed of decades ago. The following snapshots give but a small sampling of growing grassroots movements.

We noted the founding of the Sudanese Women's Voice for Peace in 1994, in that war-torn central African country.[12] Committed to nonviolent means of achieving peace and justice in the Sudan, the group is mobilizing women in particular to take leadership positions in the peace process. As this book was going to press, we reacted with sadness and anger at the U.S. bombing of Khartoum. Though Bill's home in Tanzania was relatively near to the bomb which hit the U.S. embassy there, we cannot condone the actions of a superpower which reacts to one terrorist attack by making a terrorist attack of their own.

We watched as gay liberation organizations emerged revitalized, struggling vocally for their civil rights against a wave of repression and harsh rhetoric in Zimbabwe. These efforts take place in a country where, ironically, many of its most strident U.S.-based supporters in the days before ZANU took power were, in fact, lesbians committed to the politics of liberation through participation.

In Lesotho, we joined in celebrating the Transformation Resource Center's ten-plus years of campaigning for peace and democracy. Their quarterly newsletter, *Work for Justice*–now over fifty issues old–suggests that "part of the process [towards peace] is changing what people understand as security. Walls, guns, barbed wire are not signs of security.... Security comes when people are employed, when they till their own land, when there is social contentment."[13]

A five-week training of trainers seminar was held late in 1996 in Sierra Leone, focused upon "community-based reconciliation and trauma healing." Noting that "every war has roots that are unique to it," the seminar attempted to transform some of the conflicts into peace and healing, recognizing that this can only be done once "those unique roots and issues are named, and ways are found to deal with the issues and bring people together into new relationships."

Catholic Archbishop Christophe Munzihirwa, attending to the over one million Rwandan refugees that were part of his diocese since 1994, wrote a pastoral letter read throughout the churches of the region at the end of September 1996. "Courage asks for solidarity and discipline," he urged. "Our forefathers have never cultivated hatred or vengeance. When the war was over and peace agreed, the fighters of yesterday met in the same market .... We have to be welcoming to everybody, and we will be enriched by the values carried by different ethnic groups and races." Assassinated one month after that letter was written, the work of Archbishop Munzihirwa carries on–through the churches and the communities he touched.[14]

In 1997, a Pan African Conference for Women, held in Kigali, Rwanda, put together a far-reaching Declaration on Peace, Gender, and Development. Pledging to work for the prevention and peaceful resolution of continental conflicts, the Declaration asserted that "peace can only be built on the basis of equality, liberty and justice." Calling on international bodies and governments to respect the basic tenets of human and women's rights, the Kigali Declaration helped make clear the links between justice and peace.[15]

In Nigeria, the Pan-African Reconciliation Council-like the Kenyan-based *Chemi Chemi ya Ukweli* (Wellspring of Truth) and others–develop trainings in nonviolence and empowerment. Supported by local communities, church groups, and global organizations like the International Fellowship of Reconciliation, which now produces a quarterly newsletter on training initiatives in Africa, these efforts have brought about a renewed sense of the culture of peace.[16]

In Burundi, we learned of the efforts of peace educators Karerwa Mo-mamo Modeste and David Niyonzima, who helped set up a House of Peace, Peace School, and Kalimba Peace Community in one of their country's centers of conflict. Noting that change could begin once people from different ethnicities and perspectives were brought into the same room, Niyonzima commented that "we know the solution–the heart to search for peace–will come out of these efforts." A weekly program has been developed for school children to create collages, cut-outs, and visuals documenting their ideal "histories of peace," inventing and imagining what a life without war would be like. "These images," as Modeste put it, "reflect our knowledge and our hope: that our future of peace is in the hands of our children."

The West African country of Mali was the scene of "the flame of peace"–the destruction of thousands of small arms symbolizing an end to the major civil conflict in that country. Through careful inter-governmental negotiation at Mali's urging, sixteen nations of West Africa have now signed an agreement to limit production, import and export of weapons, in what is being termed "A Peace of Timbuktu."[17]

And on the streets and in the schools of Harlem, activists and educators respond and reflect upon the situation in the Congo, in Eritrea, and throughout the Diaspora. Memories of Mandela's visit to "the capital of Black America" following his release from prison still linger, as a new generation of "one million" youth march to the call for economic and political freedom. Hugs of solidarity created lasting images, as Winnie Mandela embraced Betty Shabazz, the widow of Malcolm X, and Nelson embraced Dhoruba bin Wahad, the former Black Panther Party member who had just been released after spending nineteen years in U.S. jails as a political prisoner. Shouting "we shall not give up the fight"–for the freedom of the over one hundred political prisoners still incarcerated–the struggle for freedom, to free the land, and to bring power to the people, shows significant sparks of vibrancy and revitalization.

The Pan-African spirit continues.

NOTES

1. A review of the MAI, and what has been and can be done to stop it, can be found in Mark Vallianatos' *License to Loot: The MAI and How to Stop It,* Friends of the Earth, Washington D.C., 1998. *Other campaigns working against multinational capital–specifically the debt crisis–include the IMF/World Bank: 50 Years is Enough!, U.S. Network for Global Economic Justice, 1247 E Street, Washington D.C. 20003, [www.50years.org], headed up by South African poet laureate Dennis Brutus. The Jubilee 2000 networks [coord@J2000USA.org] are coordinating educational forums around canceling existing debt by the year 2000.*
2. From the proceedings of the Seventeenth International Peace Research Association General Conference, "Meeting Human Needs in a Co-operative World," University of Durban-Westville, South Africa, June 24, 1998.
3. From the proceedings of the Seventeenth International Peace Research Association General Conference, "Meeting Human Needs in a Co-operative World," University of Durban-Westville, South Africa, June 25, 1998.
4. From the proceedings of the Seventeenth International Peace Research Association General Conference, "Meeting Human Needs in a Co-operative World," University of Durban-Westville, South Africa, June 26, 1998. *See also Naidu's Peace Research: The Canadian Journal of Peace Studies, Brandon University, Manitoba R7A6A9; IPRA's International Peace Research Newsletter, M. Kumar, 1715 Outram Lines, Kingsway Camps, Delhi 110 009, India; COPRED's Peace and Change, Blackwell Publishers, Boston, special Africa Peace Studies issue Volume 25, Number 1, January 2000.*
5. From Bill Sutherland's unpublished "Pan Africanism: An OAU Program," a proposal for an OAU-initiated effort to revive and extend the concept and practice of Pan-Africanism, 1990

6. Denise Slabbert, "Wave On, Magic Mama," *Sawubona*, South African Airways, June 1998.
7. See *Truth Talk*, the official newsletter of the Truth and Reconciliation Commission, November 1996, 106 Adderley Street, Cape Town, South Africa.
8. Interview/dialogue between the authors and Zenzile Khoisan, Cape Town, July 3, 1998; discussion between the authors and Archbishop Tutu, July 1, 1998.
9. The International C.O. Meetings (c/o The Norwegian Association of Conscientious Objectors, P.O. Box 8831, Youngstorget N-0028 Oslo, Norway) take place every two years. The Eighth ICOM, hosted by Tchad Non Violence (B.P. 1266, N'Djamena), took place in August 1996.
10. From the proceedings of the Eighth International Conscientious Objectors Meeting, N'Djamena, Chad, August 6, 1996.
11. From the proceedings of the Eighth International Conscientious Objectors Meeting, N'Djamena, Chad, August 7, 1996.
12. As reported in *African Women for Peace*, newsletter of UNIFEM's African Women for Conflict Resolution and Peace project, P.O. Box 30218, Nairobi, Kenya, [www.unifem.undp.org].
13. *Work For Justice*, No. 49, Transformation Resource Center, P.O. Box 1388, Maseru 100, Kingdom of Lesotho.
14. As reported in *AfricaNews: News and Views on Africa from Africa*, Koinonia Media Centre, P.O. Box 8034, Nairobi, Kenya, [listserv@peacelink.it, then type "subscribe afrinews"].
15. The Kigali Declaration, and other related news, was reported in the annual International Women's Day for Peace and Disarmament bulletin, published by the International Fellowship of Reconciliation (Spoorstraat 38, 1815 BK Alkmaar, The Netherlands) and the International Peace Bureau.
16. As reported in *Nonviolence Training in Africa*, occasional publication of the IFOR. *See also Voices from Africa 8: Conflict, Peace and Reconstruction, UN*

Non-Governmental Liaison Service, Palais des Nations, CH-1211, Geneva 10, Switzerland.

17. Robin-Edward Poulton and Ibrahim Ag Youssouf, *A Peace of Timbuktu: Democratic Governance, Development and African Peacemaking,* United Nations Institute for Disarmament Research, New York, 1998.

CHAPTER 9

THE FUTURE OF NONVIOLENCE, ARMED STRUGGLE, AND REVOLUTION IN AFRICA

The end of the millennium has gotten everyone talking about the lessons learned over the past hundred years of struggle; for pacifist and Pan-Africanist movements, our own inquiry into five decades of our movement seemed most appropriate. We discussed and debated how liberation victories in the countries of Africa had affected the lives of ordinary people, and how people could strive to build their own free societies, allowing for the greatest opportunities of creativity and human dignity. How could the strategy and tactics of nonviolent revolutionaries and guerrilla fighters motivated by love and a passion for justice contribute to our own wholistic understanding of the next steps on the road to social change? How appropriate and successful were the political and economic structures adopted from various Northern models and accepted by many new leaders? A review of our talks reveals some basic commonality: it can be taken as a given that mistakes have been made by progressive partisans from all philosophical viewpoints. It is clear that efforts against global domination, especially from an economic perspective, must continue and be strengthened. What themes for future work, then, emerged from our dialogues?

One topic, which we brought to the table–the focus on the effects of nonviolence and armed struggle–appeared to reemerge as a theme: the relationship between pragmatism and principle. Though no clear arguments were put forward for a strategic understanding of how nonviolent and armed-struggle approaches have functioned as successful parallel actions, those closest to the actual circumstances of revolutionary change were consistently the most open to redefining and rethinking old philosophical assumptions. A narrow philosophical purism has created a false dichotomy between those who cling to one or the other approach as the only way forward. Those furthest away from experiencing some form of revolution–be it geographically or practically–seemed most intent upon maintaining strict ideological divisions.

In Ghana, for example–where nonviolence was used as the primary strategy to bring about independence, but was not forcefully developed to protect the country against regressive military coups–our discussions demonstrated a fairly sophisticated strategic understanding, especially amongst those who had grown up in the struggle. Kwesi Botchway, a leading intellectual and Minister of Finance at the time of our 1992 visit, noted that, from his perspective, "there is no doubt at all that the methods of struggle have a very important bearing on the outcome. I think that in all real-life situations, people have used both violent and nonviolent forms of struggle, even when the major tendency has been one or the other."[1]

If tactics relate to outcomes, then, why not a more deeply considered analysis of the effects of a diversity of tactics? Botchway alluded to one side of the myths and misconceptions that prevents people from building more united movements. "Not everybody understands nonviolence," he commented, "in all its dimensions and ramifications. In the late 1960s and early 1970s, nonviolence was seen as the opposition to a struggle that turned more violent. At the time, it was seen more or less as a betrayal, an Uncle Tom method. There was much ideological baggage that came with nonviolence."

Some of this baggage must be laid at the doorstep of the many nonviolent activists who were afraid of tactical escalation and who, in some instances, did oppose the revolutionary momentum of the times. The misconception that nonviolence must always and only be used for reform has been born of the well-funded and vocal nonviolent advocates who speak loudly and arrogantly of their moral authority, while simultaneously criticizing the violence of some revolutionaries, remaining quiet in regards to the violence of the status quo. In our view, this brand of false nonviolence is not merely reformist; in working against fundamental change it contributes to the violence of continued oppression. But it is far from the be-all-and-end-all of nonviolent social change.

The flip side of the coin of misconceptions suggests that armed struggle is always the only path towards true liberation. Yet many with whom we spoke, especially those who were actually engaged in armed struggle, understood all too well the long-term limitations. The Mozambican example is most striking in this instance. As a nation engaged in a people's war of liberation during the late 1960s, FRELIMO founder Eduardo Mondlane accepted the possibilities of alternative tactics. Thirty years later, Graça Machel spoke most eloquently of the effects of prolonged war on the consciousness and psyche of the people. Never suggesting that another path to liberation should have been taken, Machel nonetheless has articulated through personal experience and statistical analysis (as in her noted UN report on children) that armed action in her country was waged with high cost.[2] While carefully not placing the blame of Mozambique's terror on the freedom movement, Machel's and present Prime Minister Pascal Mocumbi's sensitivity to the effects of militarism and military structures has, in our view, a greater depth of understanding than many Western anti-militarist activists we know. The search for nonmilitary alternatives in this instance, not based primarily on any pacifist philosophy, will hopefully provide useful paradigms for revolutionaries of all types throughout the world.

Esi Sutherland-Addy, speaking generally about strategy and tactics in the African liberation process, suggested that, in struggle, "violence is inevitable." In any true confrontation of revolutionary proportions, we cannot disagree;

oppressive forces are unlikely to give up their wealth and power peacefully. All revolutionaries–whether engaged in violent or nonviolent tactics–must be prepared for an inevitable outbreak of directed violence. But just as we organize for survival in a world filled with the indirect violence of poverty, racism, sexism, heterosexism, and authoritarianism, so must we decide when and how to respond to the most direct forms of repression and oppression. Nonviolence is often seen as a simple one-shot tactic, which can be judged a failure if but one casualty is lost. Yet in war, many casualties occur before either side declares victory or loss. As we have stated before, the nonviolent revolutionary, like their armed counterparts, must be trained and disciplined to anticipate and deal with these losses. If the violence of oppression is inevitable and ever-present, it is up to the true revolutionary to weigh the long- and short-term political and psychological effects of any action they take, to judge their own circumstances, strengths, and weaknesses. Too often in these instances, only theoretical constructs are considered; a balancing of one's principles with the pragmatic of a given situation has too rarely been a feature of modern struggle.

Pragmatism, by itself, was the dominant theme of most of our dialogues. South Africa is arguably the grand example of the complexities regarding methods of struggle. From mass nonviolent strikes to armed attacks by small groups, there have been strong elements of principled nonviolent philosophy, as in the case of Luthuli's or Gandhi's own early campaigns, and committed strategies of the liberation armies, as in the ANC military command structures led by Joe Slovo and Chris Hani. Elements of a pragmatic balance, however, seem to be most prevalent, including the philosophical approaches put forth by leaders like Biko and Tutu, or the MK limited focus on solely material targets. Nowhere can we find examples of either "pure" nonviolence or "pure" armed struggle; people's war–it must be remembered–called for many acts of nonviolent propaganda and education. In direct action, it has always been a matter of which form of struggle has been predominant.

Perhaps the tactical pragmatism we heard from all sectors in both South Africa and Namibia has mainly to do with a weathering of the struggle from visionary and hopeful times to times of repression or of economic determinism. In South Africa, for example, it is interesting to note–given the range of philosophical and strategic approaches–the very small number of people who are currently committed to nonviolence as a way of life. Similarly, few people in that country would today support a world-view that includes people's war as a chief means of winning victories. We are left, then, with the question: Does it make a difference whether people act on principle, or upon strategy alone? Did pragmatism make a difference in governance after independence?

On the theme of pragmatism and principles, of the strategy and tactics of nonviolence and armed struggle, one troubling concern strikes us as a partial answer. Without some philosophical principle to guide us, without some broad vision that includes–but is not limited to–the general goals of peace and justice, the spiritual aspect of socioeconomic and political change can easily be lost. Our own hope, as liberation movements evolve and grow, is that a revolutionary spark be maintained through hard times. *Satyagraha*, an understanding of the soul force that lies between so many power relationships, may well provide a part of that spark.

* * *

The economic recolonization which had been spreading throughout the so-called "developing" world at the time of our first dialogues, and which has intensified especially on the African continent, suggests itself as our second major theme. With a similarity of concerns evident across national and political lines, most leaders we spoke with indicated a basic desire for mass participation and redistribution of resources, but indicated no strong confidence that this would be possible in any short-term time frame. Mwalimu Julius Nyerere's assertion that the great independence struggles of the twentieth century resulted in little more then "flag independence" echoes our own concern that the promises of freedom have not been met, as institutionalized poverty remains enforced by transnational corporations.

A common problem faced by those working to mobilize people around broad economic change is how to make the continued struggles for construction and development–for the building up of a country–as dramatic and exciting as the struggle against the often more obvious enemy of foreign domination and colonialism. Though corrupt business and governmental structures have proven equally as destructive for the common African as European domination, organizing peoples movements against the subtler forms of neocolonialism has proven difficult in almost all circumstances. Even in those instances where activists we spoke with had an understanding of and commitment to waging these battles, the "how to" aspect of our discussions were left vague at best.

Part of the vagueness, we suspect, has much to do with the relative disunity–or at least the lack of vigorous discussion–on the political and economic implications of neocolonialism. Most of those with whom we spoke agreed strongly on the need to maintain the current structures of the nation-state, though the related issues of nationalism, ethnic divisions, and the international nature of capital were barely addressed. The growing hegemony of the nations of the north, especially economically and especially with regard to relations with the south, would seem to us to necessitate a strong analysis of the role of national and state entities in organizing for social change. Though there was strong across-the-board agreement in our dialogues about the damaging effects of continued external intervention, there were many differences on the question of how to effectively build African movements against the forces of imperialism.

One concrete problem–facing all of the finance ministries of newly independent nations and effecting all people on the grassroots level–is the often confusing issue of how to deal with the international debt and with the structural adjustment programs of the International Monetary Fund (IMF) and World Bank. Ghana, whose founding father Kwame Nkrumah focused much of his later life on defining and exposing the evils of neocolonialism, was long considered a model adherent to the austerity programs mandated by the IMF. With certain politicians calling "the Ghana model" a modern miracle, it was hard to accept this positive outlook for a country, which still faces massive unemployment, and labor problems.

Ghanaian intellectual Dr. Eboe Hutchful, in assembling the documents for *The IMF and Ghana: The Confidential Record,* called into question the history of Africa's apparently most successful marriage with the forces of international capitalism. Looking at the role of the IMF immediately preceding and following the 1966 coup ousting Nkrumah from power, Hutchful argued that the disagreements between the Fund and the Ghanaian government had less to do with Nkrumah's vision of socialism and more to do with the perceived threats that Nkrumah's broad international popularity and presence would have had on the "primitive imperialism" of the 1960s. The monitors of international capital at that time, Hutchful suggests, had to develop a better understanding both of the methods of manipulating African governments run by radicals and of the means to exercise flexibility in their drive to continue to extract profits. By the time that Jerry Rawlings took power in Ghana, these lessons had been well learned. [3]

Activist and scholar Walden Bello painfully recounted the costs of those lessons in his essay "Ghana: Beacon for Africa?" A chapter in the insightful book *Dark Victory,* published by Food First: The Institute for Food and Development Policy. Since 1983, Bello noted, Ghana has undergone sixteen stabilization and structural adjustment programs. Quoting from the *Financial Times,* the statistics on Ghana's compliance with the IMF are clearly summarized. The *Times* reported that Ghana gained "a real growth rate of five per cent a year, reduced inflation from an annual rate of 123 per cent in 1983 to eighteen per cent in 1992, restored confidence and stimulated investment and the return of millions of dollars held overseas by Ghanaian nationals." In addition, debt arrears of $600 million were erased by 1990. The quietly kept social impact of Ghana's structural adjustment, never the concern of the *Times* or northern economic analysts, was the primary focus of Bello's report. The informal sector of the economy was most drastically and suddenly cut, effecting and sometimes eliminating the incomes of small vendors–usually women. In addition, at least 50,000 workers in the civil service sectors lost their jobs permanently, with others facing cuts and wage reductions. Possibly fifteen per cent of the entire labor force has been affected this way, while simultaneous increases in the price of food and other basic goods–to match international levels–has affected the entire population. Bello's conclusion, an obvious one in light of this data, is that Ghana has faced "increasing inequality, declining food self-sufficiency and rising absolute poverty."[4]

Ghana, of course, is hardly the only example of places where IMF-induced structural adjustment has led to widespread continued injustice and the maintenance of unequal distribution of resources. It's significance lies in the attention it's received as a classic success story, a perception which has helped President Rawlings in building a populist and–with ceremonies in tribute to Nkrumah–a leading Pan-Africanist image. It must be clear that while Rawlings can take credit for helping to ease his country out of a history of military rule, the success of his government in domestic economic matters is little better than that of any African country struggling to deal with the transnationals. Much of Zambia's modern monetary misfortunes, for example, can be traced directly to the economic and political destabilization of the IMF/WB. Our talks with Kaunda, who went back and forth trying to arrive at a creative balance with the northern elites, bears out his high personal cost of struggling with the money lenders.

We have found it noteworthy that, while searching for grassroots answers to the hard economic challenges facing revolutionaries in Africa, our own thoughts and dialogues have not always been in direct keeping with traditional "class struggle" leftists. A U.S.-based founder of the Committee for Academic Freedom in Africa, Silvia Federici, has suggested that the problem of economic dependency in the 1990s has been "misdiagnosed" by both the right and the left.[5] The international debt crisis, Federici asserts, has been a crisis neither for the right-wing forces (who allegedly worry that the defaulting of major "Third World" debtor countries has or will disturb the international banking system), nor for the leftists (whose concerns have focused upon the debt as chief obstacle towards "Third World" development). "The debt crisis," she wrote, "has been a productive one for the capitalist classes of both the debtor and the creditor nations,"[6] where the major losers have been those subsistence farmers whose very working of the land for non-corporate interests provide the key, though unorganized, resistance to capitalism.

We agree with Federici that, in all these cases, the question of land is central–especially as at least sixty per cent of the African population continues to live by subsistence farming, done mostly by women. Federici has considered African villages as potential "bases of resistance," criticizing a popular leftist tendency to see African traditionalists "either as helpless victims of government corruption and natural disasters or as protagonists of backward struggles revolving around tribal allegiances." This concept parallels the thinking that went into the early construction of the Ujamaa village structures in Tanzania. Indeed, Nyerere alone amongst our dialogue participants spoke directly about the impact of globalization. We cannot help but recollect that the call by Gandhi–for the Indian Congress Party to stay out of governmental power and remain a grassroots force strengthening the village republics–was seen as primitive, unrealistic, and anti-modernist by many progressives.

If, however, the economic policies of debt and multinational development provide the major forms of recolonization–a new "neoliberal" approach to world domination–then all of these notions seem to hold substantial validity. From resistance to census taking or tax collection, to more direct refusal to cooperate in land expropriations, the economic combativeness in, for example, Nigeria, indicate clear signs of hope. There, the struggle of the Ogoni people against both military dictatorship and the machinations of the Royal/Dutch Shell Oil Company has only been heightened by increased repression. Movement for the Survival of the Ogoni People (MOSOP) Vice-President Noble Obani Nwidari, quoted in the April 1997 issue of *The Nonviolent Activist*, proclaimed that "peace and truth are the instruments for success."[7] The strengthening of these initiatives will help subvert the overall interests of the transnational corporations of the north, and help build resistance to the process of globalization. Making political freedom or democracy meaningful for the ordinary people, after all, depends directly upon our ability to resist.

* * *

"Think Globally, Act Locally"–a phrase that characterized so many of the diverse progressive efforts of the 1980s and '90s–was reiterated by many of the nongovernmental, community-based organizers with whom we spoke, making it our third major theme. The efforts to strengthen civic society in the post-independence era have been on the agenda for much of the continent, especially as the dissolution of civic structures took place in Zambia, Tanzania, and elsewhere. In Mozambique and Angola, where the Portuguese colonists attempted to destroy all aspects of those country's infrastructures before the liberation movements took state power, overt and covert wars prevented revolutionary internationalists from building the societies of their dreams. Even in South Africa, where United Democratic Front and other structures maintained an alternative local community apparatus inside the apartheid state, most of these structures were dismantled after the liberation movements were unbanned. The task of the future–as discussed in our dialogues–is clearly to rebuild.

From a peace perspective, the role of the armed forces in civic society was one question raised throughout our travels. Most participants felt that the maintenance of some military was necessary, while agreeing that militarism itself was a problem. Whether armed groupings in civilian governments could ever play a socially useful role was a matter of some debate. The majority believed that a positive role could and should be created, and though very few accepted the radical suggestion of nonmilitary defense, many agreed that coercive recruitment tactics, such as the draft, were inappropriate. Laurie Nathan, the former national coordinator of South Africa's End Conscription Campaign, helped insure that no conscription would be allowed in the new South Africa. As a conflict resolution specialist, he now helps lead sensitivity trainings for the integrated police force.

* * *

High on the list of most of our dialogues–our final major theme–was the need to work towards reconciliation and peace. Just as justice–in economic and political terms on the local and global levels–was a concern for all discussants, the connection between these themes and the perceived "cycle of violence" was brought up in most countries we visited. This cycle of violence, or social violence in more general terms, was addressed passionately by Mocumbi and Machel, by Zimbabwe's Nathan Shamuyarira, by Yash Tandon and Salim Salim and so many others. Indicating great interest and forethought about the effects of violence on society, both governmental programs and grassroots campaigns were at least in the development stages for breaking the patterns of outwardly manifested social strife. Attempting to balance an acknowledgement of the root causes of the violence of the past with a program for dealing with the challenges of the future, South Africa's Truth and Reconciliation Commission was always faced with an almost insurmountable task. It is no surprise, then, that many on both ends of the political spectrum were made uncomfortable with its final report. It should also come as no surprise that the TRC report is viewed by many as an historic document–charting new waters in the world of international and domestic affairs–and that Archbishop Tutu has suggested a truth and reconciliation process for the countries of the North.

Indeed, the cycle of violence is hardly unique to the movements or societies of Africa. IPRA analyst Kumar Rupesinghe has noted that many more people have died through violence in situations not traditionally defined or recognized as war, and that all evidence points to the likelihood that this trend will continue to increase. In the United Nations University–published *The Culture of Violence*, Rupesinghe outlined the role of the modern nation-state in supporting this trend. Seen almost universally as the "best vehicle for the evolution of human civilization," the centralized state, according to Rupesinghe, "has been the vehicle, upon which violence has been mediated," and state structures have held onto a "monopoly of violence."[8] Our own concerns, about the "Black man's burden" of the nation-state in Africa, led us to raise questions about peace in the context of currently structured society. Recent books on African-based anarchism and on challenges to the nation-state in Africa have suggested, as was done throughout our dialogues, that any "reconstruction of the nation-state" would have to involve recognition of the pluralistic, multicultural nature of African society. "The decentralization of power and the recognition of minority rights," wrote Adebayo O. Olukoshi and Liisa Laakso, "would have to be integral to the democratization project."[9] The building of a lasting peace, connected for us to the building of a revolutionary soul-force with the power to engage masses of people in radical change, will–we believe–take a strong dialogue between socialists, anarchists and others. It will take a principled unity based upon a commitment to radical reconciliation, to an ending of the cycles of violence by an ending of the root causes of violence, to a radical shift in power.

Power, after all, and the shifting and balancing of power dynamics on all levels, is what revolutionary change must be about. As we've tried to describe, a common misconception of nonviolent struggle is that it naively ignores power dynamics in the hopes of a utopian peace. Religious and ethical beliefs that lead individuals or groups to abstain from violence, while important to note and often at the core of pacifist organizations, are nevertheless not the same as the strategic and philosophical commitment to pro-active nonviolent techniques used for engaging in revolutionary struggles. Gene Sharp, a colleague of Bill's who went on to lead the Albert Einstein Institute at Harvard University, maintains that nonviolent action is "capable of wielding great power, even against ruthless rulers and military regimes, because it attacks the most vulnerable characteristic of all hierarchical institutions and governments: dependence on the governed."[10] This understanding of the sometimes slow, but necessarily mass-based, disciplined, and populist workings of the weapons of nonviolence–namely, noncooperation, boycotts, strikes–is often neglected by revolutionaries of all stripes.

An example lies in the strategies and tactics developed in South Africa after Sharpeville, when, as was stated, many felt that the apartheid government was on the verge of collapse. Most grassroots activists were ready for an increase in militancy–but militancy need not have simply meant the beginning of small-scale military actions. Massive and militant nonviolent actions–facing down those machine-gun-wielding policemen on the rooftops as demonstrators marched on the capitol–might have been equally effective in creating the international moral climate to block the eventual Chase Bank bail-out of the racist regime. Though hindsight and the safety of geographic distance always makes it easy to second-guess any situation, our concern is chiefly with a clear sizing-up of power dynamics. As we return to the question of how to break the cycle of violence at its roots, we must also return to an understanding of the power we hold onto–even in reactionary times–as fighters against injustice and oppression.

* * *

We have long lost count of the number of times when pacifists have accused us of being dupes of the advocates of armed struggle, defending their right to arms more than our own commitment to nonviolence. Conversely, some of those involved in liberation movements–and more commonly, their allies in the north–have accused us of being soft in our commitment to the cause, unwilling to fully embrace the only true path to change. These critics, more than anything, have assured us that, in fact, a certain unity of purpose exists, which has long been overlooked.

Buried in a false dichotomy of tactical and strategic purity, a true and clear analysis of the pros and cons of both armed struggle and nonviolent direct action has been lost, losing along with it the chance for a dialectical revolutionary perspective that brings people together rather than pulling them apart. Such a perspective might mean the giving up of long-held puritanical beliefs in search of a philosophy of revolution that includes the spiritual as well as the strategic, that connects the means and the ends, and that understands the constant, ongoing, multi-leveled efforts required for lasting, radical, mass-based social change.

Fundamentally, we believe that it is up to each movement and each people to determine their own ideologies and methods of struggle. As internationalists, however, we do believe that there are some common lessons to be learned, and as grassroots practitioners we certainly know that people can and do affect conditions and circumstances, and can shift a given dynamic of struggle by the methods used–whatever the social conditions of the moment. We are frustrated when our own long-term colleagues from the north and the south–and from both sides of the nonviolence/armed struggle debate–find it unfashionable to speak of the need for one group to learn from the other. Those of us who believe that there are more points of commonality than difference, it would seem, must be missing something important. The methodology, to these people, represents the revolutionary cause itself.

On the contrary, we believe that these distinct groupings of progressive people not only can study and work together–but must do so. There are greater technological possibilities then ever before for the south-north divide to be shattered. But economic injustices and long-held prejudices still prevent meaningful communication from taking place. The business world, out of abject necessity, has begun to understand the opportunistic merits of a multicultural and multinational approach, albeit skewed towards power remaining in the hands of the few. For those seeking to turn these power imbalances on their head–to make revolution–it is imperative that we all take appropriate responsibility for building bridges. Appropriate responsibility, for our part, does not mean pretending that we are all equal partners coming together with equal resources. Some groupings–even within our low-budget grassroots movements–must be willing to give up some power and resources, while others must be ready to take on leadership positions. First and foremost, our movements must be willing to take a critical and realistic look at history, and be willing to learn some hard lessons across dogmatic ideological lines.

A summary of the themes of our dialogues, and of the methods used to bring about peace and justice in modern-day Africa, shows that, in several countries, there was a conscious use of Gandhian nonviolence as the principal means of struggle. In Ghana, Nkrumah changed the name to positive action, but credited Gandhi in his writings and speeches. In Zambia, Kaunda was the most explicit in his use of principled nonviolent action. The first experiments by Gandhi, and the influence of Nobel laureate Albert Luthuli, were evidence that nonviolence in South Africa had some consideration beyond simple pragmatism. In these cases, as well as Tanzania and Namibia, where Nyerere and Nujoma engaged in nonviolence on a pragmatic basis, the example of India's struggle was an inspiration. This was also because there had been a connection between the Pan-African movement leaders, such as George Padmore, and the leaders of the Free India movement in London.

Most countries that turned to armed struggle, earlier had engaged in some form of nonviolent action. This was true of Algeria, South Africa, Namibia, Mozambique, Zimbabwe, and in Kenya's Mau Mau experiences. Even after being committed to armed struggle, nonviolent actions proved to be quite effective. We recall that the FLN in Algeria was losing militarily when it's nonviolent response to Red Hand action kept world pressure on France. It was Black Consciousness action and the United Democratic Front in the 1980s that gave focus to the external support afforded the anti-apartheid freedom fighters. External support–the pressure of worldwide public opinion–has always been an essential element in successful nonviolent action, and certainly played a major role as northern powers used newly independent African nations as pawns in the Cold War game. People-to-people solidarity, against political and economic domination, is the foundation for a positive globalization.

So often, in societies which have undergone dramatic change, the structures which brought about the changes were disbanded because people felt that they had achieved their goal, whether political independence or socialist revolution. History indicates that once leaders take state power, divisions often develop between the ruling party and the people. This has been true in countries that have followed Western capitalist, Eastern socialist, and non-aligned political models. Nyerere's Ujamaa, Kaunda's humanism, South Africa's freedom charter–all attempted innovative changes and faced with difficulty the traps set by the neocolonial and neoliberal northern powers. There has, throughout the world, been a gulf between radical theory and practice; the question now is how to work the system between a rock and a hard place.

In looking at strategies for the future, several points stand out. First, the most effective forms of struggle have always involved mass participation. This is true whether the struggles are nonviolent or armed, whether based on mass action (as in Ghana or South Africa) or on people's armies (as in Algeria or Zimbabwe). Secondly, no struggle has ever been entirely nonviolent or military in nature, and support for revolutionary movements must not be contingent on these elements. Finally, it must be understood that, in one sense, the matrix for revolution is never peace; it is static violence. Colonialism in Africa and segregated society in the U.S. constituted classic examples of static violence, of basic social injustice where peace could not be possible. It should be no surprise, then, that the primary agents for change were fundamentally inter-related, with Malcolm X and Martin Luther King having their effects on one another as they did on African society, even while Lumumba, Nkrumah, Haile Selassie, and Nyerere were having their effect upon movements in the United States and the rest of the Diaspora.

In a world of globalization, the Pan-African movement must also be global. As it continues to work for the unity of people of African descent throughout the world, it must also unite with other movements seeking peace and justice. Connections between Pan-Africanists must be made with environmentalists, feminists, human rights advocates, and those seeking economic justice. No struggle is won without allies. Our movements must learn not simply to unite or merge, but to build cooperation through parallel action.

In a world of institutionalized militarism as well as war, where there is an inextricable mix of physical, psychological, and spiritual violence, one may well find more love and creativity in people engaged in armed struggle than in those who refuse to risk violence yet remain inactive in the face of injustice. But while nonviolent resisters must not be rigid in promoting their method of struggle, we do not accept that the tragedy of taking life–even in the struggle for a just cause–is somehow cathartic or without negative social consequences. The connectedness between the means and the ends, like the links between the personal and the political, suggests that nonviolence must be a leading part of any constructive social movement.

In a world of turmoil and reevaluation, we have been looking for answers from our positions on Pan-Africanism and Gandhian nonviolence. We have tried to redefine "soul force" to encompass both spiritual power and the original African American definition of soul: breathing genuine warmth and human feeling into western materialism and eastern asceticism. In our theory of nonviolent revolution, the goal is a society with structures that will encourage and promote maximum opportunities for individual as well as group expression. It recognizes that no governmental system can be responsible for individual motivation and choice, but relies upon the creativity that comes from voluntary group associations. By spirit and soul, we do not seek to push a theological, religious, or New Age agenda; we refer to the very source of human strength for continual creative struggle, for lasting social change.

What "soul force" means for each of us, or how it can and should be appropriately used, is indeed a unique and personal proposition. As we struggle for unity across yesterday's ideological and strategic lines, it seems to us that this question–the quest to find a mix of the spiritual and the political, the means and the ends–is key to addressing tomorrow's hurdles. Revolutions don't have clear beginnings or endings. The more we try to finalize our definitions or strategies or tactics–putting simple prescriptions for complex situations–the less we seem to understand about the building for truly revolutionary change. In the meantime, as we stumble together through high times and low, our own simple suggestion is to not get trapped by our own rhetoric or dogmas. We must better understand the gray areas, with no set or simple answers based on theories of the past. Our experiences suggest complexities beyond the white and the black, like the shadows and the cracks between the keys on a piano.

Now is the time to write new tunes for a new tomorrow. When and wherever possible, we must try to play in the cracks.

NOTES

1. Interview/dialogue between the authors and Dr. Kwesi Botchway, Accra, July 19, 1992.
2. See Graça Machel's *Impact of Armed Conflict on Children: Report of the Expert of the Secretary-General of the United Nations,* UN Department of Public Information and UNICEF, New York, 1996.
3. Hutchful, *op. cit.,* p. 3.
4. Walden Bello, *Dark Victory: The U.S., Structural Adjustment and Global Poverty,* Pluto Press with Food First and Transnational Institute, London, 1994.
5. The Committee for Academic Freedom in Africa publishes an occasional newsletter analyzing various aspects of African affairs, and can be contacted c/o Federici, New College, 130 Hofstra University, Hempstead, New York 11550-1090.
6. Silvia Federici, "The Debt Crisis, Africa and the New Enclosures," in Midnight Notes' *Midnight Oil: Work, Energy, War, 1973-1992,* Autonomedia, Brooklyn, 1992.
7. ---, *Nonviolent Activist,* April 1997, 339 Lafayette Street, New York 10012, USA..
8. Kumar Rupesinghe and Marcial Rubio C., *The Culture of Violence,* United Nations University Press, Tokyo, 1994.
9. Adebayo O. Olukoshi and Liisa Laakso (ed.), *Challenges to the Nation-State in Africa,* Nordiska Afrikainstitutet, Uppsala, in cooperation with the Institute of Development Studies/University of Helsinki, 1996. See also Sam Mbah and I.E. Igariwey's *African Anarchism: The History of a Movement,* See Sharp Press, Tucson, 1997.
10. Gene Sharp, *Social Power and Political Freedom,* Porter Sargent Publishers, Boston, 1980, see especially "What is Required to Uproot Oppression? Strategic Problems of the South African Resistance," p. 161.

INDEX